LIVE
loved free full

365 daily reflections
to draw you deeper
into the desires
Jesus has for you

Wayne Jacobsen
Compiled and edited by Jessica Glasner

International Standard Book Number
978-1-7340153-6-2

Copyright © 2021 by Wayne Jacobsen
All Rights Reserved

This book or parts thereof may not be reproduced in any form, stored in a retrieval system, or transmitted in any form by any means—electronic, mechanical, photocopy, recording, or otherwise—without the written permission of the publisher, except as provided by United States of America copyright law.

Except where otherwise indicated, all Scripture quotations are from the Holy Bible, New International Version. Copyright © 1973, 1978, 1984 by the International Bible Society. Used with the permission of Zondervan Publishers.

Scripture taken from The Message (MSG) Copyright © 1993, 1994, 1995, 1996, 2000, 2001, 2002. Used by permission of NavPress Publishing Group.

Scripture quotations taken from the New American Standard Bible® (NAS), Copyright © 1960, 1962, 1963, 1968, 1971, 1972, 1973,1975, 1977, 1995 by The Lockman Foundation Used by permission. (www.Lockman.org)

Blue Sheep Media
BlueSheepMedia.com
2902 East C Street | Torrington, WY 82240
p. 201.240.7106 | 213.408.9322
email: publish@bluesheepmedia.com

Cover and Interior designs: Nan Bishop, nbishopsdesigns
Background Photo by Annie Spratt on Unsplash

Printed in the United States of America
Original Printing January 5, 2021

To my three delightful grandchildren
Aimee, Lindsay, and Austin
who make my heart happy every day.
I pray you'll always know the wonder of
exploring the God who Created you
and that you'll have lots of adventures
with him as your life unfolds.

SECTION 1
Living in Love

JAN 1 — First Love

God never intended you to move on from there.

You remember that first moment you knew God loved you? Do you recall the euphoria of knowing that the Almighty God who spoke worlds into existence took note of you too, and even genuinely cared about you and every event in your life?

If you are like most, that reality probably became clear to you in the midst of great pain or failure. His love captured your heart. Everything about the world around you paled in comparison to him. Every day was an adventure. Even through the most challenging circumstances, you knew you were safe in his care and that all your struggles were just part of a larger plan.

All he wants is for you to remain there or, if you've left it, to return there. That's why Scripture calls it first love. We were never meant to leave that place but to live in its joy every day.

First love is not how much you loved him on that day—first love is how much he loved you then, and how much he still loves you today.

> *I've loved you the way my Father has loved me.*
> *Make yourselves at home in my love.*
> JOHN 15:9–10 (MSG)

JAN 2 — Settle for No Substitutes

Isn't the record of most of our lives littered with significant periods where we wandered away from his love, seeking other things to carry our spiritual life?

Devoid of his presence, we are hounded by fear, guilt, and the delusion that we can earn that love by just trying harder. So easily, we find ourselves living with love-substitutes. We double our efforts to be responsible, committed, or disciplined. But these efforts don't produce love; they can only flow out of it.

If the Lord's love seems distant for you, let him draw you back to himself. Find a quiet place and wait in silence before him. He will rekindle your affection. Don't try to go on without it. God never intended you to live even one day outside the wonder of his love. And don't make the mistake of trying to earn it, either.

You can't earn points with someone who is no longer keeping score. Jesus already filled up your card with maximum points. You don't have to earn what he has already freely given; you simply get to receive it.

> *See what great love the Father has lavished on us,*
> *that we should be called children of God!*
> *And that is what we are!*
> 1 JOHN 3:1 (NIV)

JAN 3 — There's No Fear in Love

Fear and love cannot exist side by side in the human heart. Though the Psalmist tells us that the fear of the Lord is the beginning of wisdom, it is only the beginning.

John discovered that perfect love casts out fear and that true wisdom is gained inside of your growing confidence in his affection. If you don't love God, you would be well served to fear him. Once, however, you learn what it really means to love him, you will never need to fear him again.

As you grow secure in his love, you will come to know

who God is. And knowing him, you will want to be like him. Discover that, and your calamities will never again drive you to question God's concern for you or whether you've done enough to merit his affection.

Instead of fearing he has turned his back on you, you will be able to rest in his love in the moments you need him most.

There is no fear in love. But perfect love drives out fear...
1 JOHN 4:18 (NIV)

JAN 4 — A Father Like No Other

God's desire for you since the first day of Creation was to invite you past your fear of him, so you can discover what it means to love him. He offers you an intimate friendship that will transform you as he becomes the all-consuming passion of your life.

He will be the voice that steers you through every situation, the peace that sets your heart at rest in trouble, and the power that holds you up in the storm. He wants to be closer than your dearest friend, and more faithful than any human being.

I know it sounds too good to be true. How can mere humans enjoy such a friendship with the Almighty God who created all that we see with a word? Do I dare think that he would know and care about the details of my life? Isn't it presumptuous to even imagine that this God would take delight in me, even though I still struggle with the failures of flesh?

It would be, if it were your idea. It was his, however, long before you even considered it. He's the one who offered to be your loving Father—loving you and caring for you in ways no earthly father ever could.

He knows you better than you know yourself; he loves you more than anyone ever has; he knows that when you relax into that reality, you will discover that all of your fears, including your fear of him, will be destroyed.

> *But perfect love drives out fear, because fear has to do with punishment. The one who fears is not made perfect in love.*
>
> 1 JOHN 4:18 (NIV)

JAN 5 — Who Is He Really?

Scripture paints two seemingly contradictory portraits of God. As the holy God, he is shown to be unapproachable in his purity, willing to mete out unspeakable torment on his Son, and ready to consign the unrepentant to eternal agony in hell. He is also portrayed as a tender Father, so loving that the most wayward sinner could run to his side in absolute safety and find forgiveness and mercy.

If you cannot resolve these images into a coherent view of God, you will end up playing the he-loves-me-he-loves-me-not game. Like the schizophrenic child of an abusive father, you'll never be certain which God you'll meet on a given day—the one who wants to scoop you up in his arms with laughter, or the one who ignores or punishes you for reasons you don't understand.

Here is why so few believers ever discover the depths of friendship God has offered to them. They see God's holiness as a contradiction to his tenderness. Unable to reconcile the two, fear wins out, and intimacy with him is forfeit. Vacillating between loving him and fearing him will keep you from ever learning to trust him.

You cannot love what you fear, and you will not fear what you love.

> *For you did not receive a spirit that makes you a slave again to fear, but you received the Spirit of sonship.*
>
> ROMANS 8:15 (NIV)

JAN 6 — Why Follow After God?

"Would you follow God if there was no hell?"

Someone asked me that a few years ago, and my immediate reaction was, "Of course I would."

If he had asked me that when I was younger, I doubt I would have answered with such certainty. Back then, my relationship with God was more confused. We would have said God was loving, but only for those who did everything he wanted. But whoever did that?

His holiness was his most terrifying feature, and the best reason I was given to follow him was my fear of the consequences if I didn't. Threatened with eternity in flames was all the motivation I needed to do everything I thought required to stay in his good graces. More than anything, I wanted God to like me, protect me, and bless me.

Looking back now, I realize I was not in an endearing relationship with my Creator as a beloved son. I was caught in the Stockholm syndrome with God; like the victim of a kidnapping, I sought to ingratiate myself to the one I feared, confusing that with love.

For the past twenty-five years, however, I've come to rely on his love. It has made all the difference. God never wanted our indentured servitude but to share his life with his grateful children.

> *For you did not receive a spirit of slavery to fall back*
> *into fear, but you received a spirit of adoption,*
> *through which we cry, "Abba, Father!"*
>
> **ROMANS 8:15 (NASRE)**

JAN 7 — Fear or Shame Won't Help

In the early days of my journey, fear and shame were constant if unwelcome companions. I was constantly afraid I wasn't doing enough for God to like me, and I was ashamed of my sinful desires. My shortcomings and failures were always before me since he commanded us to be as holy as he was.

However, that was not the relationship God had in mind for me, and it is not the relationship that would help know him or experience all he had for me.

Jesus didn't seem to live with his Father that way, and he was perfect. He called his Father "our Father," so that we could share in that relationship as well, and through it be transformed. So, instead of focusing his followers on their failures, he invited them to focus on his joy. He told them everything, "so that my joy may be in you and that your joy may be complete."

No one I knew in my young days lived that way. To us, God was a demanding deity, and we lived every day under threats, obligations, and a constant demand for perfect performance. Jesus pointed us down a different road because those who live like that cannot experience his fullness, and they won't effectively share his love in the world.

Fear and shame will not produce the work of God in us. Jesus showed us his Father was not a terrifying presence in the world, but the most endearing. Love is the coin of his realm, not fear and shame.

> *Therefore, there is now no condemnation for those who are in Christ Jesus...*
> **ROMANS 8:1**

JAN 8 — A More Compelling Reason

So, back to our question of a couple of days ago: Would you want to follow God if there were no hell? Fear of hell was just about the only reason people got saved when I was young. No one wanted to jump through all those religious hoops unless the consequences of not doing were far worse.

Whatever hell turns out to be, it is the place where sin devours its prey. As tragic as that might be, the fear of it was never meant to be our motivation for following God. If we're going to sustain a journey in him, we need a more compelling reason than fear. And our friends and family need to hear an invitation that inspires them to consider God's reality better than this: "You're a horrible person and God is going to torment you if you don't repent."

That's what engages the Stockholm syndrome, rather than a real journey of love and affection. Besides, I'm not convinced fearing hell will be enough to save anyone. Oh, it might hold them in check for a few months at a time, but when the fear fades, as it always does, they will be back to their old self-destructive ways.

God's love for you is the only source of salvation and the only motivation that will untwist all sin wrecks in this world and the one to come. Taste that, and you'll follow him to the end of the age.

> *Taste and see that the Lord is good;*
> *blessed is the one who takes refuge in him.*
>
> **PSALM 34:8**

JAN 9 — God, the Rescuer

Many people misunderstand the Old Testament—they conclude that God is the executioner in the redemption story. Stories like Noah's Ark, Sodom and Gomorrah, and Canaan's Conquest are enough to convince people that God is a terrifying presence out to destroy in anger the world he created.

Nothing could be further from the truth. There are times God intervenes in human history in ways that hold severe consequences for those who resist him, but if you look at the whole story, you'll see he is always the rescuer. His judgment is like the surgeon's scalpel—it sets things right in a broken world.

Sin is the destroyer, not God. Using our self-preferring nature and preying on our limited knowledge, it draws us into the darkness like captives. Because we go so willingly, we see God's actions against the darkness as actions against us. But God wants to break through the bondage and draw us back into his light and his healing.

Salvation, according to Jesus, does not come to those who try to appease an angry deity with their offerings or sacrificial needs. Salvation is found inside an affectionate relationship with the Creator of all. It is less about fixing our circumstances than it is about rescuing us from the lies of darkness.

Unfortunately, too many people confuse God himself with the religion we've created in his name. That makes it difficult for them to connect with him. People in relative ease often keep God at a distance. They take in just enough Christianity to soothe their conscience and to satisfy their fears about the afterlife, but they don't want too much of him because he might intrude on their pleasures.

Other people, caught in tragic circumstances or deep pain, call out to him, seeking relief by promising God they will do anything he wants. Neither of these will lead to a long and satisfying connection with him.

Do you need to be rescued? Ask him and let him do it however he decides is best.

> "Because he loves me," says the LORD, "I will rescue him;
> I will protect him, for he acknowledges my name."
>
> **PSALM 91:14**

JAN 10 — What If?

I sat on a deck in the High Sierras surrounded by pine and cedar trees with a young man who did not grow up with any kind of spiritual influence in his life. He and his fiancée had asked me to marry them, so we were talking about what kind of involvement they wanted from God in their wedding and their marriage.

"I know nothing about him," the young man answered.

I paused a moment thoughtfully, then pointed to the beauty of the forest all around us. "What if there is a God who made all of this, who loves you more than anyone else you've ever known, and he wants to walk with you as you explore your life in his Creation?"

He looked up at me and smiled, his eyes misted with tears. "I would love that."

Who wouldn't?

If you don't know him that way, ask him to show you. Resist any expectation to what that has to look like and watch what he does.

> How great is the love the Father has lavished on us,
> that we should be called children of God!
> And that is what we are!
>
> **1 JOHN 3:1**

JAN 11 — Following God Without Fear

Some Christians tell me that people will not serve God unless we terrify them with the possibility of hell. I disagree. I can think of five great reasons anyone would want to follow God that have nothing to do with fear. Let's look at two of them today and three more tomorrow.

First, because God is the most engaging presence in the universe. He is full of life, laughter, joy, and wisdom more precious than wealth. Far and away he is the best friend I have. Oh, I don't always understand what he's up to, but I know in time he'll show me what I need to know.

I'd rather talk over things with Father, Jesus, and the Spirit more than anyone else in my life, and I love the conversations I have with others. If you haven't experienced him this way, I'm sure I got a bit of an eye roll there, but honestly the things he adds to my life fill it with wonder and wisdom.

Second, because this world makes no sense without him. All that is real is not visible. I see his glory in the Creation and his hand in the seeming coincidences of life—meeting a person at just the right moment or having an insight drop into my heart from a conversation, a sentence in a book, or a song lyric.

Even failures or the betrayal of others turns out to have meaning in the larger scheme of things that he understands so well. A seemingly silly choice in one moment will open opportunities down the road I would never have foreseen.

I sensed his calling to me at a very young age. Inside his reality, I find the courage and resources that hold me through life's most painful seasons.

Let us draw near to God with a sincere heart and with the full assurance that faith brings, having our hearts sprinkled to

*cleanse us from a guilty conscience and having
our bodies washed with pure water.*

HEBREWS 10:22

JAN 12 Three More Reasons

Let's continue our discussion of the reasons that you might want to follow God that don't include fear of the afterlife.

The third reason for me is because navigating successfully through a broken Creation is beyond my best resources and wisdom. Self-indulgence leads to the corruption and injustice that not only diminishes my life, but it also stains our world and harms others. How do you navigate circumstances you can't control that seem unjust? How do sickness and tragedy make sense inside God's love and his ultimate purpose to redeem the world back to himself?

Without his active input in my life, I only consider how things affect me, and that's a painful way to live in this universe. He has a way of causing the sufferings of this world to fold into a larger plan of our transformation and his redemption. I wouldn't want to live without it. He has given me insight to make decisions I wouldn't otherwise have made, and though he often invites me down more difficult roads, they always bear better fruit over time.

Fourth, I am powerless to resist my destructive appetites and desires if he does not give me the wisdom to untangle them, the strength to refuse them, and the fullness to displace what they prey on in my twisted soul.

Without him, I'm adrift in a world of indulgence; with him, I can learn to say no to those things that add more pain in the world and yes to a path that leaves more grace in it.

Fifth, because I want to be part of something bigger than myself and my own existence. God not only created this planet but now moves it to its ultimate redemption. By showing us what it truly means to be loved and to love, I can become part of that unfolding purpose and encourage others on that path as well.

> *To them God has chosen to make known among the Gentiles the glorious riches of this mystery, which is Christ in you, the hope of glory.*
> COLOSSIANS 2:27

JAN 13 — The Most Engaging Invitation

Far from being the kill-joy that religion makes God out to be, or the excuse for our injustices to others, God becomes a valued companion in this journey called life. When you know who this amazing God is, "Be holy as I am holy" is not the most onerous command in Scripture, but the most engaging invitation. When you know him, you will want to be like him.

And if you want to be like him, it's great to know he has provided everything for that to happen. There's no way I could do that on my own. All I have to do is learn to live in his love, and he's the one who teaches us that, too.

Now, I know some of you reading this are frustrated that your relationship with God doesn't feel like that. Despite your prayers, Bible reading, church attendance, and trying to be good, God still feels like a distant deity rarely involved in real circumstances of daily existence. I lived a long time there myself, so I understand. The five things I've described above are the fruit of a long trajectory in learning how to live in his love. It doesn't happen overnight, with a snap of the fingers or an ecstatic Jesus encounter.

Learning how to lean into his reality and recognize his fingerprint around us is a lifelong quest, perhaps the greatest adventure our humanity offers. Our appetites can betray us, our intellect often deceives us, and the world so easily distracts us with its amusements and its fears. Cultivating the inner life to become increasingly sensitive to the ways Jesus makes himself known does take some focus and participation from us.

> *But one thing I do: Forgetting what is behind and straining toward what is ahead, I press on toward the goal to win the prize for which has called me heavenward in Christ Jesus.*
>
> **PHILIPPIANS 4:13–14**

JAN 14 — Where to Begin?

What do you think? Do you want a relationship with God based on fear or the endearment of his own character and love?

If you don't know how to do that, find someone who does and ask him or her if they will help you. Don't look for someone to tell you exactly what to do, but who will instead help you see God's fingerprints in your own journey and the realities his Spirit is offering to invite you farther down that path.

Let them share their journey with you, but don't try to copy theirs. Instead, learn to listen in your heart as God shows you how he wants to make himself known to you. Then watch how he does that. Share your journey with them and let them help you lean into those things that seem genuine and recognize those things that smell of self-effort.

Try not to get discouraged when it doesn't happen quickly or as easily as you might hope. Look for others who have a similar hunger. Please don't give up, because learning to find your footing on a journey with him does take a while. This life is not like going to Disneyland; it is a real engagement with the Maker of heaven and earth.

Knowing him starts in small ways and over time grows to become the most valuable part of your life.

> *The kingdom of heaven is like a merchant looking for fine pearls. When he found one of great value, he went away and sold everything he had and bought it.*
> MATTHEW 13:45–46

The Fatherless Epidemic

"I think my dad hates me," she said through her sniffles, choking back the sob that hung in her throat. Then she detailed the fight they'd had the night before. Her dad was upset about the provocative way she often dressed, and she was certain he had no respect for her choices.

I walked her back through the conversation, a surrogate dad who suggested that her father's fears were less about judging her than they were about trying to protect her from men with less than honorable intentions.

"So you think my dad doesn't hate me?" she asked at the end.

"Nicole, I have no idea. He's your dad, but I would be surprised if he didn't love you very much. However, can I ask how things are with your heavenly dad?"

Her twisted face told me my question had confused her. A moment passed. "Do you mean God?"

I nodded. "I grew up in church," she said. "I hate him."

I smiled as I looked at Nicole and whispered to her as if sharing the most incredible of secrets: "As wrong as you might be about your earthly dad, I can tell you you're dead wrong about your heavenly one."

Her eyes lit up. "What do you mean?"

"Nicole, you have a father who loves you more than anyone on this planet ever has or ever will."

The hope that we all have a Father who knows us completely but loves us extravagantly is all but lost in our day. It might be time to uncover it again.

> *This is how God showed his love among us: He sent his one and only Son into the world that we might live through him.*
> JOHN 4:9 (NIV)

JAN 16 — A Girl and Her Daddy!

"Majesty, worship his Majesty..." The familiar words rolled off my lips as I sat among a group of believers from all over the western United States who had gathered to share their experiences in relational church. It was Sunday morning and we were just beginning with a chance to sing songs of praise and thanksgiving to God. I felt unsettled.

Sitting next to me that morning was a three-and-a-half-year-old girl, cradled in the arms of her father, Jim. Nyssa struggles against the complications of Freeman-Sheldon syndrome, a genetic muscle disorder that has caused severe scoliosis (curvature of the spine) and disfigured fingers. She is fed through a tube in her stomach and the disorder renders her unable to talk, walk, or play like other children. In fact, she can only lay cuddled in her father's arms, cooing and slobbering. The connection between her and her father and the love and adoration that beamed from his face as he whispered to her and jiggled her in his arms was mesmerizing.

That's what I want! The words sailed through my mind so quietly I almost missed them. I had to stop a minute and ask not only what I had heard, but where it had come from. Certainly, this wasn't my thought. After a few moments of meditation, however, I recognized Father's voice in it and suddenly it dawned on me why my heart had been so unsettled that morning.

We were exalting God, joining the great throng of angelic beings that surround the throne with praise and adoration to God. He was just wanting us to enjoy a moment in his lap, like that father and daughter; with an intimacy that no moment of adoration could rival.

> *Yet to all who did receive him, to those who believed in his name, he gave the right to become children of God—children born not of natural descent, nor of human decision or a husband's will, but born of God.*
>
> JOHN 1:12–13 (NIV)

JAN 17 He Has Chosen You

Nyssa was adopted into her family. Her parents first laid eyes on her when she was eleven days old and knew her entire condition before they threw wide the doors of their home and invited her in.

Jim told me he was initially reticent to adopt a child with so many special needs. But the moment he first laid eyes on Nyssa, all that changed. "As soon as I had her in my arms," he said, "she looked up at me and sighed. My heart just melted, and I knew I had to say 'Yes.'"

She was chosen in the same way Father has chosen you. He was fully aware of all the brokenness he would love you through.

Her father reminded me that she couldn't even crawl into her own father's lap that morning. If her father hadn't scooped down and picked her up, she would never have been there. I'm certain our plight is similar. Who of us can really claim to crawl into God's lap by our own power? He is our only source, and there would be no intimacy if he did not make it happen.

Perhaps the most we do is just lift our arms to him in surrender and desire. But our place on his lap is all his doing.

> *You did not choose me, but I chose you and appointed you so that you might go and bear fruit—fruit that will last—and so that whatever you ask in my name the Father will give you.*
> **JOHN 15:16 (NIV)**

JAN 18 — We Are All Beautiful in His Eyes

Though our flesh can be seduced by the adoration of others, our Father doesn't share the same ego. I know many people who sacrifice the affection of their family for their success in the workplace, but God isn't wired that way. I think he would treasure affection over adoration any day of the week. He is the God of love, remember?

Nyssa's brokenness didn't diminish her father's affection. If anything, her brokenness made her more endearing. We have the tendency to diminish our worship when we are aware of our own failures and weaknesses.

Don't great crowds of adoration always push the so-called "beautiful people" and the "power people" to the front while shunning those deemed "lesser" to the back? But in a father's lap there are no greater and lesser. Parents delight equally in their children and only see points of brokenness as cracks into which more love can be poured.

Can we dare to believe that our Father sees us the same way Jim sees his daughter Nyssa? I can assure you he loves you far more than that.

> *But he said to me, "My grace is sufficient for you,*
> *for my power is made perfect in weakness."*
> **2 CORINTHIANS 12:9 (NIV)**

JAN 19 — Do You Love Me?

It makes more sense to me now, why Jesus asked Peter the question he did after the resurrection: "Do you love me?" He didn't want to know if Peter adored him, feared him, or was ready to serve him in the face of any conceivable threat.

He just wanted to know he had Peter's love. Having that, he knew everything else would fall into place. Lacking that, nothing else would matter.

If the cross accomplished its purpose, even this one—who had betrayed him so painfully—would find his way back into his love. After all, Peter never stopped loving him, but simply let his fears overwhelm him when the pressure was on.

His failure did not disprove his love. Jesus knew that. For the moment, Peter didn't. But he would soon enough and then he would be free to live out the rest of his days with growing affection for his resurrected friend.

Don't think your mistakes prove your lack of love. Find a love bigger than your failures and you'll find a life that grows increasingly free from wanting to go your own way.

> *And I pray that you, being rooted and established in love,*
> *may have power, together with all the Lord's holy people,*
> *to grasp how wide and long and high and deep is the love of*
> *Christ, and to know this love that surpasses knowledge—*
> *that you may be filled to the measure of all the fullness of God.*
> **EPHESIANS 3:17–19 (NIV)**

JAN 20 — Affection or Adoration?

What do you think? Would I rather sit on the couch with my children while they tell me what an incredibly awesome father I am, repeating the same words again and again so I am sure to get the message; or would I rather take a walk with them, talking about their joys and fears?

The latter, of course. Far more than their praise, I'd rather have my children's presence. I want to be with them in their laughter and to comfort them in their tears. Why would it be any different with God?

The fact is, you can praise someone you don't love, holding him at a distance, feeling left out and alone. However, I don't think you can love him and not also be completely overwhelmed by how worthy he is of your praise.

Just make sure your adoration never displaces affection. Give him all the adoration and praise he deserves. Just don't be confused that to him your praise means more than our love.

You are my friends if you do what I command. I no longer call you servants, because a servant does not know his master's business. Instead, I have called you friends, for everything that I learned from my Father I have made known to you.

JOHN 15:14–15 (NIV)

JAN 21 — In the Eyes of a Son

"Everything God is calling me to right now seems wrapped up in this picture," Glenn told me as he laid the black and white photograph of father and son on the table.

This was the first time I had been in Glenn and Elaine's

home. We sat down for breakfast a few hours earlier and hadn't yet moved from the table. We were talking about the awesome relationship that God extends to each of us through his son.

The photo was carefully framed and matted, an obvious treasure. I could see why immediately—I was captured by the interplay of this father and son standing beside a sapling birch tree that had already lost its leaves for winter. The clothes they wore spoke of a previous generation.

The delight of a father looking down at his son and the obvious pride of a two-year-old looking back was captured perfectly by the photographer. The connection between this father and son was profound. As Glenn cradled it in his hands, he told me he is just beginning to see his relationship with God in the same way. So should we all.

> But whoever did want him, who believed he was who
> he claimed and would do what he said, He made
> to be their true selves, their child-of-God selves.
>
> JOHN 1:10–12 (MSG)

JAN 22 A Dad and His Son

The father and son in the photo are obviously delighted with each other and the photo perfectly captures the joy, wonder, and affection that God wants to share with his children.

"I'm a long ways from that," Glenn admitted after I had a chance to let the picture sink in, "but I know he is calling me to be just like that little boy."

I know what he meant because I'd been down that road. Learning to be so at peace in the Father's presence, so secure in his care, and so ready to enjoy the day with him, was a long journey for me.

"That's me!" Glenn finally said. "The little boy there! I was two years old." My head shot up in surprise. I had not even considered that this was a family photo. "My father died of a heart condition within two months of that picture. I have no memory of him, only this picture. Now I want to know my heavenly Father with the same simplicity and joy."

No this isn't the relationship God asks of us, but the one he had already been at work to produce in us. "We know love," John wrote, "only because he loved us first."

God is love. Whoever lives in love lives in God, and God in them.
1 JOHN 4:16 (NIV)

JAN 23 Wrong Father!

Some of the craziest stories show up in my email.

"My wife's best friend is a real-life episode of the Jerry Springer Show," a friend wrote. "She hadn't been talking to her dad for a few years. Bad situation. He's a pretty terrible guy."

I can't imagine worse pain than having a father who is too broken to love his child and pour that love into them in their most formative years. But the story got better.

"Anyway, she found out a month ago that he isn't her actual dad, and that her real dad has been trying to find her for twenty-two years, ever since he found out that a one-night stand had produced her. He had prayed for her nonstop since coming to know Jesus along the way.

"Once he found her, he and his family immediately traveled a long distance to meet her. She has a new dad! Just like that, everything she thought to be true about her father was completely wrong and she had a dad! And her newborn, their first, now has a grandfather! Beautiful."

Not all stories turn out this well, but this much is true: No matter how awesome or despicable your earthly father was, we all have a Father who made us, whose love for us far exceeds what even the best fathers could give his child. Find that Father and you will find great joy and security.

> *But while he was still a long way off, his father saw him and was filled with compassion for him; he ran to his son, threw his arms around him and kissed him.*
>
> LUKE 15:20 (NIV)

JAN 24 Your Real Father

Many of us have been taught that the God of religion is an angry and demanding presence in the Creation. If we don't please him, he will make horrible things happen to us. But try as we might, we can never seem to be good enough, and we wind up feeling frustrated with ourselves, rejected, and all alone.

But that isn't your Father. That's someone masquerading as him to exploit your love, devour your joy, and destroy your life.

The Father, who is your real Father, has been searching for you all your life. He has been closer than your breath, and yet you may have missed him for all the illusions religion has created to keep you afraid and working hard for him.

When you discover your real Father, the fear will evaporate in his great delight over you.

> *Suppose one of you has a hundred sheep and loses one of them. Does he not leave the ninety-nine in the open country and go after the lost sheep until he finds it?*
>
> LUKE 15:4 (NIV)

JAN 25 — When You Get Father Wrong

She grew up genuinely loved by her father. He took great delight in her and treated her with great affection. But as she grew, she began to ask things of him that he knew would only hurt her. When he expressed his concerns and regret over not being able to give in to her, she grew increasingly frustrated and distant. Soon she even questioned whether he loved her anymore, or ever did.

As that played on her mind, she began to see his every act of affection through jaded eyes and concluded he only acted like he loved her to get what he wanted from her. His acts of affection were dismissed as tools of manipulation.

Her disappointment grew and eventually gave way to anger. She stopped asking of him and demanded instead. When she didn't get her way, she pouted.

Her wants became more important than the relationship with her father and she blamed him for being a bad father. In her mind, her desires were "needs" and his refusal to meet them only proved what an uncaring person he was. She ended up saying horrendous things to him and about him to her friends, all to justify her own bitterness and anger.

The father, however, knew better. Her words stung, but he knew they weren't true. Even in the face of her anger and manipulation he responded with sorrow, not anger. He knew she was sliding into the dark space of her own selfishness where lies rule the day, and he was powerless against her false accusations.

No matter what he did, she would only belittle him and dismiss his attempts to love her. There is no greater bondage than believing your own lies to be the truth. Even Jesus warned us that when our "light" is really darkness, there is no greater darkness!

> *Your eyes are windows into your body. If you open your eyes wide in wonder and belief, your body fills up with light. If you live squinty-eyed in greed and distrust, your body is a dank cellar. If you pull the blinds on your windows, what a dark life you will have!*
>
> MATTHEW 6:22 (MSG)

JAN 26 You Can Always Go Home

Continuing our story from yesterday, eventually another came along who promised to meet all her "needs" and do for her what her father refused to do. Of course, he only did it to get what he wanted from her, but she thought she had found true love. At the beginning she got what she wanted from her boyfriend, even though he only wanted to use her, and turned her back on her dad, who loved her.

Of course, over time his motives became evident as he started demanding his way with her. He pampered her less and abused her more. He was just exploiting her needs to fulfill his wants and as that reality sunk in she slid into despair. The freedom she thought he offered turned out to be a prison of her own making.

Then she knew that she'd made the poorest of choices. She wondered if she had burned so many bridges that she had no choice but to keep on her course no matter how painful. In her honest moments, however, her heart longed for home, a bit wiser about her father's love. Unfortunately, she was too embarrassed and scared to face the father she rejected so casually. She was sure her father hated her after all she had done, not knowing that she was only projecting her emotions on him.

This is actually the moment—if she takes the risk—

that she can discover how amazing true love really is.

Regardless of how faithless Israel was, God was always ready to draw them into his love whenever they made the slightest turn back toward him, and even at times when they didn't!

He will always be there for you, too, no matter how far into the weeds you have wandered.

> *"Come, let us return to the LORD...*
> *(so) he will heal us;"*
> **HOSEA 6:1 (MSG)**

JAN 27 Coming Home

His father looked longingly down the road every day, hoping against hope that this would be the day he comes home. His heart had been broken by his son's waywardness and by the price he'd paid, but neither made him angry or ashamed. He only wanted his son to come home.

Then one day he saw him down the road, plodding toward home with his head hung down. The father burst through the door with great joy and rushed to his side, welcoming him back inside the affection that had only grown in his absence.

You can always go back to the place where you were truly loved and find yourself smack dab in the middle of the affection you may have spurned before.

Love always prevails over failure.

> *"Quick. Bring a clean set of clothes and dress him. Put the family ring on his finger and sandals on his feet. Then get a grain-fed heifer and roast it. We're going to feast! We're going to have a wonderful time! My son is here—given up for dead and now alive! Given up for lost and now found!" And they began to have a wonderful time.*
> **LUKE 15:22–24 (MSG)**

JAN 28 — God in the Shower

After a gathering in Ohio, a professor visiting the United States from India on an exchange program approached me with a question. He loved the informality of our gathering but was bothered by the casual dress. "If I was going to meet the President of the United States today, I would dress up in a suit and tie. Should we offer God any less?"

"And so would I," I responded. "But there are those who would feel no need whatsoever to dress up if they met the president today." He looked at me quizzically. "His children. The president wouldn't want them to dress up because he's their father and no formality is needed."

Sons and daughters need no pretense in Father's presence. He invites us to enjoy him, not impress him.

But this question bothers me in another way. Its hidden premise is that God is somehow more present at a gathering of believers than he is when we take a shower in the morning or when we're hot and sweaty from a hard day's work. And he's not, you know?

> *Is there any place I can go to avoid your Spirit? To be out of your sight? If I climb to the sky, you're there! If I go underground, you're there! If I flew on morning's wings to the far western horizon, you'd find me in a minute—you're already there waiting!*
>
> PSALM 139:10–12 (MSG)

JAN 29 — Simple Love

In my travels, I met a couple who had moved to America sixteen years before, but after meeting Jesus, they felt like they should return to Japan to witness to people. As they expressed it, "Our old ideology was we had to do something significant, to be a part of something for God," and felt guilty that they weren't.

Shortly after my trip I got an email from them about the work God had done in their heart in the interim.

> *"He showed us that my family and I haven't had the close relationship with God that we once had. We all felt we had to pay God back for what he had done and in trying to do that we missed the most important thing— God simply loves us."*

> *"I am significant; you are significant; every person is significant to God. When we discovered that, we couldn't hold our tears back."*

If you are feeling pressure to pay God back, let it go. You don't have to do something great for God in return. Let love lead you, and you will find that he may take you to the ends of the earth, but not for payback; simply because he's invited you to go with him.

But because of his great love for us, God, who is rich in mercy, made us alive with Christ even when we were dead in transgressions—it is by grace you have been saved.
EPHESIANS 2:4 (NIV)

JAN 30 Just a Phone Call

Guilt hung over her for years, like thick fog. She had come to the United States for an education. When she left home, her grandfather had offered to help her with tuition but she was supposed to return and get a job to repay him.

Her life took a different turn. She got married, stayed in the United States, and for a long time was not able to work due to immigration issues. She hadn't kept her promise and whenever her mother needed a dig, she would needle her daughter about it.

After years of embarrassment and avoiding her grandfather, she finally called to apologize for not keeping her promise. He simply responded, "That's okay, honey." He had let it go a long time before and was more concerned with her visiting him than paying him back. He even offered to pay for her trip home.

"The reconciliation was sweet," she said when she wrote me.

Can you imagine all the years of lost relationship simply for the lack of a phone call? Sometimes all it takes is a phone call to shine the light of God's healing into the most troubling of circumstances and disarm the attempts of the enemy to drive people further apart and deeper into their own darkness.

Not only can it promote healing with those we've cut out of our lives, but it will reveal some wonderful insights about Father's love for us. I hope her story can encourage you to see what God might do with some of your broken relationships.

> *If it is possible, as far as it depends on you,*
> *live at peace with everyone.*
> **ROMANS 12:18 (NIV)**

JAN 31 Living Loved

The joy of this journey comes not in convincing ourselves that God loves us but in actually learning to live as one of his beloved children!

And as you grow to know him, you'll realize that he is not a "warm fuzzy" grandpa in the sky. He is the transcendent, holy, all-powerful God of the universe who has offered to be my Abba, the most affectionate term that a first-century toddler would call his or her dad. Yes, his affection is outrageous.

But that affection also seeks to win me into increasing arenas of light so that I can be transformed by truth, not just coddled in my deceptions, lies, and broken coping mechanisms. That's why I rarely use the term "unconditional love"—not because I think God's love has conditions, but because the reference is so static. God's affection is transformational, allowing me to know him while also changing the core of my being.

The invitation to live loved is not to buy into a new doctrine but to embrace a new way of living. I can increasingly live inside the Father's affection instead of all the fears, anxieties, and ambitions of my flesh. And so can you! It is both joy and freedom of the highest order.

It is not something you turn on or off in a moment; it is a lifetime journey of being shaped a bit more every day as you learn to be at home in his love. Don't just believe in his love, live loved! Ask him to help you because this is way above what any of us can produce on our own.

> *We have come to know and have believed
> the love which God has for us.*
> **1 JOHN 4:16 (NAS)**

FEB 1 — Knows Me Best, Loves Me Most

Most people live with the fear that if people really knew what was inside them, they wouldn't have any friends. An old chorus I sang as a child ended with a different sentiment—the one who knows us best loves us most.

He who knows every doubt I have, every failure I've made, every temptation I struggle with, and every side-tracked journey I've fallen into, loves me more than anyone else ever has. He doesn't define me by my weaknesses but sees me as the person he created me to be when I live in the freedom of his love.

That's not always true of other people, which is why we hide our pain and spend a lot of effort pretending to be better than we are. But, there's really no need to with God. He does know you best, and he does love you most.

> *You have searched me, Lord, and you know me.*
> *You know when I sit and when I rise;*
> *you perceive my thoughts from afar.*
> PSALM 139:1–2 (MSG)

FEB 2 — The Authentic Life

The world teaches us that in order to be liked we have to pretend to be someone we aren't. We have to fit into people's expectations or risk their rejection, which is why we walk away from so many conversations regretting things we said or didn't say because of what others might think of us. We're convinced that people will only like us when they don't really know us.

If we really knew that the one who knows us best loves us most, we'd be free to be ourselves around others. As with our Father, true fellowship only begins where people are free to be authentic, not when they pretend to be someone they think others want them to be. We no longer have to project an image and can let others in on our weaknesses and struggles.

Of course, with people there is always risk in that. Some may not like us, but real friends will. We will find our relationships deepening with them because we're not having to pretend any more.

Our security in Father's love opens the door for us to live simply and honestly before others, and that will do more than you can ever imagine in helping you taste of the kind of friendships God wants us all to know.

An honest answer is like a warm hug.
PROVERBS 24:26 (MSG)

FEB 3 — Mistaken about Love

"Simon, do you love me?" The betrayed turns face to face with his betrayer.

"Yes, Lord; you know that I love you." Peter's response is not flippant—it is measured. He doesn't respond with the word for divine love, *agape*, that Jesus had used, but with a lesser word, *phileo*, used for the companionship of friends. Jesus then tells him to tend his lambs.

Jesus asks again and again Peter answers the same way. Finally, Jesus asks one more time but ends with Peter's word: "Peter do you like me as a friend." *Phileo*.

And now Peter, grieved at the third question, answers in agony, "Lord, you know all things. You know that I like you."

What a difficult conversation this had to be. Peter wasn't ready to say that he deeply loved his friend, even though he did. He mistakenly thought his failure a few days before proved otherwise and I suspect he was trying to be honest about that.

Fortunately, he would soon discover that it didn't.

This is love: not that we loved God, but that he loved us and sent his Son as an atoning sacrifice for our sins.
1 JOHN 4:10 (NIV)

FEB 4 — Beyond Failure

Peter, so confident that night that his love would prevail, boasted that he would die for his friend. But

Jesus knew better. He knew the fear in Peter would overwhelm his faith and that by the next dawn Peter would be devastated by his greatest failure.

But if the cross was going to be worth anything, it would have to demonstrate God's love so completely that it could usher a man from his worst failure into the fullness of the Father's love.

Jesus wanted him to know that his failure was not a measure of his love. Perhaps Peter didn't understand it completely. Perhaps this was just the seed, or maybe he couldn't grasp it until the fullness of the Spirit captured his heart at Pentecost, but we know he eventually got it.

Whenever he refers to the love of God in his own epistles, *phileo* is no longer on his lips. It is *agape* and *agape* alone. Peter came to know not only the depth of God's love for him, but also his love for God.

Though you have not seen him, you love him; and even though you do not see him now, you believe in him and are filled with an inexpressible and glorious joy.

I PETER 1:8 (MSG)

FEB 5 Looking for Love

Our Father is a God of love. It was love that invited men from fishing boats and tax booths into an awesome friendship. It was love that devised a plan for our salvation for which he would be the sacrifice. And it was love that held him through the brutal agony of the cross until our redemption was won.

His love prevailed through it all. Was this the final test of the cross—not just that God loved us, but that the sacrifice itself might produce love in our hearts for him?

I think so, for this was what God wanted with us from the very beginning and he has done so much to win us into that realty.

> *Give thanks to the Lord, for he is good.*
> *His love endures forever.*
>
> **PSALM 136:1 (NIV)**

FEB 6 — Live the Love

Love is the very essence of God's nature, and it is the means by which everything in his kingdom is transacted. He knew we are ill-equipped to understand that. Life in a fallen world is based around power, not love. We live by seeking to acquire the power or means necessary to guarantee our own survival, happiness, or safety. We primarily understand love only in terms of what we get out of it—a good feeling, a friendship, or some other need.

God's love is self-giving. It doesn't seek its own glory or advancement, and in fact makes one only more vulnerable in a hostile world. But this love is the most powerful force in the entire world, able to transform the most broken lives and able to carry us through unimaginable pain.

Jesus lived in that love every second of his life, and in doing so he sought to share it with his disciples. All he asked them to do was stay in the love he had given them. If they did that, everything about their lives would bear fruit, but he warned them that if they wandered away, they would whither up and die.

His call to love was not just for them, but also for all who follow him. That is the only basis for life in this kingdom.

> *As the Father has loved me, so have I loved you.*
> *Now remain in my love.*
>
> **JOHN 15:5 (NIV)**

FEB 7 — Helping Others See His Love

You already have his affection! The great lie in the universe is that you are not loved by the Creator.

If you don't realize how deeply loved you are, that's where the journey begins. He wants to show you and, in the process, untwist all that has distorted or blinded your perception of his love.

I am meeting more people on this journey who are learning to live loved and who also have a heart to help others live there as well. How can they help others if they don't hold a position, write a book, or speak at conferences?

Surely, the best way to equip people is by being an example to them when you're not even trying to be. Your life can make them hungry for the same experience. Where they want your help, just share with them what God has taught you. Help them recognize God's fingerprints in their own story and pray with them that the eyes of the heart will be opened to see the Father's love.

You can instruct people without putting it into a lecture or reducing it to a set of principles. This is an adventure, where God is the lead character and you are just pointing out the ways in which he works. The most important kind of teaching, more so than ever comes from a pulpit, happens in a conversation around a table.

That's why Jesus said he needed far more workers to help people embrace the reality of living loved. People need to see it as well as hear about it.

Then he said to his disciples, "The harvest is plentiful but the workers are few. Ask the Lord of the harvest, therefore, to send out workers into his harvest field."

MATTHEW 9:37–38 (NIV)

FEB 8 — I Had No Idea!

It's amazing how long we can miss God's reality in the midst of all the hard work we are doing for him. I received this email recently from someone who had just come to that realization.

> I went out to eat with some friends tonight and they were talking about a recent message they'd heard about Christ on the cross with the two thieves and how we destroy our lives through sin. One repents; one does not.
>
> But…tonight as we shared that story, I saw something incredibly awesome for the first time. I saw two men hanging next to Jesus that He loved with every bit of his being and one of them knew it and the other did not! I am telling you my eyes are seeing more and more clearly.
>
> I had no idea. After thirty-two years of trying to love Jesus with everything I had in me, I am beginning to get sight of what lies ahead! He already loves us. There are no words to describe it!!!

No, there aren't.

You would think the one thing thirty-two years of living hard for Jesus would produce would be a security in his affection. It can't. Religious performance makes us busy trying to earn his love. We keep falling short, so we have to work harder and we only end up exhausted. We miss who he really is.

When you realize you already have his affection, you can wake up each day at rest in him. Then, you'll be ready to follow him not because you have to, but because you get to.

> *When they came to the place called the Skull, they crucified him there, along with the criminals—one on his right, the other on his left. Jesus said, "Father, forgive them, for they do not know what they are doing."*
>
> LUKE 23:33–34 (NIV)

FEB 9 — The Fruitfulness Trust Produces

Somehow religion gives us the mistaken idea that there are some people—those who work hard to please him—whom he really loves. Those who don't, he hates.

But that isn't true. He loves all of us! The question is whether we'll embrace that reality or deny it to our own destruction.

And don't try to tell me that those motivated by the fears of religion do more for God than those who rest secure in his love. I know better than that. Those who respond to the fears of religion may be caught up in a frenzy of activity they think is for him, but in the long run it is only for their own self and their personal hope of earning what he has already given. While I will always acknowledge his graciousness to use even our misguided efforts for his glory, they can also waste a lot of time and resources while hurting others in the process.

The people I see who do the most for his kingdom are those who live each day in the security of his affection. They do what he puts on their heart *with* him, instead of trying to do a bunch of stuff *for* him.

If it takes two days, ten years—or even thirty-two, I pray you come to know just how loved you are and learn the fruitfulness that comes from growing trust in his love.

> *I do not set aside the grace of God, for if righteousness could be gained through the law, Christ died for nothing.*
>
> GALATIANS 2:21 (NIV)

FEB 10 — Where Transformation Begins

"Living loved" puts the focus where it belongs—on how it shapes the way we live.

Letting God teach us how to live inside of his affection may be the most difficult lesson any of us will learn: our flesh wants to earn it. Religion constantly challenges that reality by putting us on a performance treadmill so we think we can only trust God's love when we've done enough to earn it.

That's why it is easier for many of us to believe that God is disappointed in us, or even ashamed of us, because of our failures and misguided priorities. We think the more righteous we can be the more of his love we can have.

Who has ever done enough to earn his good graces? Being righteous won't earn you more of his love. The reality is he already loves you. That doesn't change—whether you believe it or not makes all the difference for you. The more you live in his love, the more righteousness you'll experience.

Living loved is not the reward of a well lived journey; it's the trailhead. It's where transformation begins!

> *Therefore, as God's chosen people, holy and dearly loved,*
> *clothe yourselves with compassion, kindness,*
> *humility, gentleness and patience.*
> **COLOSSIANS 3:12 (NIV)**

FEB 11 — L-Cubed

I enjoy hearing how God weaves people and their experiences together to invite them into his love. I got this one morning from a lady in Arkansas.

> *My idolatry was my Bible, the church, certain leadership, and my deepest wanting to be "used" in any capac-*

ity by God for His kingdom. All the while, believing if it's less of me and more of Him, I am successfully positioning myself for His plan. So why, then, was it not working?

Unfortunately, I was living within a duplicitous belief system. On one side I was living in "faith" that God would provide in all areas. The other side, I was focused on what "I had to do" to stay in His grace, mercy, and promises.

And in what can only be called an amazing whirlwind of life, my once unseen shackles to religion, religiosity, and all things idol were cast off. I didn't spend hours, days, or weeks fasting or repenting to have this revelation. I didn't have to tithe or abruptly alter my lifestyle. I didn't have to be miserable or homeless. I simply became open to a Life Lived Loved.

Hence, I have used your expression of a life lived loved—or "L-Cubed"—for nearly every conversation I have had since. It is a wondrous moment to behold when Father takes such a simple line and moves mountains right in front of you.

That it is. I hope his journey encourages your own. L-Cubed: Life Lived Loved! It is why Jesus died, so you would know that and relax into its reality.

But now he has reconciled you by Christ's physical body through death to present you holy in his sight, without blemish and free from accusation—if you continue in your faith, established and firm, and do not move from the hope held out in the gospel.

COLOSSIANS 1:22–23 (NIV)

FEB 12 Loved

I met this man and his wife last month. He is a relatively new believer, but incredibly passionate for the life of God. Here's a bit of his story.

> Why is it still amazing to us when the simplest of messages become the most profound? There are no deep philosophical or theological debates needed. No perpetual diatribe on the whys and hows of God sending his Son to take care of my sinful self. Instead, there is only the love, peace, and power that only Father in heaven can manifest in and through His children.
>
> What I have come to understand is that I can break away completely from the standards of measurement both Christians and the lost have come to rely on so heavily and simply focus on a journey that has no specific outcome or finish line while I am in this body.
>
> That consumes any need to be right or in control, especially with my wife. I recently shared with a group of men that the greatest assessment a husband can share is this: "My wife is growing in and with her Father—joyfully!" What is in place in me so that this can take place signifies a freedom in Christ.

I love the way God opens eyes and invites us further in.

> *And now these three remain: faith, hope and love.*
> *But the greatest of these is love.*
>
> **1 CORINTHIANS 13:13 (NIV)**

FEB 13 — The Standards of Love

I was in an internet exchange the other day where I was asked, "Do we meet God's standards of love? If not, what can we do to improve?"

The question doesn't even make sense to me anymore. It used to, when I thought of love as a command whose expectations I had to meet. Then, I had to consider if I was doing enough to love others. Trying to do that, however, was exhausting and unworkable.

At the end of the day, I wasn't really loving people; I was only pretending to love them. Now I see love as a reality God invites me to live in with him. He *is* love; if we respond to his love, we'll find ourselves loving as he does.

Otherwise, we're just reduced to actors trying to follow a script. God invites us into a relationship of love that would transform us from the inside out. As I grow to know him, I will find increasing love in my heart for others.

I don't have to conjure it up. I don't have to pretend to have it. When it's there I can live out of that love. When it's not, I go to him, sit at his feet, and ask him to teach me more of his love.

"Father, win more of my heart into your love, so that I can love others the way you love me."

If I speak in the tongues of men or of angels, but do not have love, I am only a resounding gong or a clanging cymbal.
1 CORINTHIANS 13:1 (NIV)

FEB 14 — Love As a Journey

As I relax into the reality of his love for me, I find love in my heart for others, even when they are being spiteful toward me.

Love is now a journey for me. It begins inside my

relationship with him, and he invites me into its flow. Little by little, one day at a time, I get to see how his reality begins to shape mine. When I am at rest in his ability to love through me, my heart is at peace. It's amazing how I see relationships around me differently.

When I don't embrace that reality, I get worn out, self-focused, and anxious. As I sit here today, I see the ocean of God's love as the world's greatest resort, and there is no better place to live. That doesn't require one thing of me, except that I grow in my awareness of his love. That will change everything in me that he desires.

I have come to want nothing else. No other trinket or ambition in this world compares to the joy of living loved. But be prepared: the learning curve can be fairly steep for those of us who lived most of our lives as if we weren't loved.

But the fruit of the Spirit is love, joy, peace, forbearance, kindness, goodness, faithfulness, gentleness and self-control... Since we live by the Spirit, let us keep in step with the Spirit.
GALATIANS 5:22–25 (NIV)

FEB 15 — You're in Safe and Certain Hands

She was only a few months old when Aimee, my new granddaughter, came over with her parents one Sunday. I got to feed her from a bottle and then she fell asleep on my shoulder for two and a half hours while I watched a Green Bay football game. What a special time! My heart was so filled with joy just to be near Aimee and watch her breathe, smirk, and rest. She had one hand on my chest and the other around my side.

She's pretty helpless, you know. She really can't do a thing for herself and must depend on those around her to take care of her.

Jesus encouraged us to the same kind of relationship with his Father. "Unless you become like a little child…"

You don't need to be anxious for anything because he will take care of you. Wouldn't it be great to trust that?

> *What I'm trying to do here is to get you to relax, to not be so preoccupied with getting, so you can respond to God's giving.*
> MATTHEW 6:31 (MSG)

FEB 16 You Are His Delight

I was reading Song of Songs a few weeks ago. I wondered if the bridegroom's delight over his lover is like Jesus's delight in his Church. I know how I feel when I've been gone from Sara for a few days—the ache in my heart just to be near her again and hold her in my arms. Could this be how God feels about me?

I've concluded that what it means to come to be his delight is that God feels for me similarly to what I feel for Sara. His, however, is a billion times greater than mine. He is God and, after all, he has more love in his heart than I can possibly fathom.

And if I really knew he delighted in me like that, wouldn't it be so much easier to rest in his certain arms, even in the places where I'm most broken and helpless?

I am at my best when I am at rest in his love, and less so when I'm anxious about how he feels about me. If you only knew he looked at you with delight, how much would that change how you go through this day?

> *You've captured my heart, dear friend. You looked at me, and I fell in love. One look my way and I was hopelessly in love!*
> SONG OF SOLOMON 4:8–15 (MSG)

FEB 17 — When Grace Gives Way to Hope

Several years ago, I was in San Francisco helping my eighty-three-year-old father go through a critical surgery. It was a two-week ordeal to correct a previously botched surgery.

The second surgery was an arduous and tenuous procedure demanding a top-notch specialist, which is why they had moved him to San Francisco. He came out of it as well as the doctors had hoped but having had two major surgeries in the last two weeks took an obvious toll on his body.

I love the way God slips in little things even at a time like this to let people know he's around. One night the nurse came in to introduce herself. "I am Grace," she said, "and I'll be with you through the night." That was pretty cool. Maybe all nurses should be named Grace, especially those who follow a major surgery.

The next morning a new nurse took over. "My name is Hope and I'll be taking over from Grace today." It made me smile and reminded me of the grace and hope God pours into my life every day.

May our Lord Jesus Christ himself and God our Father, who loved us and by his grace gave us eternal encouragement and good hope, encourage your hearts and strengthen you in every good deed and word.

2 THESSALONIANS 2:16–17 (NIV)

FEB 18 — And Hope Gives Way to More Grace

Later the next afternoon, Hope came in and informed my dad, "Grace will be taking over again tonight."

Even through the pain of his recovery, he smiled.

Incredible! Surrounded by Grace and Hope right around the clock!

We all are, you know. It just usually isn't so obvious. But it would be my prayer for you that you would find expressions of God's hope and grace in whatever challenges you face today.

He's there, you know, as certain as the sun rises!

And who knows? Maybe Joy will come in the morning.

And God raised us up with Christ and seated us with him in the heavenly realms in Christ Jesus, in order that in the coming ages he might show the incomparable riches of his grace, expressed in his kindness to us in Christ Jesus.

EPHESIANS 2:6–7(NIV)

FEB 19 And We Beheld His Glory!

God became part of his own creation in the form of a human being to show us exactly who he is and how he feels about us. He took on the helplessness, vulnerability, and limitations of human flesh so that he could experience life just as we do, from infancy through adulthood to his tragic but glorious death on a cross.

Isn't that the most awesome miracle?

He was here! In flesh and blood, experiencing the same sorrows, stresses, joys, and affections! Through the eyes of those who knew him best, we get to read all about him in the Gospel accounts. He faced every temptation we face and endured the vitriol of those who opposed him. He showed us that he could overcome anything along with the Father who walked with him.

The miracle didn't end there. By his death and resurrection, he opened a door whereby he could come and live in us, so we would have his comfort and help in any circumstance we face.

*The Word became flesh and made his dwelling among us.
We have seen his glory, the glory of the one and only Son,
who came from the Father, full of grace and truth.*

JOHN 1:14 (NIV)

FEB 20 — The Word Made Flesh

The Word of God entered the Creation, just like all the rest of us, as an infant. As he grew in stature, he grew in wisdom to understand his Father and his purpose in the world.

Though Jesus ascended to the Father after his resurrection, the Word of God still lives in the world—through us. He is no less present with us or in us today than he was around a fire on the shore of Galilee or at Lazarus's home in Bethany. In you, he continues to experience all the joys and pains of humanity navigating a broken world. And, through you, he can demonstrate the love and life of the Father in whatever situation you find yourself. Ask him to show you how you can reflect his glory today.

What a miracle. Today, in you the Word wants to become flesh yet again. Christianity is not primarily a theology, a ritual or an ethic. It's a way of life—us in him, him in us!

*On that day you will realize that I am in my Father,
and you are in me, and I am in you.*

JOHN 14:20 (NIV)

FEB 21 — Transformation Flows Out of Love

For too long religious tradition has used the fear of God's punishment to terrify people to live according to what they say are God's rules. That's why religion has to paint God like an angry ruler, demanding conformity or doling out consequences to the disobedient. Yet, we have thousands of years of history to prove that fear doesn't work for lasting change.

Even though we talk about God loving us, most believers grow up as unloved children, trying hard to perform the way they think God wants them to. What amazes me so much about the Gospels is that Jesus talks about a Father who loves us and who invites us into his house so that he can transform us.

This transformation only happens when people are secure in their Father's affection for them. I think this is the biggest battle that must be won in our hearts to experience the life of Jesus. We have to stop living to appease him and live as the beloved children we are. Nothing will transform us faster or more deeply.

With the Incarnation, God was putting all his eggs in one basket: to win by love and affection what fear never could.

> "A new command I give you: Love one another. As I have loved you, so you must love one another. By this everyone will know that you are my disciples, if you love one another."
> JOHN 13:34–35 (NIV)

Secure in Father's Affection

Because we don't know how to live as his beloved children, we have no idea how to relate to our brothers and sisters. Often we act like competitors—we tear each other down to feel better about ourselves or we try to get to the top of the authority pyramid so we can lord over others. Beloved children don't live that way. They don't need to.

In living loved, we love in return and experience the fullness of New Testament community without the need for rules and rituals. That's why I am convinced that getting our relationship right with God is far more important than finding a right way to do church.

For Christ's love compels us, because we are convinced that one died for all, and therefore all died. And he died for all, that those who live should no longer live for themselves but for him who died for them and was raised again.

2 CORINTHIANS 5:14-15 (NIV)

SECTION 2
Embracing His Freedom

FEB 23 Mad, Sad, or Overjoyed!

"I've heard that there are two kinds of Christians in the world," the young woman said, perched on the couch of a home I visited recently. "Christians who either see God as mad or who see him as sad." On a normal day, that would have sounded fine to me. Either he is mad at our sin and wants to blast the world into oblivion, or he is sad about our sin and hopes to rescue us. Of those two, I'd choose the latter.

But as God would work things out, earlier in the day I'd had breakfast with a group of men and one of them said that he began his spiritual journey when he'd heard someone say that God is the most joyful presence in the universe.

So, when I heard the young woman claim that God was either sad or mad, I was already alert to a third alternative—he could be filled with joy.

Mad or sad still focuses on us and our sin. Isn't it interesting that we are taught to view God through our sin, rather than beyond our sin? Instead of celebrating the essential nature of God at work in a broken world to rescue us, we're left to sulk in the brokenness and failures of this temporal age.

Instead, I have called you friends, for everything that I learned from my Father I have made known to you.

JOHN 15:15 (NIV)

FEB 24 — To Make Our Joy Full

The night before he died, Jesus told his disciples that everything he had said to them was so their joy would be full. This is his passion: to see us find the same joy in the Father that he knows.

When Jesus said that, he was only hours away from his trial and crucifixion. He said it despite the fact that his countrymen lived under the repression of Roman rule. He said it in the face of a world still devastated by sin, disease, war, and great pain. He said it knowing his closest friends would desert him that night.

And yet, he showed us that God's prevailing thought over Creation is not anger or sorrow. He is the most joyful presence above it and inside of it. Everything he does is for one purpose: to give that joy back to his creation.

This is the joy he wants you to have—a joy that consumes any pain, trial, failure, or struggle we might be in at the moment. It is a joy deeply based on the pleasure of God, his desire for us, and his unfolding purpose in the world. He invites us to live in that space with him and let it prevail over the temporal pain and grief of the world we live in.

Paul called them "momentary, light afflictions"

producing in us an "eternal weight of glory." This was the apostle who'd been stoned several times, shipwrecked three times, robbed on his journeys, and lied about by close friends. Obviously, he was focused on something far greater and far grander than his immediate circumstances.

The joy Jesus spoke about is not temporal and thus does not swing with the fickle tides of circumstance. This joy goes deeply into his own character and purpose unfolding in this broken world. That's where I want to live—every day, in every situation.

> *I've told you these things for a purpose: that my joy might be your joy, and your joy wholly mature.*
> **JOHN 15:12 (MSG)**

FEB 25 — Every Day, Every Moment

There was never a moment in the last seven days of your life when Jesus wasn't present with you—fully aware of everything you were doing.

Think about that for a moment and ask yourself whether you see that as good news, or bad news?

For most of my spiritual life that kind of thinking was a bit disconcerting to me. The very thought of him seeing everything filled me with guilt at every lapse of good judgment. The thought of him seeing all my failures and indulgences was not reassuring.

What's more, when I thought of him being present with me, I felt badly about how little I'd been aware of him. Even the good things I'd attempted were the result of my best wisdom, not necessarily his leading. Eventually they would collapse under the weight of the human wisdom they were built on and I'd feel like a knucklehead.

The fact that he is always with us is not something we need to fear—but celebrate. He is with us not to condemn us, but to rescue us from all the places we get lost.

For God did not send his Son into the world to condemn the world, but to save the world through him.

JOHN 3:17 (NIV)

EB 26 The Richest Treasure

The words of that perennial Sunday school song would replay in my head: "Oh, be careful little eyes what you see, for the Father up above is looking down in love."

I know it's a fun song for kids to sing as they get to point to various body parts, but it makes a horrible connection between God's love and an image of him as the divine cop shaking his finger at us whenever we falter or fail. This is certainly not the image of his Father that Jesus passed on to his followers.

Jesus's presence with us is not meant to police, condemn, or harass. It is, rather, to lead us into the fullness of the Father's life. Growing in our awareness of and dependence on him as our greatest joy is the richest treasure of the Christian life.

You know everything I'm going to say before I start the first sentence. I look behind me and you're there, then up ahead and you're there, too—your reassuring presence, coming and going. This is too much, too wonderful—I can't take it all in!

PSALM 139:3-6 (MSG)

EB 27 He Lives!

It is easy to celebrate the fact of the resurrection and miss the most important implication of the fact that

Jesus *is* alive. He is right here with you today, wherever you are reading these words.

All his friendship, wisdom, strength, and love are available to you inside that relationship. As you come alive to his presence and learn to settle in on how he makes himself known to you, you'll find that you're not alone in anything. No matter what happens around you, he has a way to navigate you through it and come out more like him.

He didn't come to start a new religion but to invite us to participate in the relationship that Father, Son, and Spirit have shared for all eternity.

It's one of the most incredible offers ever made and, yes, it does take some time to learn how to live inside of him. It's not natural for us, but it is so incredibly wonderful!

> *Before long, the world will not see me anymore,*
> *but you will see me. Because I live, you also will live.*
> **JOHN 14:19 (NIV)**

FEB 28 — A Relational Reality!

If we are going to be God's people on earth, we not only need to embrace the theological fact of the resurrection but the relational reality of it as well. He is alive—no longer just with his followers, but in them.

Many act as if he isn't, except in abstract terms. They do the best they can to read, interpret, and follow the principles they derive from Scripture. But that will only take you so far. As powerful as Scripture is to keep our hearts on track with his, it is no substitute for Jesus living in us. He wants to be a voice that guides us, the strength that gives us courage to follow, and the wisdom to help us navigate whatever circumstances we meet.

The risen Christ wants to take shape in you. Think of that! What could describe our life in him any better? Not only is it a joyful hope, but it also reminds us how incapable we are of producing that by our own power or ingenuity.

> *...until Christ's life becomes visible in your lives...*
> GALATIANS 4:19 (MSG)

MAR 1 — He Is Still with Us

Among the last instructions Jesus left his followers were to remain in him, and to love one another. He didn't want them to mistake his teaching as an ethic to be observed or a set of traditions to follow.

They had been with him for at least three years. They had seen him in all kinds of circumstances, from being overwhelmed with crowds to seeking out his Father in the quiet place. They had watched him heal the sick, endure the hostility of religious leaders, and pour himself out on behalf of the world's outcasts.

They had seen the impish look in his eyes and felt the weight of his sorrows. They were insiders and he wanted that to continue even after he was no longer visible to them in their realm.

He knew it wouldn't be easy. How do we stay aware of that which we cannot see in a world that seeks to distract us every day? We all know how easy it is to live significant chunks of our lives without even thinking of Jesus being with us, much less hearing his voice direct us, or seeing his power equip us.

And yet, the offer is still there. Take some time daily to close your physical eyes and let your body come to rest. Gaze on him with the eyes of your heart. He will show you how, if you ask him and are patient enough to learn.

My sheep listen to my voice; I know them, and they follow me…
JOHN 10:27 (NIV)

MAR 2 — Ethics Are Not Enough

How do we develop a relationship with someone we cannot see?

We have too clear a picture of what it means to be a good Christian today. It means going to church, reading our Bibles, trying to live moral lives, and sharing the gospel with others. We know what we should do, think, or say in any situation, and yet, we can't always bring ourselves to do so.

It is easier to chase expectations than it is to cultivate a meaningful relationship with him. The sad truth is most of us have had far more training in religion than we have had in relationship.

It's time to change that, don't you think? There's no way we can live in his ways without actually walking with him.

To do that we'll have to look beyond our principles and rules and learn how to see him and let him live his life through us.

Remain in me, as I also remain in you. No branch can bear fruit by itself; it must remain in the vine. Neither can you bear fruit unless you remain in me.
JOHN 15:4 (NIV)

MAR 3 — "Remain in Me"

How do I rest in the security of Father's love, even though I still fall short of my own expectations?

How can I cultivate an awareness of his presence with

me all the time, and not just when I'm afraid or in need?

How do I identify Jesus's voice when he speaks and how can I know what he's doing in my life through the circumstance I'm caught in?

How can I really draw on his power and not just give it my best effort?

Those are relational questions. This is what every new convert should learn in their first five years of deciding to be a follower of Christ.

We shouldn't hasten them on to get them to look and act more Christian so quickly. We'd do them a great favor by urging them to learn how to live out a real friendship with Jesus every day of their lives. If we did that, everything else that needed to happen in their lives would happen—they would grow increasingly free of sin, they would bear God's fruit before the world, they would love others, and they would see God answer their prayers.

Without that relationship, Jesus warned us, we would not be able to do anything that would be fruitful for his work in us or those around us.

> *If you remain in me and my words remain in you,*
> *ask whatever you wish, and it will be done for you.*
> *This is to my Father's glory, that you bear much fruit,*
> *showing yourselves to be my disciples.*
>
> JOHN 15:7–8 (NIV)

MAR 4 — How Do I Do That?

Building a relationship with Jesus—where you quiet your heart and let him teach you how to be aware of his presence and how he is making himself known to you—takes time. For me, this works best when my heart is open and pliable to whatever his will or purpose might be, especially when I can't see it.

Read all the books you want—you won't find that in any of them. You can't learn this in seminars but only as you focus on him.

He modeled what that would look like with the disciples. It's a friendship. The disciples walked with him every day. They knew his laughter and rebukes, argued with him and listened to his wisdom, called to him in their fears, and shook their heads when his words confused them.

They grew to know God as a friend, and what a friend he was too—the transcendent God of the universe!

Jesus wants no less for you. He can take you right where you are and lead you into that friendship that can fill every day with his presence.

> *This time I'm writing out the plan in them,*
> *carving it on the lining of their hearts.*
> *I'll be their God; they'll be my people.*
>
> **HEBREWS 13:10 (MSG)**

MAR 5 — Be Honest with Him

One of the best ways to grow your relationship with Jesus is to be honest with him about your struggles to know him as a friend. For the transcendent Creator of the universe to connect with humanity is an amazing reality and we shouldn't expect it to be an easy one to make from our side.

He's doing everything he can from his end, but the distractions of the flesh and the illusions we live by make it hard to see him. So, yes, it can be frustrating in the early days of learning if you're in a hurry.

Tell him the hungers on your heart and the disappointments of past attempts. Ask him to teach you to know him better and to recognize him through the normal course of daily life.

His presence is not something we experience only in Bible studies and worship services. He wants to be no less real in all the other places we inhabit the rest of the week—offices, houses, schools, cars, airplanes, and fields.

> ...anyone who comes to him must believe that he exists
> and that he rewards those who earnestly seek him.
> HEBREWS 11:6

MAR 6 He's Really Good at This

If you'll just pause even a few seconds throughout your day and recognize that Jesus is speaking to you all the time, you'll find yourself engaging in a conversation with him that will run through the course of your life. He will show you things you would easily miss and teach you how to love people around you like he loves you.

He can teach you how to do that better than anyone else. He has been building friendships with people since the world began and he is wonderfully good at it. It may be a struggle at times but cultivating that relationship is the gift that keeps on giving.

Now I realize that there is not one moment of my life that Jesus is not there, completely aware of everything going on around me and at work to lead me to the fullness of his Father's life. Even where I stumble, I have no pangs of shame, because only he can change me and he is well on the way to doing that!

> I'm an open book to you; even from a distance, you know what
> I'm thinking. You know when I leave and when I get back;
> I'm never out of your sight...
> PSALM 139:2–3 (MSG)

MAR 7 — He Enjoys the Process

After I taught about how Father extends his grace to us while he reshapes our lives, a friend shared something he had just discovered: "I think I finally understood something today. I had thought that God was only pleased by my perfection. Since I never measured up to that, I have always struggled. But I am beginning to think he not only wants me to be whole, but that he actually enjoys the process of getting me there."

What else explains why Father just doesn't wave his arms over us and make us all perfect overnight? He wants us to reflect his glory from the inside out. He patiently shapes our lives until Christ is fully formed in us. Like a potter spinning a new pot, he's not just excited about getting it done, but he actually enjoys the whole process—softening the clay, kneading it in his hands, and fashioning it with great care.

If we think he is satisfied only when we get it all together, I'm afraid our lives will be filled with frustration for both others and ourselves! But if he enjoys the process, shouldn't we also? He is fashioning you so that Jesus can take shape in you. Can you see how he's doing that? If we can enjoy the process of him allowing Jesus to take shape in us, then we can be more patient with our still-glaring deficiencies.

> *Yet you, LORD, are our Father. We are the clay, you are the potter; we are all the work of your hand.*
>
> **ISAIAH 64:8 (NIV)**

MAR 8 — We Can Only Imagine

I can't begin to comprehend what it would be like to wake up tomorrow morning and find myself free of everything that hinders or distracts me from life in Jesus.

Can you imagine no longer having to grope through the fog of your own selfishness to get a fading glimpse of God's presence?

Can you imagine no longer entertaining, even for the briefest moment, doubts about his love for you or his ability to draw you into the fullness of his life?

And, can you imagine no longer having the ravages of fleshly appetites that lure you into bondage that can suffocate you in your own amusements?

You would have nothing to hide, nothing to prove, and nothing to gain, because you would be so fully satisfied by God himself and totally at rest in whatever he gives. What would it be like to have no needs to harass you, no conflict to afflict you, no pain or disease to limit you, and no sorrow to wound you?

You would see God's face as clearly as he sees yours.

That's the journey I'm on. It becomes increasingly real with each passing day in this life and will one day be the only reality in the age to come.

Let us then approach God's throne of grace with confidence...
HEBREWS 4:16 (NIV)

MAR 9 — A World without Restraint

What a day that will be when every appetite for sin falls suddenly silent and all I want is what God wants for me! How would it be to live without a hint of fear, self-pity, or envy because the demands of my fleshy self have been swallowed up in the greatness of God?

Then, I would enjoy unrestricted insights into the beauty of God's nature and the wonder of his person. I could finally search out just how high and wide and deep his love runs for me and enjoy forever his infinite creativity and his boundless wisdom. What a life that would be!

Of course, no one reading these words has any idea what that would be like. But each day we can taste a bit more of that reality. The day of its fullness is fast approaching for all of us and it is closer now than when you began to read these words.

It is what God made you for and what he draws you toward with unrelenting grace.

> *Now that we have actually received this amazing friendship with God, we are no longer content to simply say it in plodding prose. We sing and shout our praises to God through Jesus, the Messiah!*
> **ROMANS 5:10–11 (MSG)**

MAR 10 — Beyond Death's Door

This world spares no expense to try and convince us that this is all there is. It beckons us to seek fulfillment in this age, as if it were designed to provide it. The truth is, however, it will never provide what our hearts long for most. Thinking it can will send us down a path of continued frustration and will make you doubt God's intentions toward you when things you want most don't work out as you think they should.

Life in this age is a mixed bag. At times we see the magnificence of God's glory in Creation and experience marvelous and refreshing moments of his blessings. At other times, we come face to face with the suffering and chaos of a world out of synch with its Creator.

Though the world was painted in God's glory, it was marred by sin and is now hemmed in by death. That's why God drove Adam and Eve out of the Garden after they had sinned. If they had eaten from the Tree of Life in their sinful state, they would have been victimized by a broken world throughout eternity.

> *He has made everything beautiful in its time. He has also set eternity in the human heart; yet no one can fathom what God has done from beginning to end.*
> **ECCLESIASTES 3:11 (NIV)**

MAR 11 — Death as a Doorway

How can you rescue someone from a broken world if that state is eternal? You can't. If I'm eternally shipwrecked, how can you save me?

God rescued us by condemning sin and its devastation to this finite age. The soul that sins shall die wasn't punishment but the first act of redemption. By doing so, he preserved eternity as pure and undefiled—a safe harbor to which he could rescue us and allow us to share in the fullness of his glory.

Though death is the tool God uses to keep eternity unstained by sin, it is not his friend. Paul calls it God's enemy (I Cor. 15:26) and the last one to be destroyed. He never wanted us to face death, neither the physical death that stalks our bodies in this age, nor the spiritual death that magnifies our selfish ambitions and hides us from the Father's love. We see it clearly in the devastation brought on by war, terrorism, crime, tragic accidents, and disease. With each death of a loved one, or the growing aches and limitations of age we are reminded that everything in this age is destined to perish.

But for those who yearn to know God in his fullness,

death has no sting. It is simply a doorway through which we will find our final freedom. It is not the dreaded end of our life on earth, but a passageway into the last, great adventure: the freedom to know him without limitation or distraction. For us, death will mean waking up on some tomorrow morning finally free of this broken world and our sin-scarred bodies.

> *We are confident, I say, and would prefer to be away from the body and at home with the Lord.*
> **2 CORINTHIANS 5:8 (NIV)**

MAR 12 This Life is Only the Prologue

On the last page of the last book of his Narnia tales, just when the reader thinks the story is over because the world has ended, C. S. Lewis pulls back the curtain even farther as he writes of the four children:

> *For them it was only the beginning of the real story. All their life in this world…had only been the cover and the title page: now at last they were beginning Chapter One of the Great Story, which no one on earth has read: which goes on forever: in which every chapter is better than the one before.*

Lewis gets it exactly right. The time between our birth and our death is only a small slice of your story.

When we look back from eternity, we will know that the whole of our life in this age, that seems like everything to us now, was only the beginning. I suspect we'll remember it much like we remember kindergarten, which is to say, not so well.

That's how God looks at our life in this age, and Scripture encourages us to as well. It repeatedly says that this world and our life in it are as brief as the dew on the morning grass, or a vapor of smoke that hangs briefly in the air.

If we knew that, we wouldn't be so devastated by our struggles or despair at life's disappointments. And we wouldn't fear death because we would not see it as the tragic end to life, but the beginning of life as God truly meant us to live it.

So, we fix our eyes not on what is seen, but on what is unseen, since what is seen is temporary, but what is unseen is eternal.
2 CORINTHIANS 4:18 (NIV)

MAR 13 — Caught between Two Worlds

If you want to understand God's unfolding work in you, look beyond the prologue and include the rest of the story. If not, you'll miss what God is doing and sail adrift in seeking fulfillment from an existence that cannot deliver it.

This world exists in the brokenness and chaos of sin, and just because you believe in him doesn't mean you are immune. Your circumstances will never play out perfectly. You'll never have everything you want, and you'll regularly face moments of conflict, struggle, and pain. Even the best of times will not provide enduring satisfaction because you will never quite be at home here, try though you might.

Your home is in Father's heart. Though you won't experience that fully until the end of the age, you don't need to stop enjoying the first fruits of it in our present everyday life.

The early apostles didn't think of eternal life only as life that would last forever, but as a quality of life lived in him. Eternal life is available now in Jesus. No wonder we feel caught between two worlds—we live in one but draw our life from another.

> *Fight the good fight of the faith.*
> *Take hold of the eternal life to which you were*
> *called when you made your good confession in*
> *the presence of many witnesses.*
>
> 1 TIMOTHY 6:12 (NIV)

MAR 14 — Master of Illusions

When Jesus prayed for his disciples in John 17 he specifically said his prayer was not that God would take them out of the world, but that God would keep them in the midst of it. They would be *in* the world, but they would no longer be *of* it. Tapping into God's reality supersedes everything about this age and clarifies how we can live freely in it.

But we all know that isn't easy. How distant the eternal can often feel when we get lost in our responsibilities at work and at home and by the myriad of amusements that our world offers. We think we'll find greater joy in a better job, a nicer home, or a bigger bank account. We are constantly bombarded in news stories and TV shows, advertisements, and movies that life in this age can fulfill our deepest dreams. It creates in all of us the frustration that if we could just strike it rich in business or luck out in the lottery, find the right soul mate, write that best-seller, or get a decent break for our creativity, then we would finally find the fulfillment we desperately seek.

We so easily forget that the media sells illusions, and not reality, like the endless contraptions that promise to take inches off our waistline with minimal effort from us. These illusionists aren't just in the world, they are also among God's people, co-opting the reality of God's life by promising that if we just follow their program, prayer formula, or other scheme, God will make our wildest dreams come true.

Of course, their wares sell well. Lies always do. But what happens when they don't work? The dream-merchants fly off in their Learjets while the people who paid for them are left wondering what is wrong with them or with God that he didn't carve out an easy and prosperous life for them. This frustration at God and jealousy for the world's goods has shipwrecked many believers.

See to it that no one takes you captive through hollow and deceptive philosophy, which depends on human tradition and the basic principles of this world rather than on Christ.
COLOSSIANS 2:8 (NIV)

MAR 15 The Myth of a Pain-Free Life

God will often give us moments of joy and refreshing even in the chaos of a sin-stained world. Those are great days. Enjoy them while they last.

But God's life in us does not guarantee that we won't also experience seasons of great hardship, sorrow, and pain. Anyone who says otherwise is trying to sell you an illusion, and that will fade away like the dew in the midst of real life.

That's why Paul blasted the false teachers who said that godliness could lead to financial gain (I Timothy 6). He went on to say that the follower of Jesus would be content merely with food and clothes.

Those who seek the fulfillment of wealth have never experienced the treasure that no amount of money can buy. Find your life in him and no circumstance can ever rob that from you.

> *Two things I ask of you, LORD; do not refuse me before I die:*
> *Keep falsehood and lies far from me; give me neither*
> *poverty nor riches, but give me only my daily bread.*
> *Otherwise, I may have too much and disown you and*
> *say, 'Who is the LORD?' Or I may become poor and*
> *steal, and so dishonor the name of my God.*
>
> **PROVERBS 30:7–9 (NIV)**

MAR 16 — Life Abundantly

Jesus offered an abundance of life to those who follow him, but he never defined that in material terms. I've seen people live in the fullness of that life even as they endure dire poverty, fight debilitating diseases, and face persecution for their faith. They didn't live out of the circumstances that assailed them, but instead out of God's presence that filled them.

Our home can never be in Newbury Park, California, or Lagos, Nigeria. Our home is in the heart of the Living God. The life that really is life comes from him alone; it isn't measured in convenient or easy circumstances. It can lead you through the most difficult circumstance and give you a peace that is beyond understanding.

That's what he meant by life abundantly—the overwhelming sense of fullness and belonging that comes from being his and recognizing his presence in every moment as our day unfolds. It allows his voice to guide us, his comfort to hold us, and his strength to transforms us as we become a bit more like him with each passing day.

> *You do not belong to the world,*
> *but I have chosen you out of the world.*
>
> **JOHN 15:19 (NIV)**

MAR 17 — An Oasis of Eternity

Through the lives of his followers, God continues to invade this sin-stained world. Though he does not fix every circumstance to conform to my comfort, he has offered to share all of his life with me.

He will hold me in times of suffering and laugh with me in times of joy. He will give my life meaning not by what I gain in this world, but by making me part of his unfolding purpose: to win the world back to himself through his overwhelming love.

His reality in you and your cooperation with him is the only well that can sate your quest for fulfillment. This is eternal life and it began for you the day you received him. As you let him live in you he can become more real than the world you touch, see, and hear every day.

He will create in you an oasis of eternity in the midst of the barren wasteland of our culture.

> *Therefore, we do not lose heart. Though outwardly we are wasting away, yet inwardly we are being renewed day by day.*
> 2 CORINTHIANS 4:16–17 (NIV)

MAR 18 — Greater than Anything

The only way to live in this world without becoming part of it is to continually gaze into the face of our gracious Father. That's how we set our heart on things "above" instead of getting sucked in by the illusions of this age, or think the answers we need can be found in its systems.

Seeing him, however he makes himself known on a given day, will leave us free to cooperate with his working in our own lives and in the lives of others around us.

That's why Paul could look at perilous circumstances and rise victorious through them. And this was a man who faced shipwrecks, stonings, beatings, and danger with some regularity.

His presence in you is greater than anything anyone can hurl at you. With our eyes fixed on him you do not have to surrender to the world or retreat from it. We can fully embrace whatever unfolds, knowing that God's greater purpose will go forward in our lives.

This is living in the eternal: to taste of his rich presence every day, his glorious presence that will not only guide us but will also overflow us and splash out onto a thirsty world.

Since, then, you have been raised with Christ, set your hearts on things above, where Christ is seated at the right hand of God. Set your minds on things above, not on earthly things. For you died, and your life is now hidden with Christ in God.

COLOSSIANS 3:1–3

MAR 19 — The Pause that Transforms

Look to him early and often throughout your day.

As you start your car, the moment before you pick up a phone call, or as you're prepping dinner, take a pause. Focus on him and see if he has anything to show you.

He will become increasingly real, and you'll begin to see things that are easy to miss when we just keep pressing our way through the next demand on our life. Let him show you how to follow his voice and to see where his hand is moving in your life at that moment.

Don't think this can only happen in special devotional times that you try to cram into all the other demands of the day. God wants to invade your world and walk with you through it, not wear you out with religious demands.

You'll find your values shifting from the temporary things that are destined to fade away to those things that live on through eternity. Possessions, amusements, and achievements will all come to nothing at the end of this age.

You can enjoy what God gives you without being possessed by it. You can delight in the recreation God gives without being held captive by it. And you can do what he's asked you to do in this world without keeping score that exalts yourself over others.

> *Now this is eternal life: that they know you, the only true God, and Jesus Christ, whom you have sent.*
> JOHN 17:3 (NIV)

MAR 20 Living in the Eternal

Keeping your eye on what's eternal will help you navigate through the distractions of this world.

When I took flying lessons as a teenager, my instructor taught me to trust the instruments on the cockpit panel rather than my feelings. To drive the point home, he told me to close my eyes and hold the airplane straight and level. After a few seconds he asked how I was doing.

"Fine," I answered.

"Are you flying straight and level?"

After I answered in the affirmative, he told me to open my eyes. The plane was in a steep bank and diving for the ground.

He made his point. My feelings could so easily deceive me. By keeping my eyes on those instruments, I could keep the plane level even if I couldn't see the horizon.

That's why God wants us to keep our eyes on him and glance at the world, not the other way around. The temporal world will trick us into thinking we're straight and level when we are headed for certain destruction.

By keeping our eyes on him, we'll have the orientation we need to navigate freely through the challenges of life.

> *We have our eyes peeled for the City about to come. Let's take our place outside with Jesus, no longer pouring out the sacrificial blood of animals but pouring out sacrificial praises from our lips to God in Jesus' name.*
>
> **HEBREWS 13:15 (MSG)**

MAR 21 Reconciliation not Punishment

The crucifixion story most often told paints God as an angry, blood-thirsty deity whose appetite for vengeance could only be satisfied by the death of an innocent—the most compassionate and gracious human who ever lived.

Am I the only one who struggles with that? The case could be made for God being not much different from Molech, Baal, or any of the other idols that required human sacrifice to sate their uncontrollable rage.

Many of the Old Testament writers did look forward to the cross as a sacrifice that would satisfy God, and they used the language of punishment to explain it. That's all they knew. But the New Testament writers looking back through the redemption of the cross saw it differently. They didn't see it as the act of an angry God seeking restitution for our failures, but the self-giving of a loving Father to reconcile his children back to himself.

It's good to know those false gods of our own creation are not anything like the Father of our Lord Jesus Christ.

> *"He himself bore our sins" in his body on the cross, so that we might die to sins and live for righteousness; "by his wounds you have been healed."*
>
> **1 PETER 2:24 (NIV)**

MAR 22 — A Dose Larger Than We Could Bear

The New Testament's picture of the cross does not present God as a brutalizing tyrant expending his anger on an innocent victim. Instead, it paints a picture of an affectionate Father taking the devastation of our failures and holding them in the all-consuming power of his love. There, sin could be destroyed and a portal opened for us to reengage a trusting relationship with the God who created us.

The cross was not a sacrifice God needed in order to love us, but one *we* needed to be reconciled to Him.

One of my best friends died of melanoma almost two years ago. Doctors tried to destroy the cancer with the most aggressive chemotherapy they could pour into his body. In the end, it wasn't enough. The dose needed to kill his melanoma would have killed him first.

That was God's dilemma in wanting to rescue us from sin. The passion he had to cure our sin would overwhelm us before the cure could be completed. Only God himself could endure the regimen of healing that our brokenness demanded.

That's why he was the only hope for our redemption.

Instead, immense in mercy and with an incredible love,
he embraced us. He took our sin-dead lives
and made us alive in Christ.

EPHESIANS 2:1–3 (NASB)

MAR 23 — It's Not What You Think

He took our place. He embraced our disease by becoming sin itself, and then he drank the antidote that would consume sin in his own body. This is substitutionary atonement. He took our place because he was the only one who could endure the cure for our sin.

God's purpose in the cross was not to defend his holiness by punishing Jesus instead of us, but to destroy sin in the only vessel that could hold it until sin was destroyed in him.

Perhaps we need to rethink the crucifixion in line with those early believers. God was not there brutalizing his son as retribution for our failures; he was loving us through the son in the only way that would set us free to know Him and then discover how we could become like him.

Now that's a God worth knowing.

> *God made him who had no sin to be sin for us,*
> *so that in him we might become the righteousness of God.*
> CORINTHIANS 5:21 (NIV)

MAR 24 — The Power of the Cross

For most of my life in the faith I have seen the cross only as the substitutionary sacrifice that allowed Jesus to pay the price for my sins. For the past two decades, I have been discovering that it is so much more. The cross not only qualified us for salvation, but also provided the basis for our confidence in his love. What transpired there between a Father and his only begotten son forever secured our place in his affection.

He wasn't a substitute for our punishment, but a substitute for the cure we needed from the power of sin. By taking sin into himself and destroying it there, he healed all who come to him.

There's only one place you can go to find a love so powerful—the cross on Golgotha. His death opened the door for you to have an eternity-long, love-relationship with the Lord who made you.

That is the love God invites us to live in every day. Fear paralyzes, but love will free you to come to him, even in the midst of your worst failures. Fear makes you work harder to prove your worth to him; love teaches you to trust his work in you.

This is love: not that we loved God, but that he loved us and sent his Son as an atoning sacrifice for our sins.
1 JOHN 4:10 (NIV)

MAR 25 Insecurity Does Not Lead to Life

For too long organized religion has sought to teach us that fear and shame will make us better Christians. It is not so.

Insecurity about your place in him will do far more to separate you from your loving Father than to ever draw you to him. Jesus knew that. He taught people how to live securely in God's love every moment of every day so that he could transform them in ways they never could on their own.

For those who think grace offers us the luxury of throwing token acknowledgment to God while we continue to live to our own desires, you greatly misunderstand it. Grace frees us to live in relationship with God while he teaches us how to live according to the way he made us. When you learn to live in Father's love, you will discover how to love him with all your heart. And I dare you to do that and not be transformed into an authentic reflection of his glory.

Drink deeply of his love every day. Engage him daily in conversation. Ask him to reveal himself and his love to you and watch him do so in the most unlikely places.

He wants you to walk with him that way every day, for the rest of your life—never fearing him again.

*If you keep my commands, you'll remain intimately at home in
my love. That's what I've done—kept my Father's commands
and made myself at home in his love.*

JOHN 15:9-10 (MSG)

MAR 26 How Do You Picture God?

Throughout church history, most depictions of God in art have imagined a distant and exalted older man, often with a look of anger in his eye. Interestingly enough, most depictions of Jesus (except when he is cleansing the temple) show him in softer and more compassionate moments. If Jesus was the exact representation of the Father's nature, why do so many people see them so differently?

Most images I had of God growing up were scary. They were never engaging or inviting. Jesus was the good guy. He'd fixed things with Father, or so I was told, but that didn't make Father any less scary. If I was going to be around God, I always pictured myself hiding behind Jesus's robes.

Paul, however, had no such image of God. He understood that the cross fundamentally changed how we get to view God—no longer as terrifying judge, but as he really is, our *Abba* Father.

Abba is the endearing, safe connection a small child has with his or her doting dad. When that recognition sinks in, watch out. Life will change.

And by him we cry, "Abba, Father."
ROMANS 8:15 (NIV)

MAR 27 Whatever May Come

"When you grow old…someone else will dress you and bring you where you do not wish to go."

The words Jesus used were precise and abundantly clear. No one standing in that huddled group on Galilee's shore that morning misunderstood what he had just told Peter. He would one day be imprisoned and executed for his friendship with Jesus.

The surprise breakfast on the beach with the Resurrected Lord suddenly turned ominous. Peter must have just stared, his mouth wide open with shock. The rest of the disciples might have glanced at one another with that "poor Peter" expression on their faces, completely unaware that most of them would die in the same way.

Jesus knew he had just dropped a bombshell on them, and certainly he knew the distress that would have been filling Peter's heart. He was not that many days away from his own anguish that had sent him to the Garden to pray on the eve of his crucifixion.

Whatever Peter was feeling in that moment, Jesus brought his life back into focus. "Follow me." He needn't worry about what is to come. Life isn't lived in fear. Instead just keep following Jesus one day, one step at a time.

If they persecuted me, they will persecute you also.
If they obeyed my teaching, they will obey yours also.
JOHN 15:20 (NIV)

MAR 28 What about Him?

"Follow me," Jesus said after foretelling Peter's death.

That's the same thing Jesus had said to him on the same lake some years ago. It had changed everything in

Peter's life. How much he had been through in the few short years since and how much he had learned!

Perhaps this was the best lesson yet. Jesus's invitation to him was still the same. He didn't have to be brave or strong or possess great ingenuity. He just needed to follow, to center his eyes on the one who loved him so much and stay close to him wherever it might lead.

Nothing more simply expresses the essence of what it means to be a follower of Christ. Followers follow. We complicate life when we focus on anything else. The secret to thriving through the ups and downs of life is to draw close to Jesus, doing whatever he does and going wherever he goes.

In the last days before his Ascension, Jesus wanted Peter to know that the same thing that had held him the last few years could hold him the rest of his life. Jesus would still be with him no matter what, and all he needed to do was simply follow.

So then, just as you received Christ Jesus as Lord, continue to live in him, rooted and built up in him, strengthened in the faith as you were taught, and overflowing with thankfulness.

COLOSSIANS 2:6–7 (NIV)

MAR 29 — The Silliness of Competition

Isn't it interesting that our idea of fairness always has to do with comparing ourselves to others? Every human relationship we've ever known has been steeped in competition. It seems our society can only measure worth, success, even beauty, in relative terms.

How do you compare to those around you?

Sibling rivalry competes either for the affection or attention of parents as we grow and go out in the world and try to be successful. From the day you started school, you found yourself in competition with all the other students. The infamous bell curve based education purely on competition. We don't have to know everything, just a little bit more than most of the others in the class.

In the work world, your application competes against that of everyone else looking for the same job. On the job your performance review is based on how you compare to others before you or those who have similar responsibilities in the company.

Even in church, the competition continues. Ministers count heads as a measure of success. We compare our blessings (or our trials) with others, fearful that they will say something about how well we are doing spiritually. We even use competition as one of the primary tools to raise children to be good Christians. We put gold stars on attendance charts so kids who fill up their row can feel good about themselves, and those who don't might feel guilty enough to come more often.

But in the kingdom? That's a different story. Any need for competition has been swallowed up in the affection of Jesus for us all.

Instead of competing with everyone around us, we can celebrate our uniqueness and theirs.

> *We do not dare to classify or compare ourselves*
> *with some who commend themselves...*
> 2 CORINTHIANS 10:12 (NIV)

MAR 30 — Losing Our Need to Compete!

I was pretty poorly wired to competition when I was younger. I remember a Scripture memory contest my church held when I was in elementary school. Whoever could memorize the most verses in one quarter would win a new Bible. I didn't even need the new Bible, I already had one. But I memorized 153 verses in three months. How good was that? Second place managed only thirty-seven.

Obviously, I won the contest, but looking back I think I lost something far more valuable—the freedom to not measure my spiritual life against others. For most of my life since, I have taken my spiritual temperature by comparing my life to others. As long as I studied more, prayed more, or attended church more, I could feel good about myself whether or not those things had actually led me to know Jesus better.

Am I saying competition is some great evil? Not in the world. Competition is one of the "elementary principles of this age," that Paul writes about in Colossians. Without it our world would collapse into chaos, for it is one of the most powerful motivating forces for unredeemed humanity.

However, Jesus invites us to be motivated by love alone and that frees us from reliance on our own self-effort. Now we can just follow him, without any need to compare ourselves with any other person on the planet.

In the world we may still find ourselves competing, but in Christ we are free from the elementary principles of this age.

> But, "Let the one who boasts boast in the Lord."
> For it is not the one who commends himself who is approved, but the one whom the Lord commends.
>
> **2 CORINTHIANS 10:18 (NIV)**

MAR 31 — Compare No More!

I find it very difficult to follow Jesus as long as my focus is on others.

And it doesn't matter whether I'm battling an inferiority complex based on viewing my own failures and other people's strengths, or from a superiority complex of accentuating God's grace in my life while I focus on the flesh in others. Both distort my view of him and what he has for me.

The fact that I'm even trying to find wisdom in comparing myself to others is the deeper problem. My perception of what seems to be happening to me and what seems to be happening to others will lead me to deception—either that I am exceptionally blessed (because I deserve it, of course), or that God is unfair by not doing for me what he's doing for others.

There is nothing valuable to learn in comparing yourself to others. It can only break the trust you have in him with false conclusions. Instead, keep leaning into his goodness and how it is taking shape in you.

> *When they measure themselves by themselves and compare themselves with themselves, they are not wise.*
> 2 CORINTHIANS 10:12 (NIV)

APR 1 — Comparing Does Not Help

Is it fair that the gifted young evangelist, Stephen, was stoned to death during one of his first sermons, while the young man, Saul, later to be known as Paul the Apostle, holding the coats of those tossing the stones went on to make Jesus known throughout the Mediterranean world?

You wouldn't think so, would you?

That's how limited our human perspective can be. That conclusion misses out on the marvelous purpose of God as it unfolds around us. Both Stephen and Saul had pivotal roles in that period of time. It just wasn't the same role.

Jesus watched with concern whenever his disciples competed over who would be first in the kingdom, who could be closest to him, or who wouldn't have to wash the others' feet.

He knew learning to follow him is the exact opposite of everything we have learned in this world. He knows that our proclivity to compare and press for what we think is best for us will disrupt our trust in him.

Comparison always leads to confusion. Lose the need to compare, and you'll find yourself having greater clarity about his work in you.

> "Lord, what about him?" Jesus answered, "If I want him to
> remain alive until I return, what is that to you?
> You must follow me."
>
> JOHN 21:22 (NIV)

APR 2 The Cross Makes Us Equal

The cross was God's work for us when we were powerless to do anything for him. Nothing about us made us acceptable to him, except his love for us, which is greater than our flaws and mistakes.

At the foot of the cross, we know that we could not have done anything to make God love us more than he already did. Any boasting we might portion out for ourselves is rendered ridiculous, as is any blame we render out to others.

At the cross, battling over comparative significance is exposed as the farce it is. As much as the disciples seemed to squabble about that before the cross, they never did so after.

The cross makes us all equal in the eyes of the Father. When you understand that you will never have a need to exalt yourself over others or tear them down by focusing on their weaknesses.

> ...the same Lord is Lord of all and richly blesses all who call on him, for, "Everyone who calls on the name of the Lord will be saved."
>
> ROMANS 10:12-13 (NIV)

APR 3 — A New Way to Live

At the cross, Father's love was so completely demonstrated that no tragedy in our lives can erase the reality of his love for each one of us. Having loved us at the ultimate price, how absolutely silly is it for us to doubt that love just because something doesn't work out the way we want.

Also, at the cross all the righteousness of the law was met on our behalf. We no longer have to live by law, rules, guidelines, and expectations. We are now free to serve in the newness of the Spirit, where a relationship with him reshapes everything in us from the inside out.

The only rule now is, "Follow me!"

Even that is less a command than an invitation to the best that life has to offer. For the one inviting us to follow him is the one who loves us more than anyone else in all the world.

> Consequently, you are no longer foreigners and strangers, but fellow citizens with God's people and also members of his household, built on the foundation of the apostles and prophets, with Christ Jesus himself as the chief cornerstone.
>
> EPHESIANS 2:19-20 (NIV)

APR 4 — Since When Do We Know Best?

Adam and Eve made their choice in the garden, certain they were acting in their own best interest. *We will become like gods*, they thought. Unfortunately, they did not appreciate all the ramifications of that choice until it was too late.

I've often wondered why God was not a bit more specific about the trees he'd planted in that garden. He did warn them they would die if they ate from the forbidden tree. But why didn't he tell them all of it? Why didn't he tell them that if they ate of it, they would subject themselves and thousands of generations to the horrible atrocities of sin, disease, depression, broken relationships, abuse, and death?

If he had, and told them all they had to do to avoid these things was to go over and eat of the Tree of Life, don't you suppose they would have done it?

Of course they would. But why? Because they loved and trusted him? No.

They would have done it only because it would have been in their best interest. They would have still chosen control of their own life and by doing so would have missed out on the relationship that would make them complete.

Thus, they came to know good and evil without the trust in him that would empower them to choose the good.

Learning to trust him and not use him for our own desires is the only path to fullness.

> *Jesus turned and said to Peter, "Get behind me, Satan! You are a stumbling block to me; you do not have in mind the concerns of God, but merely human concerns."*
>
> MATTHEW 16:23 (NIV)

APR 5 — Why the Law Could Never Work

God knew from the beginning what Adam and Eve's choice would be, and he had already prepared to use their failure as a stepping stone to their redemption.

Immediately after their fall, he prescribed conditions where their bent for choosing in their own best interest could be utilized to help hold their sin in check until the Savior would come. That's why God used rewards and punishments to make his ways appeal to our self-interest.

We do the same thing when we discipline our children. Their flesh will always choose self-interest over what is truly best for them. When we discipline them, we try to make disobedience less attractive. This is how our world conforms behavior. Your teachers used it; your boss does too.

Anyone who has ever used self-interest as a motivating tool knows ultimately it will not work. God never expected his own law to work because our flesh was just too weak.

While the Law could conform external behaviors in the short term when the punishments are severe enough, it could not ultimately transform us. When the fear fades, we go right back to our self-interest even if it is destructive to us.

God's love, however, is powerful enough to invite us into the freedom that Law never could.

> *Now choose life, so that you and your children may live*
> *and that you may love the LORD your God,*
> *listen to his voice, and hold fast to him.*
> **DEUTERONOMY 30:19 (NIV)**

APR 6 — Leaning Away from Conformity

We obey traffic laws for fear of getting a ticket. The military makes people conform to their standards through an exhaustive set of rewards and punishments. Grades in school and incentives in business all appeal to greed and fear to make us do what they want.

All designs to use self-interest as the motivating force for us to be better.

So, it's no wonder that religious leaders would use the threat of hell and the promise of eternal life to conform our behavior in God's kingdom. That's why so much fear and guilt—or promise of God's blessing or leadership positions—are used to get believers to do what's right.

It's a trap, and all the more because the intentions are to get us to live better. But righteousness doesn't flow out of fear or bribery. In this kingdom, living in his love is the only hope of enduring freedom from our misguided notions of self-interest to truly discover the life God wants to give us.

If you want to seek his freedom, lean away from fear and guilt and into a growing trust that you are loved and that Jesus knows what is best for you.

> God didn't go to all the trouble of sending his
> Son merely to point an accusing finger,
> telling the world how bad it was.
>
> JOHN 3:16 (MSG)

APR 7 — Observing Law Made Him a Sinner

Children who have been constantly motivated only by fear will end up rebellious teenagers. Fear can never change us from the inside.

Having been taught all their lives to respond to their

self-interest, what will children do when their interests child's interests are better served by going along with their peers instead of following the hopes of their parents?

Even Paul blamed the same process that made him a Pharisee and faultless in legalistic righteousness as the very process that also made him the chief of sinners.

On the outside, his life conformed to God's law. Inside he was filled with pride at how good he was and raged with hate toward those he thought were a threat to his religious interests. So, he slaughtered God's people in God's name and by doing so became a murderer and a blasphemer.

Righteousness alone can never be the goal. The goal is only the righteousness that comes from a growing trust in who God is and a growing knowledge of how he works in us. As it did for Paul, it always begins with our recognition of his mercy.

> *Therefore, since we have been justified through faith, we have peace with God through our Lord Jesus Christ, through whom we have gained access by faith into this grace in which we now stand...*
> ROMANS 5:1-2 (NIV)

APR 8 — The Danger of Religious Arrogance

Much of our orientation to the Christian life is incredibly similar to the Pharisees. We might call them "New Testament principles" instead of Law but they still are a set of dos and don'ts that we try to package to appeal to people's self-interest. Regrettably, the results are the same.

Externally, we may be doing a lot of good things while the most despicable of sins devours us from within. Scripture and history show us that even the most religious of us will only end up using our traditions and principles to maximize our own best interests, like tax-lawyers groping for loopholes.

Even worse, pride in our performance will lead to a religious arrogance that is toxic to real fellowship and destructive to people around us who might want to know the God we know.

How do you view people around you who are not as committed or devoted as you consider yourself to be? If you view them with disdain, you have fallen for this trap.

Fortunately, we always have the option to take a different path where love makes us more compassionate for people who have yet to discover the freedom God wants to offer them.

I will put my laws in their minds and write them on their hearts. I will be their God, and they will be my people.

HEBREWS 8:10 (NIV)

APR 9 — A Demonstration of Love So Powerful

God's ultimate plan to deal with self-interest was not going to come through law or obligation. He knew our flesh was too weak for that. The only way we could find life was for self to be swallowed up in the immensity of Father's love.

So Jesus came to die—not because God needed an innocent victim on which to expend his wrath, but because sin needed a host to be consumed by the cleansing love of a victorious God. His act of obedience to endure such anguish on our behalf demonstrated a love so powerful that we would never want to doubt him again.

Now we don't have to live each day doing what we think is best—we just have to embrace his presence in us and his desires for the redemption of the world. Every circumstance becomes an opportunity to see where trusting him might lead us.

What do you hear him whispering into your heart today? The One who loves you most can guide you through whatever you're facing and enfold it into his purpose in the whole of Creation.

Because we can trust his love and care for us, we no longer have to look out for ourselves. Instead, we can follow him freely all of our days.

> *And he died for all, that those who live should no longer live for themselves but for him who died for them and was raised again.*
> **2 CORINTHIANS 5:15 (NIV)**

APR 10 — You Are Mine

When I was eighteen, I was speeding down a dark country road at close to a hundred miles an hour with five others aboard. All of a sudden, I was overwhelmed with an urge to slam on my brakes and did so without even consciously choosing to. As the car skidded to a stop, a diamond-shaped reflector sign came into view. The road was coming to a dead-end that dropped off into a cement ditch. My tires stopped within a yard of that sign.

I haven't thought about that for a long while, until one day when I was complaining to God about all the difficult circumstances that seemed to surround me. "Why can't I get away with doing what seems to work for everyone else?"

At that moment my near accident came to mind

and with it this thought in my head: "Ever since that night I've considered you mine. You deserved to die in a tragedy that would have taken five other lives, but I saved you. I own you."

That last phrase came at me with a smile and a wink. What captured my heart in that moment was the overwhelming love of God who considered me his.

Being owned by him is not bondage. He has the greatest ideas I've ever heard even though they often run counter to my own. He didn't want to use me for his gain but to encourage me to trust him to provide the best way forward. Being owned by him was not an obligation, but an invitation into a great adventure where his wisdom could supplant mine for my own good.

God was *for* me, not against me; letting him have his way in me is something I've never regretted.

And he died for all, that those who live should no longer live for themselves but for him who died for them and was raised again.
2 CORINTHIANS 5:15 (NIV)

APR 11 Living in Love Instead of Fear

"But perfect love drives out fear," John wrote, "because fear has to do with punishment. The one who fears is not made perfect in love."

Many people have told me that our holiness is derived from fear. We must be so afraid of God that we'll be scared out of sinning. That hasn't worked, however, for anyone, throughout history. John says it clearly here. Fear does not lead to perfection, only love does.

Learning to live in the Father's affection changes our perception of everything. Love invites us into his perspective and in time his love undermines the reason we are so captive to sin. Seeking our own joy with our own wisdom is a cleverly disguised march toward self-destruction.

His love frees us from the tyranny of twisting every opportunity to make it work best for what we think we want. Once we begin to see his purpose around us and become engaged with him, the impetus for sin is displaced and our freedom grows.

Obedience is no longer the onerous task of trying to keep God appeased, but the simple result of living in trust. After all, isn't sin only the result of trying to provide for ourselves what God said he would provide for us? If so, then when we are confident that God knows best, we no longer have to push for our own agendas.

We no longer have to trust our conclusions about the best way to joy or comfort. My agenda no longer needs to be served and I'll come to recognize more clearly what he has in mind. That's not only true of sinful appetites, but also for our ambitions in ministry.

There is no room in love for fear. Well-formed love banishes fear. Since fear is crippling, a fearful life—fear of death, fear of judgment—is one not yet fully formed in love.
I JOHN 4:18 (MSG)

APR 12 — The One Who Is Truly Free

We understand people who serve their self-interest. In fact, it is easy to manipulate people with fear of repercussions and bribery. But when someone ceases to be motivated by such things, they themselves become a threat to the self-interest system. Others will call them rebels and accuse them of being un-submitted.

The free person in Christ and the rebellious will always look the same to those who labor under religious obligation, because both ignore the conventions that govern men. But there is a major difference between the two. The rebel does it to serve himself and his passions, always harming others in the process and leaving a wake of anarchy behind him. The free person in Christ, however, does so because they no longer have a need to serve themselves.

If the world hates you, keep in mind that it hated me first.
If you belonged to the world, it would love you as its own...
JOHN 15:18 (NIV)

APR 13 — Let Go of Your Agenda

The free person in Christ has embraced God's love at a far deeper level than any method of behavioral conformity could ever touch, and they will guard that freedom even if it means others will misunderstand them.

They will reject the conventions of religion when it impinges on that freedom. However, they do not do so to please themselves, but the Father in whose love they rest. They'll also share that freedom with others because they want them to find that same joy.

This is the parent, coworker, brother, sister, son, or daughter who God scatters across the whole earth, and by liberating them from self-interest–based legalistic righteousness he allows them to taste the majesty and depth of all that waits for them in the Father's heart.

This is how God brings his children into his glory. As long as you seek your own best interest in the circumstances you face, you will miss the life God offers to you.

Learn to let go of your agenda and trust Father's immense love, and you will discover what true freedom and joy really are.

Since you died with Christ to the elemental spiritual forces of this world, why, as though you still belonged to the world, do you submit to its rules...These rules, which have to do with things that are all destined to perish with use, are based on merely human commands and teachings.

COLOSSIANS 2:20-22 (NIV)

APR 14 — A Beautiful Moment

While in downtown St. Louis one April evening, after an outing looking to help some of the homeless, a group took me to stand under the arch at nine o'clock. We ascended the hill it sits on next to the Mississippi River just as a thunderstorm made its approach on the city.

While we stood there, lightning flashed across the skyline, racing through the clouds and then suddenly spearing the earth with its jagged fingers while the thunder rolled in the background. It was one of those rare moments when the awesome beauty of God's creation literally takes your breath away and its memory hangs on for weeks afterward.

As great as times like that are, they pale in comparison to those moments when God lets someone see just how loved they are. Sometimes it comes with a flood of tears and at others with a simple chuckle and a shake of the head. I've seen it happen while sharing a portion of Scripture or sitting down with someone to talk or to pray.

Somehow, as only his Spirit can—when the heart is ready—he allows them to see that they are carrying far too much baggage, robbing themselves of the simplicity of knowing God as their loving Father. That's where freedom begins.

...where the Spirit of the Lord is, there is freedom.
2 CORINTHIANS 3:17 (NIV)

APR 15 — The First Moment of Freedom

Some have labored for months or years under the oppressive burden of trying to earn God's approval, trying to please abusive leadership or failing the expectations others have held for them.

The moment God's love works its way past all those things and captures them in his sheer delight is a moment that knows no equal in creation.

Once people discover just how much he loves them, and that love is motive enough to allow God to do everything in their life that he wants to accomplish, you can see the weight lift from their shoulders. You can see in their eyes the renewed hope of enjoying again their relationship with Father.

Sometimes it is an immediate realization, at others a slow awakening until that wonderful moment when the penny drops.

> *Your very lives are a letter that anyone can read by just looking at you. Christ himself wrote it—not with ink, but with God's living Spirit; not chiseled into stone, but carved into human lives...*
>
> 2 CORINTHIANS 3:1–3 (MSG)

APR 16 — I Get It!

Recently someone wrote me with huge letters, all caps: "I GET IT!!!! I FINALLY GET IT!!!!" What is better than that?

I still remember one of my moments like that years ago. I had tried to fit myself into a calling God had not given me (or anyone else for that matter), and I had tried to find a Christian response to people who were playing power games God wouldn't let me play any longer.

On a walk through a plum orchard, he spoke to me: "If you never teach another sermon, write another book, or spend one more moment counseling a broken life or witnessing to a lost soul, I will not love you one bit less!"

What a moment! I never realized how much of my efforts as a believer had been wasted trying to earn the approval he had already given me. It had devoured my relationship with him and twisted my relationships with others.

That moment of revelation freed me to follow him in ways I never had before—even though many people I knew at the time would reject me for it. It also allowed me to reorder my entire life, no longer striving to earn his affection, but simply learning to live in it every day.

If you haven't had that moment yet, it's coming. Keep leaning toward him—praying, hoping, believing.

For I am convinced that neither death nor life, neither angels nor demons, neither the present nor the future, nor any powers, neither height nor depth, nor anything else in all creation, will be able to separate us from the love of God that is in Christ Jesus our Lord.
ROMANS 8:38–40 (NIV)

CHAPTER 17 How You Use Your Freedom

As spectacular as God's freedom is, it is not the end of the journey. It's the trailhead for an adventure that can revolutionize your life.

Don't forget, it was freedom that allowed the Prodigal Son to leave his father's house and strike out on his own. He abused his freedom as an excuse to indulge his flesh, not knowing how much it would betray him and leave him broken in a pigpen of self-doubt, loneliness, and desperate need.

I've seen many people shipwrecked by freedom, but many more who have discovered that freedom allowed them to find the fullness of his life in them. For them it wasn't freedom to do whatever they wanted but the freedom to follow Jesus without guilt and shame.

God's freedom doesn't make us his disciples—it only opens the door for us to decide whether we want to be one or not.

> *It is for freedom that Christ has set us free.*
> *Stand firm, then, and do not let yourselves be*
> *burdened again by a yoke of slavery.*
> **GALATIANS 5:1 (NIV)**

APR 18 — The Failure of Rule-Keeping

Without the freedom to be authentic and to make choices based on our own free will, true discipleship cannot begin. The pressure of others will only complicate our decisions.

It is the environment Paul protected at all costs. He knew all too well how our religious tendencies make us great rule-makers. They take our best intentions for others and make them into a conspiracy that actually denies others the life they are seeking.

So when believers in Galatia sought to institute a set of "New Testament principles" that would rob God's people of the freedom to hear Jesus and trust him, Paul rushed into the breach asking why they would trade the simplicity of relationship with Jesus for rules and regulations that they would have to keep by their own effort.

That's always a bad trade.

The only thing that counts is faith expressing itself through love.
GALATIANS 5:6 (NIV)

APR 19 — The Double-Edged Sword of Freedom

Some among the Galatians used freedom as an excuse to indulge their flesh, thus conspiring with the darkness in them. But even in the face of those who abused freedom, Paul still spoke up for the necessity of it.

If people are really going to be changed by God, freedom is the only incubator in which God's Spirit can transform those who want to walk with him.

Thus freedom is not only the trailhead to the depths of God's heart, it is also the trailhead away from it. Scary isn't it?

The choice is ours. Freedom in and of itself is no virtue. Only as we use it to engage him in ever-deepening friendship and to find freedom *from* our willfulness and arrogance will freedom be the blessing God intended.

> *You, my brothers and sisters, were called to be free.*
> *But do not use your freedom to indulge the flesh;*
> *rather, serve one another humbly in love.*
> **GALATIANS 5:13 (NIV)**

APR 20 — A Life Lived in Father's Love

Religious thinking keeps us trapped in guilt and shame, harassed by obligations we can never fulfill, bored with empty rituals, and in constant pursuit of some new truth that will finally make it all come alive.

All are fruitless endeavors that will leave us empty.

Jesus didn't load up his followers with any of these things. In fact, he dismantled them at every turn. He simply demonstrated to them what a life lived in Father's love looks like.

It affected everything about the way he thought and acted, and it was so engaging that the disciples were constantly amazed at how God worked through him. They wanted to learn to live like him.

How easy it is for us to find ourselves trapped in a religious veneer of Christianity and miss the reality of it.

> ...holding to a form of godliness, although they have denied its power...
> 2 TIMOTHY 3:5 (NIV)

APR 21 — There's No Substitute for a Relationship

Given the times in which we live, we all need constant reminders that Christianity is not just a creed to confess, a set of ethics to obey, or repeating rituals to fulfill. As valuable as those things can be, they are not the substance of our faith.

When we substitute religious teaching or obligation for a vibrant relationship with him, those things will ultimately frustrate or bore us. We will end up half-heartedly attending services or observing disciplines and miss the greatest joy of belonging to him.

At its heart, Christianity is a growing connection to the Living God where we get to know him as he really is and enjoy him as he makes us a reflection of his glory. We will never learn to live in that reality by pursuing ethics, memorizing doctrine, or following rituals. These will always be woefully inadequate substitutes for the lack of knowing him.

We live in Christ by discovering how to abide in him, like a branch in a vine. He yearns to teach you how to do that. All you have to do is ask him, lean in to him every day, and watch his glory sort out in the real experiences of your life.

> *I'm no longer calling you servants because servants don't understand what their master is thinking and planning.*

*No, I've named you friends because I've let you
in on everything I've heard from the Father.*
JOHN 15:13–15 (MSG)

APR 22 — By Every Word

I stood in a beautiful cathedral in Albi, a small city in the south of France. Underneath its entrance was a dungeon. It was the focal point for a crusade launched against a group of French Christians who resisted the corruption of the papacy in the twelfth century.

The cathedral was built to intimidate those believers with the might, power, and resources of the church. The message could not have been clearer if it had been scripted in neon above the hillsides. "No one resists the power of the institutional church and survives."

And none of them did. Within fifty years, every one of those families who had dared to separate themselves from Rome were imprisoned and killed if they did not repent and rejoin the institution. And, true to Jesus's words, those who did the killing and torturing were certain they were doing God a favor.

Fortunately, our religious institutions today don't have the same power to imprison and kill, but it still amazes me how Christians can treat one another with gossip, accusation, lies, and manipulation when they feel that the occasion demands it.

Live generously with all. Enduring change doesn't come for coercion. Loving others provides the best environment for the light to shine.

*Don't tolerate people who try to run your life, ordering you to
bow and scrape, insisting that you join their obsession with
angels and that you seek out visions. They're a lot of hot air,
that's all they are. They're completely out of touch*

with the source of life, Christ, who puts us together in one piece,
whose very breath and blood flow through us.
COLOSSIANS 3:18-19 (MSG)

APR 23 — Be Careful of Substitutes

The temptation to make lunch out of stones has always been puzzling to me. Jesus was at the end of his fast. He was hungry. Changing stones into bread would have been easy for him to do and no one would have been hurt by it. There was nothing wrong with having bread. In fact, the request for it is included in the prayer he modeled for his disciples. "Give us today our daily bread."

If Jesus would have changed stones into bread, it wouldn't have been a sin by anything we know. It was not forbidden in any of the laws of the Old Covenant. It was not even that different from the first miracle he would perform a few days later at a wedding reception by changing water into wine. Of course, the fact that the enemy was offering the option to him might have been a giveaway.

"...Man does not live by bread alone..."

Now the problem comes into sharp focus.

Making bread out of stones was not in Father's heart for him to do. This was not God's idea and Jesus knew that the only way to live is by following the voice of his Father, initiating nothing out of his own desires or even need.

He put his trust in Father's provision, not the substitutes offered by a foreign voice.

Jesus answered, "It is written: 'Man shall not live on bread alone, but on every word that comes from the mouth of God.'"
MATTHEW 4:4 (NIV)

APR 24 — Breaking Free

Can someone try too hard to walk with God?

Absolutely!

I know that sounds odd, but relationship with the Living God cannot be earned by human effort, even extensive human effort. Those trying the hardest to make it happen often find themselves furthest from it.

It breaks my heart every time I talk to someone who is overwhelmed with frustration that their diligent efforts are going unrewarded. Those who trade in religious performance will never tire of telling us to try harder and giving us an increasing array of tasks to "help" us find him.

Self-effort is still a focus on us, however, and that takes our eyes off the real prize. It obscures our view of the Jesus who is right there with us to lead us into relationship with his Father.

You are too unique and Jesus is too creative to resort to familiar formulas. Following someone else's idea of what your relationship should look like is not the same as following his. He alone can carve out a relationship between you and his Father that is tangible and will grow with each passing day.

To discover that, we'll want to learn how to cease from your own labors and relax into a relationship that he desires with you more than you do with him. All you need to do is ask him and follow the nudges he'll put in your heart.

Now then, why do you try to test God by putting on the necks of Gentiles a yoke that neither we nor our ancestors have been able to bear? No! We believe it is through the grace of our Lord Jesus that we are saved, just as they are.

ACTS 15:10–11 (NIV)

APR 25 — From Frustration to Wonder

When I lived bogged down by the demands and agendas of religion, most mornings I would wake up defeated. I'd look at the clock dreading what the day might hold and wonder how I could get everything just right so God could do incredible things around me.

I loved God and was as passionate for him as I am now, but I was also exhausted all the time. There were so many things to fix, so many people to see, and so many meetings I had to prepare for.

I prayed hard each morning for God to bless this or save me from that. Most of the time my prayers didn't seem to make any difference. It was horrible. No matter how well I did on any given day, I always fell short of my own expectations. On my best days I broke even; on most days I felt incredibly frustrated, either by my own failings or, conversely, how inactive God seemed to be. But I didn't know there was any other way.

When I think back to those days now, they are a distant memory. Now I awaken every morning excited at how my unfolding adventure with him will take expression today.

Now, I'm a morning person, so not all of you will wake up the same way, but if you're following him your days will be more about wonder than they are frustration and exhaustion.

It does not, therefore, depend on human desire or effort, but on God's mercy.

ROMANS 9:16 (NIV)

APR 26 — What Might This Day Hold

The reason I'm excited to wake up each day is because I can't wait to see who God might put in my path, or how he will sort out some unresolved thing in my heart, or how he will touch someone else I know around me.

Could this be what Jesus meant when he promised us the fullness of his life? He wasn't talking about the ease of circumstance or the fulfillment of our dreams, but the absolute adventure of walking through each day with him as his purpose slowly but surely unfolds our lives.

If I begin my days focused on the troubles and challenges ahead, my day goes very differently than when I am looking for the opportunities he is creating to transform my day.

He is there in our simplest joys and in our most crushing circumstances, always inviting us closer, always transforming us so that we can live more freely in him. If this isn't at least a piece of that abundant life, it is more like it than anything I've known to date.

> *I have told you this so that my joy may be in you*
> *and that your joy may be complete.*
> JOHN 15:11 (NIV)

APR 27 Even in Prison

The freedom Jesus gives is not dependent on circumstances, but actually transcends them. Here is such a testimony from a man in prison as he shared it with me in an email:

> *I am finishing a five-year sentence for grand theft…I am learning to trust and that includes giving up my own way. I am the middle-adopted child of dysfunction and chaos. I am forty-seven years old and I am recovering from the mistaken assumption that life is all about me.*
>
> *Coming to prison has actually given me time away from the "system of religious obligation" and has freed*

me to simply know, love, and trust my Father. "Living loved" is so simple yet so life changing...I have really taken to heart the truth of embracing the process of life—even the darker shades—and I find myself less angry, unforgiving, and selfish. The veil has been lifted and I am completely loved and accepted!

I received Christ at age thirty in the ministry of a group of loveless, joyless people, teaching loveless, joyless people how to be loveless and joyless. I really believe now, in looking back, that I had to go under the law for almost twenty years to enable me to relate to and empathize with those still under the yoke of slavery. Now that I have discovered true freedom my heart aches for those being crushed by religion. I understand that I am not called to change or convince anyone, just to simply love and encourage them as Father places them in my path.

The Scripture declares, "Where the spirit of the Lord is, there is obedience." No. "There is church attendance." No. "There is law." No." It clearly states, "Where God is, there is freedom." I think real freedom is so fleeting to the body of Christ, that most would not recognize it, even if it bit them on the butt!

I am free to love, to grow and free to fail and free to make mistakes and bad choices! Now that's freedom. Love really does cast out fear.

> *Then you will know the truth, and the truth will set you free.*
> JOHN 8:32 (NIV)

APR 28 Afraid of the Light

One can easily understand a child who is afraid of the dark. The real tragedy of life is when grown men and women are afraid of the light. —Plato

As I read that this morning, I thought back through the Gospels and how many people came face to face with the light of God in the glory of the Son. Some embraced that light and all it would accomplish in them. Others sunk back into the shadows, unwilling to see God for who he really is or to comprehend his work in them.

The Pharisees refused to answer Jesus's question about John's authority because they were unwilling to confront the political risk in whatever answer they gave him. Yet, Zacchaeus embraced it even when his thievery was clear to all.

Isn't it odd that we find more comfort in the darkness of our illusions than in the light that may expose us, but will also heal us?

Jesus said, "For a brief time still, the light is among you. Walk by the light you have so darkness doesn't destroy you."
JOHN 12:35-36 (MSG)

APR 29 *Loving the Light*

It's amazing what people will do to avoid the light of Jesus. Even many theological disputes are ways to talk about the light without coming face to face with God and letting him expose the lies or coping mechanisms that keep us captive to the darkness.

When God is your loving father, however, there is nothing left to fear—even when our temptations, illusions, and failures are exposed. He would only shed light on those things because he wants to heal us from their power.

The test of discipleship is not how much you can keep up with all the disciplines or make yourself busy with God's things. The real test of discipleship is whether or not you love the light enough to keep crawling into it against all your natural inclinations to retreat into the false safety of the darkness.

Where is the light of God shining into your life today? Don't be afraid of it. True joy lies down that path.

> *If you walk in darkness, you don't know where you're going. As you have the light, believe in the light. Then the light will be within you and shining through your lives. You'll be children of light.*
>
> JOHN 12:35–36 (MSG)

APR 30 — Why the Law?

I spent a weekend in the Sierras with a group of men sharing about the transformation afforded to us through the power of the cross. We had talked about performance-based living versus affection-based living, and how the law is fulfilled in us as we live a life of love, not as we try to fulfill the law. Live loved, and love! It *is* as simple as that.

At the end of the session one of the men sat down next to me. "You know what I'm hearing you say about the law?" he asked.

He paused, staring off into the distance. "I think the law was to tell us how we should treat people we don't love."

I love that. That's why Paul and Jesus told us if we could learn to live in his love, no law would be necessary and yet it would still be fulfilled.

> *...for whoever loves others has fulfilled the law.*
>
> ROMANS 13:8 (NIV)

MAY 1 — Love is the Rescue

If you don't love God enough to walk with him as your Father, you'd be well served to follow his law. If you don't love yourself enough to embrace what God says is true and instead want to indulge your destructive appetites, the law would help you make better choices. If you don't love others enough to treat them fairly, respectfully, and generously, the law can help guide you.

The law really is an attempt to rescue you from yourself, though it rarely feels that way. We chafe under its demands, and even if we agree with its goals, we can't sustain the will power to fulfill it.

Until you discover the depth of God's love, you'll never be able to keep the law. It only shows what *must* be done to avoid punishment, not what *can* be done to embrace the life God wants to give us.

Once you discover the power of love, you will find the law a cheap substitute indeed!

And then you're ready to truly live!

> *Therefore love is the fulfillment of the law.*
> **ROMANS 13:10 (NIV)**

MAY 2 — Lessons from the Garden

One day as my daughter was leaving our home with her kids, my wife Sara leaned over to me and said, "You and Julie are funny in my garden. You are always fussing about the kids. Don't rake that, don't pick that flower, or walk there."

I had no idea where this was leading.

"I personally don't care about any of that. I want my grandchildren to really enjoy my garden and I want them to really enjoy being there with me."

As I listened to her, I thought, *I don't care about any of that either*. I was just trying to protect her garden. I know she works hard to keep it looking nice and I wanted those kids to respect that.

But I was defending something Sara wasn't defending herself. Why was that? She was more concerned about her relationship to those kids that what her garden looked like.

I knew her words reflected God's priorities more than mine did. How often I've said, "Don't do that," to other people in God's garden. He's inviting them into a relationship and I'm busy trying to make sure they don't mess anything up.

What a lesson! When you put the relationship first, keeping things neat and tidy no longer makes sense. Those things can be fixed easily enough. What God cares about is enjoying his kids and them enjoying him. In time, he knows they will come to care about the things he cares about.

> *Forget about deciding what's right for each other. Here's what you need to be concerned about: that you don't get in the way of someone else, making life more difficult than it already is.*
> **ROMANS 14:13 (MSG)**

MAY 3 — Keeping Reality Straight

Dreams are an intense experience for me. I've awoken from many a dream in sorrow over someone's death or in anxiety over a challenging circumstance. So real do they seem that the emotions often linger long after realizing it was only a dream.

However, what we see and feel when we're awake is not the real world either, at least not all of it. We so easily mistake the dictates of this world and our interpretation of them as reality itself. It isn't. The real world is in Father's heart, where what's eternal has more weight than the things we see and touch here. He has invited us to be at home in him in everything we do and in every circumstance that confronts us.

We have to live in this world, but he invites us to see beyond it. Behind every circumstance is a loving Father at work. Through every disappointment is a greater truth yet to be explored. Beyond our confusion is wisdom waiting to be discovered.

Instead of interpreting who God is through the things we see, we will be far wiser to interpret every event through that which God values. When we lose sight of that, the distractions and routines of living in this world will define our reality and diminish our awareness of him.

As this world is far more real than our dreams, so is God's reality far more significant than what we experience in this one. I'm sure you've touched it in moments of prayer and reflection where fears vanished, and you could see possibilities beyond your strength and wisdom.

That's the real world. Do your best not awaken from that one as you go about your day.

The things we see now are here today, gone tomorrow.
But the things we can't see now will last forever.
2 CORINTHIANS 4:18 (MSG)

MAY 4 Real Spirituality

When God is with you during your day it is just as spiritual to work on your car or decorate your house as it is to pray, gather with other believers, or share his life with someone who is lost. When we live as his beloved children, his glory shines through our lives no matter what we might be doing at any given moment.

Simple acts of caring as you go about your day have a profound impact on others. I'm convinced we best demonstrate God's life when we are least aware of it. When we try too hard, we are only acting, and the world sees it instantly even if we don't.

Those who are lost are not looking for actors on a stage, but people who find his joy in the simplicity of everyday life. It won't be fake or artificial because it comes from reality not pretense.

When we live with the freedom to let him take shape in us, he makes himself known in ways that will even surprise us.

Those who enter into Christ's being-here-for-us no longer have to live under a continuous, low-lying black cloud. A new power is in operation. The Spirit of life in Christ, like a strong wind, has magnificently cleared the air, freeing you from a fated lifetime of brutal tyranny at the hands of sin and death.

ROMANS 8:2 (MSG)

MAY 5 — Competition-Free Relationships

What do relationships look like when they are no longer steeped in insecurity and competition?

It's hard to imagine, isn't it? So many of our relationships even with other believers are tainted by the need to prove ourselves or by worrying about what they think of us. Those relationships are painful and awkward. I've had many like that.

Over the past few years, however, I've been blessed to have an increasing number of relationships with people who are learning to live loved by the Father. In their growing security with him, they have no need to compete with anyone or to try to impress me by acting spiritual or pretending to be in a better place than they are.

These relationships are full of authenticity and freedom; rather than making people less loveable, they make them ever-more endearing. There's a freedom to share, love, support, and serve, all without the need to gossip or tear others down to make themselves look good.

When we come to rest in the Father's love for us, just as we are, we'll extend that same love to others. Competition no longer has any power over us even if others around us are still playing that game.

We can finally value in each other what God values in them.

> *For this reason, I kneel before the Father, from whom every family in heaven and on earth derives its name.*
> **EPHESIANS 3:14–15 (NIV)**

MAY 6 — A Confessing Community

Our world values people who conform; God values people who are authentic.

Sometimes we're so busy acting right that God doesn't get to touch us where we really hurt. Jesus never chided anyone for being real. If we're angry at God, don't you think he'd rather have us be honest about it and work through it rather than hide behind meaningless words that do us no good?

Isn't the same thing true in our relationships? When someone is faking it to us by saying things we want to hear, the relationship stays superficial. Depth only comes when we get to know the person they are, not the one they want to appear to be. When people are authentic, even in their weaknesses, they become more endearing.

Honesty opens the door to relationship.

So, while our world may seem to value those who boast in their good fortune, it really isn't true. Our Father values those who confess their own weaknesses and struggles. A believing community is a confessing community. These are people who do not posture themselves to look good but find their way to a generous honesty that allows the Father's glory shine through their brokenness and failures.

> *Therefore confess your sins to each other and pray for each other so that you may be healed.*
> **JAMES 5:16 (NIV)**

MAY 7 — An Authentic Community

In a confessing community, gossip has no power. How can it, if everyone already knows one another's strengths and weaknesses? In that environment, there is nothing to be gained by exposing the failures of others.

There is great freedom in not having to pretend to be anything other than who we really are. That's one of the blessings of living loved. Knowing the Father loves us even in the midst of our brokenness frees us to love others in theirs. In our conversations and our prayers, we can freely share our struggles, celebrating his work to transform us.

When I find people who exalt their strengths and gossip about the weaknesses of others, I immediately know how insecure they are. The only way they can feel better about themselves is to point out the flesh in others. How tragic! They are still competing for their identity and that tells me how disconnected from God they are.

They might be well served to revisit the cross and remember that none of us have earned anything by how good we are; nor do we gain any advantage in how good we can pretend to be. When we understand that, we can encourage others past the most painful obstacles into the fullness of life in Jesus.

Where some feel the need to tear others down, Father values building them up. Be like Father.

Do not let any unwholesome talk come out of your mouths, but only what is helpful for building others up according to their needs, that it may benefit those who listen.

EPHESIANS 4:29 (NIV)

MAY 8 Difficult Choices

Over the years I've shared a meal or two with some incredible brothers and sisters.

All of them had been involved in successful vocations or ministries at one point, and yet all of them found it necessary to walk away. Many felt they had to walk away or compromise their conscience. Others felt that their relationship with God was being swallowed up by the institutional demands.

For all of them it had been a very painful decision, and when they made the choice none of them really knew what lay beyond it. Their friends and families didn't understand what they were doing, and they were often ridiculed. Many withdrew from them for fear they were contagious.

But they had some wonderful things in common. None of them were bitter or pined away for their "successful past." They all confessed how deeply their relationship with Jesus and their understanding of the power of God's grace had grown. All of them said that because of this difficult decision, they had discovered life and freedom in Jesus they never imagined existed.

When I ask them if they have any regrets about the choice they made, they all smile and answer, "None at all!"

> ...the freedom we have in Christ...
> **GALATIANS 2:4 (NIV)**

MAY 9 — A Mother's Redemption

Five years before her twenty-four-year-old daughter, in the midst of severe pain, had taken her own life. The grief that followed shattered her soul and left her isolated.

Even close friends from the church she had attended distanced themselves from her. Like most parents, they would rather judge her as a bad mother, than feel the vulnerability that this could happen to one of their children.

Beyond all of that, however, God still inserted himself into her pain.

When Erin died, most of me died with her. I was acutely aware that a person could be alive and yet dead—because I was. Conversely, for the first time I understood that I could be dead [unresponsive to God] and yet be alive.

I prayed, "God, I know this is not your problem. You don't produce spiritual birth defects. How did I miss the truth of knowing You? How did this happen to me? Why don't I know you? I thought I was pursuing a relationship with You, but here I am, a child of God, walking in darkness and deep trouble, hemorrhaging life and dying. I am poised to walk the same pathway to death as Erin. Show me how to know you the way you intended for me to know you; not my way, God, your way."

"Please just start with, 'Jesus loves me this I know,' and take it from there," God answered. *"You don't even know that, but it's a good place to start."*

Sometimes the simplest answer is a great place to start over.

> *I give them eternal life, and they shall never perish;*
> *no one will snatch them out of my hand.*
> JOHN 10:27 (NIV)

MAY 10 From Grief to Celebration

Continuing yesterday's story about a mother dealing with the suicide of her daughter:

I stayed with my burden of guilt (and) failure for six years. God never failed to offer his way of coming into the light during that time.

When an adult child takes their life...for the mother of that adult, Mother's Day can be messy. This was my sixth sad, messy, awkward Mother's Day and, although emotionally prepared, or so I thought, I wasn't prepared for how God would use my mess to heal another place in my soul.

A few days before Mother's Day this year, I felt God spoke to my heart that morning. "You can continue to carry a burden of guilt and your 'good mother' definition or let My light, truth, grace, and love shine on your twisted thinking."

He didn't say it's time for me to move on, that I should just get over it or just to suck it up. He told me that every time I think of Erin I should use the word "celebrate."

"Every day, I'm celebrating with Erin and every day Erin is celebrating with Me. Guess who's missing the

> *party?"*
>
> *I wish I could explain how God did it. Without changing the original experience, God somehow disconnected the painful "good mother syndrome" memory that was hardwired in my soul. The painful memory of Erin's suicide had a voice that mocked me.*
>
> *It hasn't been an on/off switch, but gradually when I think of Erin I respond to what the Holy Spirit said, and I use the word "celebrate." The painful memory and my wrong definition have been diffused [unwired?] and celebrating His Life in this situation is producing less painful and more appropriate responses to both my internal and external world.*

I love that story and, over the years since, she has told me how it has taken hold of her heart. God has a way for you to prevail in the most painful event of your life. It mostly likely won't be in the same way he touched this lady because he has an endless tool at her disposal.

> *It's wonderful what happens when Christ displaces worry at the center of your life.*
> **PHILIPPIANS 4:6 (MSG)**

MAY 11 — What's in it For Me?

People who make major decisions against their own self-interest for some higher good have always fascinated me. It's easy to understand why people do good things when there is something in it for them.

Even our pleas for volunteer help or charitable contributions are almost always linked to a personal benefit for the giver—tax-deductions or feeling good about doing their part. That's just the way our world works. You can almost always bet that a person will act in their own self-interest even to the detriment of others around them.

But that's not the way Father's kingdom works. Jesus said so in perhaps the most paradoxical statement of his ministry: "For whoever wants to save his life will lose it, but whoever loses his life for me will save it."

When we only worry about what's in it for us, and always seek to maximize our benefit—even in our pursuit of God—we will end up disappointed and empty. Life is found in the giving up of our selfishness and looking out for the interests of others as well as our own.

Trying to manipulate everything to our advantage leads into the darkness; laying down our lives for the good of others opens doors into the life God wants for you.

> *...If you love those who love you, what reward will you get? Are not even the tax collectors doing that? And if you greet only your own people, what are you doing more than others? Do not even pagans do that?*
> MATTHEW 5:45–50 (NIV)

MAY 12 · The Path We'd Rather Not Take

This is an incredible kingdom our Father has crafted. Choosing his way is undoubtedly the best decision we can make for ourselves.

However, our knowledge about what is truly best for us is so limited, that decisions we make seeking our own best interest only draw us further from him. That's why Jesus warned anyone who would come after him that he would need to "deny himself and take up his cross and follow me."

This verse has been misinterpreted by some in a way that leads to asceticism—denying every pleasure and mortifying ourselves, thinking it will lead to godliness. Jesus wasn't using it that way. He was talking about choices we make when God is leading us down a path we'd rather not follow—as he was in going to the cross. He was not advocating denial for denial's sake, but when our desires run counter to God's.

Only where we mistrust the pursuit of happiness on our terms will we discover the path that leads to true joy. For our joy comes not in attaining our desires, but in being free from our own selfish passions that keep us in the dark.

> Then Jesus went to work on his disciples. "Anyone who intends to come with me has to let me lead. You're not in the driver's seat; I am. Don't run from suffering; embrace it. Follow me and I'll show you how. Self-help is no help at all. Self-sacrifice is the way, my way, to finding yourself, your true self. What kind of deal is it to get everything you want but lose yourself? What could you ever trade your soul for?
> MATTHEW 16:24–26 (MSG)

MAY 13 — The Fellowship of Freedom

"You, my brothers and sisters, were called to be free. But do not use your freedom to indulge the sinful nature; rather, serve one another in love." (Galatians 5:13)

Doing whatever I want isn't freedom; it is slavery to self. Trying to make it on my own isn't freedom; it's independence and usually a defensive reaction to hurt.

The freedom Jesus gives disarms the power of guilt, selfish ambition, religious obligation, and our own self-preferring ways so that our friendship with him can grow. In that love, we'll find ourselves exploring opportunities and making decisions that align us with his work in the universe.

That's a tough road to go down alone. We greatly benefit from people in our lives who encourage us to aspire to that level of freedom. Find people like that and intentionally make the time to spend with them.

So, just because you have been manipulated and abused by those who claimed to be more knowledgeable (or more anointed), doesn't mean everyone will treat you that way. We are as much a prisoner when we react to hurt as we are when it overruns us. That's true of sin and of unhealthy relationships with others.

While hurt can make us more aware of how well-intentioned relationships can turn destructive, it doesn't mean we're on our own. Jesus can lead us to people who will reflect his voice and encouragement in our lives.

And let us consider how we may spur one another on toward love and good deeds, not giving up meeting together, as some are in the habit of doing, but encouraging one another— and all the more as you see the Day approaching.
HEBREWS 10:24–25 (NIV)

DAY 14 — A Fuller Perspective

I have traveled all over the world and every place I've been, I have met some of the most amazing people who are discovering who Jesus really is. I'm always encouraged to be near a true Jesus-follower, and I almost always learn something about God's ways from them.

That's his church and she is scattered all over the world. Of course, for us to see her we've got to define the church as Jesus did. He wasn't referring to the numerous groups who get together and name themselves the First Something-or-Other Church of Wherever-We-Are. He was referring to other believers who are on the journey of knowing him.

I'll admit they aren't always easy to find. Most Christians I know are distracted by all their religious activities and don't have a clue who he really is. And, they're not very encouraging to a real spiritual journey—they are more interested in conforming you to their religious views and practice.

So, while you may not always find reflections of his church in religious institutions, they are out there. And they are worth finding. But don't just look for like-minded people, because the beauty of Jesus's body in the world is that it brings us a fuller perspective of who God is.

Whenever Scripture talks about my ability to know God as an individual, it makes clear that my best view of him is a dim one, as if through a fog. But the church—*his* church—unveils him in all his fullness. We each reflect a part of him and when those parts connect in sharing and encouragement we get to see him in greater fullness.

And God placed all things under his feet and appointed him to be head over everything for the church, which is his body, the fullness of him who fills everything in every way.

EPHESIANS 1:22–23 (NIV)

MAY 15 — Authenticity and Generosity

Just because you attend the same congregation doesn't mean you're having fellowship with people. Fellowship is friendship—sharing heart and soul with authenticity and generosity.

Trying to fellowship with people who are more in love with their religion than God is nearly impossible. They are focused on conforming to rules and rituals, which is incredibly distracting and discouraging to us recognizing God's work in our own lives. You'll come away from such encounters frustrated and exhausted.

Our freedom in Christ allows us to find those who are genuinely vested in a journey of growing to know the Living God. They understand how God works, not through manipulation and control, but through grace that allows us to behold God as he reveals himself to us. The share freely without a need to convince anyone that they are right.

When I find people like that, I always come away strengthened, encouraged, and enlightened in what God is doing in my life.

But the fruit of the Spirit is love, joy, peace, forbearance, kindness, goodness, faithfulness, gentleness and self-control. Against such things there is no law. Those who belong to Christ Jesus have crucified the flesh with its passions and desires.

GALATIANS 5:22–24 (NIV)

MAY 16 — Meaningful Friendships

When I talk about relational Christianity, I use it to draw a distinction with institutional Christianity. But I'm not referring to a different way of doing church; rather it is a different way of thinking about God and his family that will allow you to experience his life with other people learning to follow Jesus—not just sit in a congregation somewhere.

People growing to know Jesus hunger for meaningful and transformational relationships with others. They just don't want to sit through a service. Many congregations over the past few decades have focused on small-group interaction, though with limited success.

Even if you go to a congregation, build a network of friends with whom you can develop deeper friendships and with whom you can share God's life with humility and tenderness.

Being loved and learning to love in up-close relationships is an important facet of the kingdom that Jesus invited us to explore. Yes, there will be fits and starts as you explore this. You'll learn the kind of people to wisely stay away from, but you'll discover the rich treasure of meaningful friendships that will provide great encouragement on your journey.

> *A new command I give you: Love one another. As I have loved you, so you must love one another. By this everyone will know that you are my disciples, if you love one another.*
>
> JOHN 13:34–35

MAY 17 — The Marks of a Free People

I also draw a distinction between relational and religious. For me, religion is the attempt to earn God's favor from my human effort. There are no bad motives in that, simply a very broken process; people caught up in it will be more concerned that you think like them than that you're exploring your own relationship with Jesus.

Throughout the past few decades, I have been encouraged by the added focus of small group interaction in homes or coffee shops as an expression of church life. However, just because a group is small doesn't make it relational. I've been in home groups with very religious dynamics, and in larger congregations that are very relational.

While I do think the home is the most natural place for us to discover life as a family, ultimately what facility we use is far less important than a host of other factors. I've noticed some common ingredients in relationships that spawn healthy body life that we'll explore over the next few days.

Though I often befriend those who don't understand many of these priorities so they might have a chance to see them in me, my greatest times of fellowship arise where people understand the nature of how God works and the freedom essential to true growth.

> Now that you have purified yourselves by obeying the
> truth so that you have sincere love for each other,
> love one another deeply, from the heart.
>
> 1 PETER 1:22 (NIV)

MAY 18 Mark #1: A Passion for His Presence

Where does the life of Jesus's church take shape? Wherever he is given supremacy in all things.

If you want to find people to grow with, look for those whose hearts are focused on him. He finds their way in their conversation as more than an idea or a good teacher, but a close friend and confidant.

They don't boast about the glories of "worship," the giftedness of their "teacher," the wonder of their denomination, or even how "relational" their priorities are. They may have those other things, but he is their only attraction. They want to know him better and follow him more closely while helping others do the same.

Cultivate this passion in your own heart. Look to him early and often throughout your day and let his words become the most important influence in your life.

> As the deer pants for streams of water,
> so my soul longs after You, O God.
>
> PSALM 42:1

MAY 19 — Mark #2: Authenticity over Conformity

Some people just want you to look good, to say the right things, and to act in a way that doesn't embarrass them. Avoid these people unless you have the grace to love them without being seduced into their way of thinking.

People who understand how Jesus builds his church value authenticity over conformity. They would rather see the rough edges in someone's life than have them put on a front. They allow people to feel what they feel, share what they think, and question what they don't understand without being judged, silenced, or called independent or unsubmitted.

People steeped in religion only know behavioral modification as the tool for personal change. You know the mantra, "If you try harder, you'll get better." Those on a real spiritual journey recognize that only Jesus can transform a life and see more fruit in encouraging us to know his love more completely than to pressure people to outward change.

They're interested in what's really going on inside of you, even if it's a mess. Rather than pressuring you to fulfill their expectations, they will walk alongside you, encouraging what Jesus is doing to set you free.

> ...no more lies, no more pretense. Tell your neighbor the truth. In Christ's body we're all connected to each other, after all. When you lie to others, you end up lying to yourself.
> **EPHESIANS 4:25 (MSG)**

MAY 20 — Mark #3: Friendships Not Meetings

People who are learning to follow Jesus are far more focused on relationships than they are meetings.

Isn't it interesting that Jesus never seemed to have held

a meeting that bears any resemblance to most of what we do in what we call church today? He got to know people at a heart level and spoke Father's wisdom into the most mundane moments. His most effective engagements with people came in homes, the marketplace, walking by the sea, or even at a well outside Samaria.

I'm not against meetings; it's just that the most important stuff doesn't happen there. Those who think it does are pursuing something different than a vital relationship with Jesus. Meetings have agendas and liturgical orders; a relationship is far more free-flowing than preplanning can ever achieve.

Encouragement is a daily reality. I've been in home groups that have met every week for years where the people don't even enjoy one another and can't even carry on a normal conversation around a dinner table.

As wonderful as it is to gather together for prayer, for worship, or to learn, without relationships that carry through the week, we can't really share the journey.

But encourage one another daily, as long as it is called "Today," so that none of you may be hardened by sin's deceitfulness.
HEBREWS 3:13

DAY 21 Mark #4: Confessional Relationships

By confessional relationships, I don't mean you go into a small booth and seek absolution from a priest or pastor. And I don't mean you are regularly focused on your failures, begging for cleansing.

What I mean is that people on a transformative journey are as honest in their struggles as they are in their joys. They don't mind being seen for who they are, and they don't put on airs to appear perfect or pass themselves off as an expert.

People who play those one-upmanship games haven't the foggiest idea what it is to share a growing friendship with the Living Jesus. Among them, you'll find far more gossip about the mistakes of others than confessions about their own.

A long time ago, I discovered I helped people far more when I was honest about my struggles and the lessons won in the school of hard knocks. Isn't it easier to love people who know they haven't arrived yet, and who are in touch with the reality of their own doubts and struggles?

Find someone like that, and you'll find a treasure with whom to share your journey.

> *Therefore confess your sins to each other and pray for each other so that you may be healed.*
> **JAMES 5:16 (NIV)**

MAY 22 — Mark #5: Not for God, But with God

People who understand body life are learning to depend on God's agenda, work, and power over human preference, effort, and ingenuity. They've given up trying to do things *for* God and they enjoy learning to do things *with* him.

Like me, they've messed up enough, hurt enough people, and fallen too short far too many times while trying to get God to bless what they want him to bless. Now, they only want to tune in to what he is doing and cooperate with him in it. For them, following God is not an onerous obedience, but a delight and joy.

Look how divided Father's family is in our day because people prefer to worship a certain way, be led by a certain personality, or because a certain program fits their needs best. Rather than being frustrated at everything they wish they could change about their lives, they're at rest in the Father's process of changing them. They realize that God is always working for their good, even when they do not understand how he may be doing that.

Life in his kingdom is not about getting all our desires met but simply to follow the Lamb wherever he goes. Ultimately what we think will make us most comfortable may be the worst thing for us. Following his ever-present nudges is the only way to know for sure.

> *Very truly I tell you, whoever believes in me will do the works I have been doing, and they will do even greater things than these, because I am going to the Father.*
> JOHN 14:12 (NIV)

DAY 23 Mark #6: Participants Not Spectators

Most people who do church life today are rewarded for faithful attendance and for being a good audience in the preplanned activities on the stage. People who are learning to follow God, however, are drawn to more interactive settings rather than just being spectators for the upfront performance.

The living reality of God's people is that everyone has a part. They would never want to see a few gifts glorified at the expense of everyone else simply having the freedom to be who God has made them to be. They can celebrate the unique contribution of each of God's people, from the oldest to the youngest, male and female, without regard to status or station in society.

They also know that worship isn't a song service to start a meeting but how we live inside the Father every day. It has nothing to do with our favorite song or whether the worship leader is anointed or not. Worship pours out of them in the way they live, with an awareness of God and a surrender to his ways.

> *"I am the light of the world. Whoever follows me will never walk in darkness but will have the light of life."*
>
> JOHN 8:12 (NIV)

MAY 24 — Mark #17: Relationally Healthy

Unfortunately, religious obligation warps relationships. It uses people as tools and rewards conformity over the reality of a relationship.

People on a better journey are learning to trust God's ability to connect them to the people they need to know, and they do not force a relationship where someone is not open. I have been with someone for only a few moments and know God is connecting us in some way for a larger purpose. I have also tried to build relationships with people that have never worked out despite our best efforts.

Be open for relationships however God brings them about, and don't be exclusive in the relationships you do have. Often the best gift you can give someone is introducing them to your friends. What God is doing in the world and even in their own locality is far larger than what you can see at any one moment. Cherish opportunities to meet others who hunger for the same God you do—even if they aren't part of the same group.

Having been loved by God, you will want to help others taste that love as well. You'll find yourself serving others in the most mundane ways, and enjoy seeing others discover the same freedom in God that you enjoy.

You can trust his Spirit to knit his body together the way he desires. He knows what he is doing, and he knows what he builds is more powerful and beautiful than anything we could possibly devise.

*...we see that God has carefully placed each part
of the body right where he wanted it.*
1 CORINTHIANS 12:14-18 (MSG)

MAY 25 — Transformation not Conformation

I went to a men's breakfast group one morning and was disappointed when the participants pulled out scorecards and each reported how many days the previous week they had read Scripture, witnessed to an unbeliever, or "hit their knees" before "hitting the shower."

They were holding one another accountable to disciplines they thought important. As sincere as they may have been, they were sincerely wrong.

These men had embraced a process of conformity, thinking it was their responsibility to motivate people to comply with their standards. Little did they realize that this process is the opposite of sharing the Christian journey. That is why accountability groups start with a wealth of zeal and quickly fade away.

Can you imagine Jesus pulling out similar scorecards to check on his disciples? Growing in relationship with God does not come through conformity, but through transformation.

*Therefore I urge you, brethren, by the mercies of God, to
present your bodies a living and holy sacrifice, acceptable
to God, which is your spiritual service of worship.
And do not be conformed to this world, but be
transformed by the renewing of your mind...*
ROMANS 12:1-2 (NAS)

MAY 26 — Don't Be Bossed Around

Real friendships are organic and therefore defy all attempts to fit us into a one-size-fits-all model. Rules, routines, and rituals are the building blocks of religion—not relationship.

People who lead religious groups will focus on obeying authority, accountability, meeting standards by human effort, finding fault, confronting failure, and blaming others. In short, conforming to these things can be quite painful, especially for those who don't have strong willpower.

People instinctively know that religious activities add stress and strain to the journey instead of helping them know God better. That is why Paul told us again and again not to have anything to do with people who wanted to boss others around, even if their aim was for greater righteousness.

Real leaders are those who encourage us to grow closer to Jesus and let him change us.

> *Who are you to judge the servant of another? To his own master he stands or falls; and he will stand, for the Lord is able to make him stand.*
>
> **ROMANS 14:4 (NAS)**

MAY 27 Sharing the Journey

The kind of people you want in your life are those who freely offer encouragement, help, service, support, love, compassion, forgiveness, and trust. You don't need multitudes of them, but a handful where sharing life and love are mutual.

People like that focus on loving God more freely and one another more openly. They trust in God's work, not their own, being real instead of repeating pat answers. They take the risk to follow God instead of meeting people's expectations. They won't force people into a mold because they know people have to have their own engagement with God so he can transform them into his likeness.

Paul was passionate for righteousness, but he knew that true righteousness only emerges out of a growing relationship of trust in God's love. His kingdom does not come as the result of our efforts, but of his.

Conforming others to what we think is best for them will only lead to frustration and exhaustion. As we encourage people to lean on Jesus they will see far more fruit than when we weigh them down with added obligations and responsibilities.

> *We continually ask God to fill you with the knowledge of his will through all the wisdom and understanding that the Spirit gives, so that you may live a life worthy of the Lord and please him in every way: bearing fruit in every good work, growing in the knowledge of God…*
>
> **COLOSSIANS 1:9–10**

MAY 28 Live Bountifully

The world turned so dark that God had to purge it with a flood. After it receded and Noah and his family had left the ark, God spoke to them. He warned them not to take the life of a fellow human because they are made in God's image. Then he told Noah to live fruitfully and bountifully.

After so severe a judgment, you would think God would warn them to be careful to live more righteously. He didn't. God gave us life to be enjoyed. It is easy for us to focus so often on what we don't have and forget to enjoy him in the midst of what we do have.

He still made it clear that violating others is against his nature. Yet, he still wanted his creation to enjoy the bounty of this earth and enjoy the life he gave them.

Is that also what it means to live righteously?

*Whoever sheds human blood, by humans let his blood be shed,
Because God made humans in his image reflecting God's
very nature. You're here to bear fruit, reproduce,
lavish life on the Earth, live bountifully!*

GENESIS 9:6–7 (MSG)

MAY 29 — Bounty in a World of Need

The needs in the world are overwhelming: sin, sickness, poverty, war, and injustice. We cannot turn our backs on such realities, less we cease to be a redeeming influence in the midst of them.

But if that's all we focus on, we will live devastated lives and be overwhelmed with guilt that we're not doing enough to help others. To survive the brutalities of this age we also have to celebrate the joys life offers. We get to hold those things in tension.

Part of living righteously is not just embracing God's holiness, but also embracing his beauty and creativity, living bountifully in whatever God gives us today. It could be as simple as an impressive sunset, the playfulness of a butterfly, or an inspiring conversation with a close friend.

Living bountifully is both embracing the joys God puts before us and staying aware of the needs that surround us. We will better play the part he's given us in relieving the suffering of others if it comes from a place of thankfulness and joy. The Creation is broken and there is great suffering in the world, but whatever impinges on our freedom to enjoy God in his creation is also part of the Fall.

Sin robs us of the true joys that life has given us, and focusing on needs alone can do the same. They will exhaust us and bring us no closer to him.

> *The heavens declare the glory of God; the skies proclaim the work of his hands. Day after day they pour forth speech; night after night they reveal knowledge.*
>
> PSALM 19:1–2 (MSG)

MAY 30 — Joy at All Times

While visiting a desperately sick woman in an impoverished township outside the city of Durban, South Africa, I watched little children laugh and play as they tossed a flattened ball around. I'm sure their playful joy lifted them above the circumstances in which they lived.

It reminded me of the day I put almost everything we owned in the trunk of my Oldsmobile Cutlass as my new bride and I departed Ohio for California to start our life together. We had very little except our love for each other and the promise of a job in Fresno.

Joy was much simpler then. We didn't have a lot of stuff to maintain or protect and we had no idea of the challenges and pain that would come as we navigated life together.

Living in Father's bounty comes one day at a time. What has he given us today to enjoy? Learn to see it and embrace it whether your circumstances are abundant or your needs desperate.

Finding joy every day will serve you well when the brokenness of this world meets you head on.

> *Oh, how sweet the light of day, And how wonderful to live in the sunshine! Even if you live a long time, don't take a single day for granted. Take delight in each light-filled hour...*
>
> ECCLESIASTES 11:7–8 (MSG)

MAY 31 — Finding Joy in Struggle

I was in the hospital with a good friend of mine whose wife was undergoing surgery to remove a tumor that may be malignant. With all the anxiety that filled his heart, we were able to talk and even laugh.

It amazes me how much joy can find its way into moments of great pain. Some of the most difficult days of my life have also had moments of uproarious bellylaughter with people who shared it with me.

Joy is not the opposite of struggle; it is often a companion to help us endure it. That's why having people with us in times of struggle is so important. Alone, we get lost in the pain and fears; someone else can distract us and even lighten our load.

There is so much that Sara and I have to be thankful for these days and with great relish we share it with others who need a friend, a smile, a shoulder to cry on.

I know this: even in the midst of great tragedies our Father makes himself known. It may be in a tender smile, a comforting arm, or a moment of levity.

Learning to share in that joy with others is part of his gift to us in a broken world.

> But rejoice inasmuch as you participate in the sufferings of Christ, so that you may be overjoyed when his glory is revealed.
> **1 PETER 4:13 (NIV)**

JUN 1 — Trying to Get God to Work

I'm sad to say that most of my life was spent in ignorance of how God works. Not knowing what he was doing or how he does it, I often felt the pressure to do something to try and spur God to action. I was taught to press in, pray through, lay hold, and to be more committed, more devoted, and more disciplined so that I could make God do what I thought he should do.

It was all so exhausting and almost always fruitless. It left me frustrated at God for not responding in the way I thought my efforts compelled him to.

In my own journey, I'm just beginning to learn how to recognize Father's fingerprints in my life and in other people's lives. It is so much more fruitful to recognize what he is already doing around me and join him there. When I see what he's up to, then I know what he is asking of me to participate with him.

That's what Paul prayed for the Colossians. He wanted them to have a thorough knowledge of the ways in which God works, so that they would know how to do their part. We are responders not initiators.

God doesn't exist to fulfill our agenda; he invites us into his.

> ...*Asking God to give you wise minds and spirits attuned to his will, and so acquire a thorough understanding of the ways in which God works...As you learn more and more how God works, you will learn how to do your work.*
> COLOSSIANS 1:9-12 (MSG)

JUN 2 You Don't Have to Do Something

"Well, we have to do *something*."

More faulty counsel has come after that brief conclusion than perhaps any other. It usually means we've given up on God working and are going to employ our best wisdom and best efforts to move things along.

If you are doing something for God because you're worried you'll miss him or that he won't respond in love to you, it will be almost impossible to recognize what God is already doing in and around you.

He is easier to recognize when we are at rest in his

presence because we know he loves us and will take care of us through whatever circumstances life brings. Instead of trying to do things for him, he will show us what to do.

He wants to give us the kingdom itself. And until we see what he is doing, we do not need to feel any compulsion to "do something." And when we do see his hand moving, we'll know exactly what he wants us to do; in doing that we'll get to taste of the fruit of his kingdom...

> *What I'm trying to do here is to get you to relax, to not be so preoccupied with getting, so you can respond to God's giving. People who don't know God and the way he works fuss over these things, but you know both God and how he works.*
> MATTHEW 6:31–32 (MSG)

JUN 3 The Relentless Pursuit of Pleasure

I like pleasurable moments as much as anyone, but pursuing our own pleasure is a trap that will never satisfy. No high will ever be high enough to match our expectations, which is why the relentless pursuit of pleasure will only satisfy for a moment and then leave us frustrated.

Jesus is the only one who knows what will bring us true joy, and he is the only one who can fulfill it in us. On his last night in the upper room, he told his followers that everything he was telling them was so that they could know the fullness of joy.

What would our lives look like if we trusted God with our pleasure, and set our focus on following him?

Seek to save your life and you'll lose it. Lose it in him and you'll find the life that really is life. Pleasure without him never lasts. Having him as your pleasure will allow you to experience the deepest joys with ever-increasing glory.

> *You're addicted to thrills? What an empty life!*
> *The pursuit of pleasure is never satisfied.*
> PROVERBS 21:17 (MSG)

JUN 4 — Following the Crowd

Wouldn't it be great if everyone around you could affirm God's voice in your life and applaud you for following it? In the real world, however, this rarely happens. People, especially those who care about you, often want the same things for you that your flesh does—whatever is comfortable, safe, and satisfying.

Paul knew that walking with an eye to the approval of others will always take you far from the reality of his kingdom. Jesus said the same thing. He said to take stock when men speak well of you, for that's how they treat false prophets. Rather, he told them you are blessed when people lie, insult, and exclude you because of your obedience to him. He knew the same crowd shouting "Hosanna" on Sunday would be screaming "Crucify him!" only a few days later.

Even our Christian culture tells us that best-selling books and growing audiences await those who obey Jesus. When he was here, however, those who sought such things missed Jesus's kingdom entirely.

Too often you'll find your well-meaning friends calling you back to the broader road thinking they are helping you follow God. Don't be fooled. Follow his nudging in your heart, even if that means you will be misunderstood by people you love.

Am I now trying to win the approval of human beings, or of

> *God? Or am I trying to please people? If I were still trying to please people, I would not be a servant of Christ.*
> **GALATIANS 1:10 (NIV)**

JUN 5 — The Danger of Religious Leaders

In our day, many who claim to lead his church are not much more than well-intentioned program managers. They have an organization to run and personal goals to meet, and they view people around them as simply part of that process. If we confuse a submissive heart with following their instructions, we will often find ourselves moving away from the path God has chosen for us.

We all know how important it is to glean God's wisdom from other believers, including those who might be further along the journey. However, make sure those are people who are on the journey to knowing God, not those who are embedded in a religious institution from which they draw pay or the fulfillment of their ego.

Religious leaders lead people into religion. Weren't these types always at odds with Jesus? Did he put their instructions above his Father's? Of course not!

How can you tell the difference between religious leaders and mature believers? Religious leaders will tell you what God's will is for you. True elders in his kingdom will instead help you grow close enough to Jesus to understand that for yourself.

> *…you have an anointing from the Holy One, and all of you know the truth.*
> **I JOHN 2:20**

JUN 6 — Being Served or Serving?

Isn't it the natural inclination of our natural mind to try and get things the way we want them, even if we disguise our ambitions by convincing ourselves it is the only right thing to do?

When God's leading seems to put you at the center and uses others to help you get what you think is best—it is time to be suspicious. All of us feel "led by God" to things we already want.

In my journey, that has mostly led me astray, and only after hurting others could I realize how selfish I was being.

If, however, his tug on your heart leads you to lay down your life for someone else's benefit, then you can feel free to run down that road. Even if you're wrong, you will still be a blessing to someone else.

> *This is how we know what love is: Jesus Christ laid down his life for us. And we ought to lay down our lives for our brothers and sisters.*
>
> 1 JOHN 3:16 (NIV)

JUN 7 — Convenience or Risk?

God's will does not—contrary to popular belief—lay down the path of least resistance. The truth is, God's will often takes us down the road of great resistance and conflict.

An open door equals great conflict! What a perspective!

When Jesus invites us to live by faith he invites us to live in the security of Father's love with an eye to his wisdom, his power, and his abilities—not our own. Often, that will take us down roads that challenge us rather than serving our own convenience.

If you are not regularly finding yourself in situations far beyond your own ability to handle, you're probably not growing. Growth comes by risking the status quo, not protecting it.

> *But I will stay on at Ephesus until Pentecost, because a great door for effective work has opened to me, and there are many who oppose me.*
>
> **1 CORINTHIANS 16:8–9 (NIV)**

JUN 8 — Where True Security Lies

Because he so desperately wants to free you from the bondage of serving yourself, Jesus will invite you beyond what feels convenient and secure. When he led Israel through the wilderness, they grew so insecure that they preferred slavery in Egypt to living as free men and women in God in the wilderness. Many make that same decision today.

In contrast, look at the list of those who walked by faith in Hebrews 11. More than eighty percent of the time, living by faith made them look irresponsible to human wisdom. But they weren't irresponsible because they were learning to follow God and rely on him, not on man's ways of doing things.

Though it took them into greater conflict and at times cost them more than they ever dreamed, it also took them into the very heart of God. They learned to rely on him and not themselves, and that is where true security lies.

When you're looking at the sign that reads "Personal Security," you're looking in the wrong direction. Turn around. Be willing to risk something so awesome at God's leading that there's no way it will work without him. That's where you'll discover what faith really is.

> *Now faith is confidence in what we hope for and
> assurance about what we do not see.*
>
> **HEBREWS 11:1 (NIV)**

JUN 9 — Content with God's Portion

"The Son of Man has no place to lay his head…You cannot serve both God and Money…But if we have food and clothing, be content with that."

You can't say you trust God's provision and then decide what it is he must provide to make you happy. Jesus didn't talk like God wanted to ensure us all with upward financial mobility. That isn't to say, however, that God won't at times bless people financially. What it means is that the best financial decisions aren't always the godliest.

How many people have not followed God's nudging because they couldn't trust him to provide for them, or because it didn't make sense financially? I've made that mistake more often than I'd care to admit.

God's path rarely makes sense if our concern for money is at the forefront, though he promises to take care of our every need. If Paul had only made decisions based on how it would secure his financial future, I'm afraid he would have missed much that God had for him. Instead he learned to be content with God's provision and realized it might vary from season to season.

Follow God or follow money, but you cannot follow both!

> *…people of corrupt mind, who have been robbed of the truth
> and who think that godliness is a means to financial gain…*
>
> **1 TIMOTHY 6:5 (NIV)**

JUN 10 — You Need a Plan, Do You?

It's frustrating at times to beg God for the five-year plan, and then only feel like you can barely see the next step. We like the long-range strategies, but what if Jesus enjoys teaching us to follow him by just giving us one step at a time?

I think of that whenever I hear someone tell me the strategy God has given them to build a ministry or a business. It hasn't worked that way for me. All of my five-year plans have come to naught, and the most fruitful things I'm involved in today came as a simple act of obedience that opened wide doors I never knew were there.

Putting our kids in public school for kindergarten began a series of circumstances where I was helping schools nationally build bridges between those with more secular interests and people of faith. I never saw that coming.

I like to say now that God's will doesn't come to us as a multiyear strategic plan. Those are usually our ideas. We like being self-reliant, able to trust sound principles and routines, rather than hear his ever-present voice.

Jesus, however, is more interested in teaching us to live with a daily dependence on his voice with a willingness to follow him even if we have no idea what the outcome might be. Following him most often means we only see the next step, rather than the next ten.

Follow anyway, and you'll see the wonder of his plan unfold in ways you could never have contemplated. That's best seen looking back at his faithfulness, however, rather than seeing into the future.

Now listen, you who say, "Today or tomorrow we will go to this or that city, spend a year there, carry on business and make money." Why, you do not even know what will happen tomorrow. What is your life? You are a mist that appears for a little while and then vanishes. Instead, you ought to say, "If it is the Lord's will, we will live and do this or that." As it is, you boast in your arrogant schemes. All such boasting is evil."

JAMES 4:13–16 (NIV)

JUN 11 Being a Light in the World

There was a time in my life that I had no meaningful relationships with people who were not Christians, and I only knew other believers who gathered in the same group as me. I looked with suspicion on those who had too many friendships with people in the world.

That's what Jesus faced when he was constantly accused of hanging out with the wrong crowd—those who were caught in sin or those who ignored the protocol of the religious crowd. Father's heart had drawn him to be with the least and the lost, helping them discover the joy of God's life.

So, don't think when God invites you on opportunities to love those who may yet be still lost that you are somehow abandoning him or his church. God has called us to be the light in some of the darkest places.

Neither do people light a lamp and put it under a bowl. Instead they put it on its stand, and it gives light to everyone in the house.

MATTHEW 5:15 (NIV)

JUN 12 Follow Anyway

Christianity is living in relationship to the Living God. You can't do that if you're not free to follow him wherever he leads you.

Of course, anyone who sets their course by trying to

be misunderstood, offending religious leaders, taking absurd risks, living carelessly, or finding company only among sinners will not necessarily be walking God's pathway. All of those can be used as excuses for arrogant and destructive acts that lead to ruin.

I'm not writing to people like that.

I'm writing to people passionate for a real life in Jesus and you won't get there by following your religious sensibilities. Instead we can learn to listen to his Spirit as he guides us and teaches us to trust him. It's easy to miss his leading when it doesn't align with the false notions we've been given about what living in God really means.

Follow the Lamb wherever he goes, so that you can be like him in the world and available for all he wants to do in and through you.

Then Jesus said to his disciples, "If anyone would come after me, he must deny himself and take up his cross and follow me..."
MATTHEW 16:24 (NIV)

JUN 13 Where Our Security Lies

In times of national or international tragedy and vulnerability it is easy to see where our security really lies. If it is placed in the illusions of our prosperous culture, you will find your stomach churning and restful sleep elusive.

As much as our government must mitigate threat however they can, our security does not lie in jet fighters, hazmat suits, or airport screeners any more than ancient Israel could rely on horses and chariots. This is a great time to discover just how much I entrust myself to the Lord's care and direction or how much I'm shaped by the age I live in.

One of my favorite phrases in the book of Revelation describes those followers who endure the trauma of the last days and overcame the power of sin and the terror of the anti-Christ's reign: "They follow the Lamb wherever he goes."

I love the simplicity of that and can think of no better words to describe how I want to live. What's even better is that you don't have to wait until the end of the age to live that way.

> *They follow the Lamb wherever he goes. They were purchased from among mankind and offered as first-fruits to God and the Lamb.*
> **REVELATION 14:4 (NIV)**

JUN 14 — It's Not the Outside that Counts

Following Jesus led Paul to be locked into prison, stoned by those who opposed him, and even to be robbed by bandits and shipwrecked on the high seas. Paul never saw these as proof that God had abandoned him, but rather as part of the challenge of walking with Jesus in a fallen world.

Though circumstances would at times press him on every side or strike him down, he said it never crushed him or led him to despair. Why?

He drew a real distinction between what was happening to him on the outside and the joy and freedom he had inside. He didn't define his existence by outside circumstances. Even calamity would only refine the treasure inside even more and be a gift he could give away to others who encountered suffering.

This precedence of inner life over outer circumstance is at the heart of what spiritual maturity is all about.

> *Who shall separate us from the love of Christ? Shall trouble or hardship or persecution or famine or nakedness or danger or sword?*
> **ROMANS 8:35 (NIV)**

JUN 15 — Trust in the Worst of Times

Paul did not see himself as the victim of his circumstances, but an ambassador of Christ in a sometimes-hostile world.

Regardless of what swirled around him, he knew that God was his refuge. Of course, he wouldn't be able to live there if he were still trying to force God to fulfill what he wanted. Can you imagine Paul praying for unchallenging circumstances every day? He would have lived in great disappointment, questioning the vitality of his prayer life.

If you can only trust God when life is easy, then you will not only miss him, but you will also miss the most valuable fruit of trust. When you set your mind on God's things and know how safe you are in his care, you can awaken to each new day not buffeted by fear, but free to see what he will do in the unfolding events of your life.

No external threat can touch his life in you—not the most painful tragedy, or the most alluring temptation. Nothing brings greater joy to his heart and more freedom to yours than to learn how to live at peace in the midst of tragedy.

He will teach you if you ask him. With your eyes more focused on him than the events of this world, you'll be able to face anything with the confidence that comes from knowing him.

> *For you died, and your life is now*
> *hidden with Christ in God...*
> **COLOSSIANS 3:3 (NIV)**

SECTION 3
Growing in Trust

JUN 16 — The Call of the Shepherd, Part 1

Do you remember the first day you knew that I loved you? Do you remember how clean you felt and how light your heart was? The air seemed clearer, the colors of my creation brighter. You felt as if you had stumbled out of a dark, dirty cave and plunged headlong into a clean, cool stream. You drank in the reality of my presence and splashed with delight in my goodness.

In that moment nothing else mattered. You knew at the very core of your being that I was real...that I had great affection for you. Even in the face of dire circumstances, you were convinced that there was nothing we couldn't walk through together. My love not only overwhelmed you, it also overflowed you with grace for others, even those who had wronged you. You woke up every morning in eager anticipation of what I'd show you that day. You delighted yourself in me as I delighted myself in you. Each day became an adventure together.

Wouldn't you like to come back to that place? Me too. That's not just where I wanted you to start. It was where I wanted you to live every day.

> ...then you will find your joy in the LORD, and I will cause you to ride in triumph on the heights of the land and to feast on the inheritance of your father Jacob...
>
> ISAIAH 58:14 (NIV)

JUN 17 — The Call of the Shepherd, Part 2

I know things got complicated. I didn't fix everything

you wanted me to fix and I know that shook your confidence in me. Others told you that you weren't working hard enough so you concluded that the success of our relationship was hinged on your effort and wisdom.

When anything went wrong you either blamed me for not loving you or yourself for not trying hard enough. Both were dead ends and the life we shared eventually faded into confusion and guilt.

But I never gave up on you. I knew your best efforts would not be enough, which is why I already satisfied in myself all my Father would ever require of you. Your righteousness is in me and guilt never has a place in our relationship.

And I know I have disappointed your expectations, but that was only because I have better things in mind for you than you have for yourself.

I work through times of pain as well as times of joy.

Though the fig tree does not bud and there are no grapes on the vines, though the olive crop fails and the fields produce no food, though there are no sheep in the pen and no cattle in the stalls, yet I will rejoice in the LORD, I will be joyful in God my Savior.

HABAKKUK 3:17–18 (NIV)

JUN 18 — The Call of the Shepherd, Part 3

I know you thought I had lost sight of you, but I never have.

It was you who lost sight of me, but I know right where you are and every place you have wandered because I followed you there. I have continued to call your name and invite you into the life that really is life. But so many other things drowned out my voice—activities you thought would bring me closer to you and the busyness you got caught in hoping to hide your emptiness.

Even when I tried to scoop you up in my arms, you recoiled, not recognizing my hand; I held back, letting you have the distance you thought you needed. I will teach you how to trust my purpose so that even times of trouble will not destroy our friendship.

Come, my Beloved, let me wash over you again like a cool fountain, cleansing all that has hurt and confused you. Let us start anew and I will show you just how much I love you and that all I ever wanted from you was you!

I'm still in your presence, but you've taken my hand. You wisely and tenderly lead me, and then you bless me.
PSALM 73:23–24 (MSG)

JUN 19 The Call of the Shepherd, Part 4

Did I not tell you that I would take care of you—that I would lead you into safe pastures and refresh you with living water?

Did I not tell you that I had rejected the shepherds who wanted to use my flock for their own purpose, battering and plundering my sheep for their own gain?

You need no other shepherd but me. I will lead you into rich pastures and watch over you so that you will never need to be afraid again. I am not going to exploit you, for I am the shepherd who gives his life for the sheep.

I did not run in the face of my own death but embraced the shame because I wanted to open the way for us to be together.

For the Lamb at the center of the throne will be their shepherd; "he will lead them to springs of living water. And God will wipe away every tear from their eyes."
REVELATION 7:17 (NIV)

JUN 20 — The Call of the Shepherd, Part 5

No one on this planet ever has or ever will love you like I do. The great lie of darkness is that you cannot trust me with your life.

Oh, but I can!

I will take care of you and teach you to follow me so that you can know the fullness of my life. I will hold you close to my heart as we walk through the days ahead. Even in the face of pain and death, I will ensure that nothing will take you out of my hand. I will draw you to myself, wipe every tear from your eyes, and through it all transform you into the person I know you want to be.

You wandered in places where you got hurt and sought out easy answers that proved false. I am not the source of your pain, but the one who has offered you healing. All the while I wanted to teach you how I work. I do not put Band-Aids over your life so it will look better. I seek to heal you at the deepest places.

Being whole is not something that you can do without me, but you can thwart the process if you won't let me show you how to yield to my wisdom and power.

You have nothing to fear. Your entire life is in my hands and my hands are sure.

> *Trust in the LORD with all your heart and*
> *lean not on your own understanding…*
> **PROVERBS 3:5 (NIV)**

JUN 21 — The Call of the Shepherd, Part 6

My sheep know my voice.

I call you by name and point the way for you to go, but you have found the voice of strangers to be more certain than my own. Those who take turns pretending to be the shepherd have destroyed your confidence in my ability to lead you. Wanting you to be dependent on them, they told you to follow them because they knew what would be best for you.

Many of them even mean well, but the end result was always the same. They could not lead you to life because life is only in me. They had no way of knowing where I wanted to lead you and they were blinded to my working by their own plans for you.

And you followed them, only to be abused and exploited. It was their vision they served and not mine. Yes, I saw your pain when they turned on you for asking honest questions and cut you off when you sought to follow me instead of them. I know how deeply it hurts to be betrayed by those you thought loved you.

I never wanted you to trust them more than me. I never asked you to follow any man or woman. They're the ones who asked you to do that.

Dear friends, do not believe every spirit, but test the spirits to see whether they are from God, because many false prophets have gone out into the world.

1 JOHN 4:1 (NIV)

JUN 22 *The Call of the Shepherd*, Part 7

I know many of you thought controlling leaders were helping you, but in the end, they only led you astray. They bullied you with their imagined authority and bloodied you with guilt and calls to loyalty.

But you knew better, didn't you?

Often, I warned you, which is why your heart was so unsettled in the things they told you. You overrode my warnings because you didn't think yourself mature enough to question people like them.

At such times you were looking to yourself and not to me. I am strong enough to lead you in my life, even beyond your doubts and insecurities.

> *They give the way of truth a bad name. They're only out for themselves. They'll say anything, anything that sounds good to exploit you. They won't, of course, get by with it. They'll come to a bad end, for God has never just stood by and let that kind of thing go on.*
>
> 2 PETER 2:2–3 (MSG)

JUN 23 — The Call of the Shepherd, Part 8

Anyone who truly knows me, will teach you to follow me.

They will not use you to build their ministry or to line their pockets. They will give freely, always pointing you to the only shepherd that matters—me! They will encourage you to trust my love for you and will teach you to follow me even when you're uncertain how to do that.

They know it is better for you to learn to follow me and make a mistake than think yourself secure in any program they could devise.

Are you tired of listening to the voice of strangers?

I want to teach you how to know my voice again. I have others who will help you learn, but listen only to those that point you to me, not the ones who would gather you to themselves. You can trust me to make clear to you everything that I want you to know and everything that I call you to do. If you don't hear my voice in what others say do not feel any obligation to follow their counsel or their instruction. You are only truly safe in me.

I am not loud and boisterous. I will not compete with the clamor of the world nor the busyness of your agenda. I gently call you by name, hold you close to my heart, and invite you to follow me.

> *...He leads them and they follow because they are familiar with his voice. They won't follow a stranger's voice but will scatter because they aren't used to the sound of it.*
>
> JOHN 10:4 (MSG)

JUN 24 — The Call of the Shepherd, Part 4

If my voice seems only to drift by for a moment and then fades into the harried pace of life, it is because your ears are better tuned to other things. I only seem distant when you trust your own wisdom instead of mine.

Often, I have shown you the way I want you to go but, instead of simply following, you looked at the challenges that stood in your way and convinced yourself that it wasn't me. One day, you will know that your safety is not in pleasant circumstances, but in being with me.

If you have forgotten how to listen, just ask me and I will show you. It is not as hard as you think. I simply want you to draw near to me and once again let your heart be mine.

The more you grow in knowing my love for you, the easier it will be to recognize my gentle prodding. I am greater than any doubt that troubles you or any voice that seeks to steer you another way. I will help you recognize my presence in all you do. I will show you how to live as a father or mother, child or student, employer or employee, neighbor or friend.

Don't banish me to a separate spiritual part of your life; I want to make all of your life spiritual and all of it full in me.

> *Come, my children, listen to me...*
> PSALM 34:11 (NIV)

JUN 25 — The Call of the Shepherd, Part 10

I know that the closer you follow me the lonelier it seems.

You even think at times that I abandoned you and you withdrew into your fears. But even there, I am with you, calling you outside of yourself to come into the freedom of being my child and to join your heart with others in my flock that live for no other.

You've been called arrogant, independent, and unsubmitted, not by those who knew my heart, but by those who wanted you to conform to their way of doing things. They can't see my flock beyond their own way of organizing it. If you only knew how many people I have scattered all over the world, you would rejoice that you're not alone.

Some of those live just down the block from you or work alongside you. I know that you don't know them yet, but you do understand the passion that courses through their veins and their desire to connect with people who share it.

I am the shepherd of all my sheep and I am not only inviting you to follow me as an individual, I am gathering my flock together from the ends of the earth—not in human systems devouring your time and energy, but in the joy of healthy friendships.

No man will own it and no system will replicate what I am building between my people. Resist the temptation to follow models devised by men that will always fail.

> *They too will listen to my voice, and there shall be one flock and one shepherd.*
>
> **JOHN 10:16 (NIV)**

JUN 26 — The Call of the Shepherd, Part 11

I will knit you into relationships with people near you and even some far away so that you can enjoy the richness of my flock. Don't try to make it happen on your own. Just live with your eye on me every day, loving those I put in your path, and soon you will find people around you who follow the same Shepherd.

But first I want your heart to be completely mine. If you try to use others in this church to get what you do not find in me, it will only ruin the relationship.

I want to teach you how to share my life together, each one receiving from my hand and sharing freely with the others without demanding anything in return. As you love that way you will find that life among my people is not cumbersome and is filled with great joy.

You will go away from encounters more aware of who I am and less focused on your needs and weaknesses. And you'll be less focused on theirs, too.

All the believers were one in heart and mind.
ACTS 4:32 (NIV)

JUN 27 — The Call of the Shepherd, Part 12

What do I need from you?

All I need is a willing heart to follow me wherever I choose to take you. I don't need great talent, great wisdom, or great abilities. If you just yield your life to me, I can teach you how to trust me beyond your wisdom and fears.

I want you to abandon your agenda for what you think your life should be—it will only distract you from what I have in mind. Even the best of intentions can lead you to desire the wrong outcomes and will encourage you down a wrong path. If you only knew the plans I have for you with a future and a hope that far outweighs your own agenda, you would abandon yours in an instant.

When the heat is on, don't try to save yourself—you will only get in deeper trouble. When trouble surrounds you, stop! Take a deep breath and turn toward me. Wait and listen until you hear that nudge in your heart that says, "This is the way I want you to go."

Don't worry about whether or not it makes sense to you. I've been here before and I know the way through your doubts and pain to greater transformation and freedom.

> *Acknowledge the God of your father and serve him with wholehearted devotion and with a willing mind, for the LORD searches every heart and understands every desire and every thought. If you seek him, he will be found by you.*
>
> 1 CHRONICLES 28:9 (NIV)

JUN 28 — The Call of the Shepherd, Part 13

As you wake up each day, open your heart to my love. Ask me to walk with you so your eyes will focus beyond your own wisdom.

Then, let me share your day with you. Don't live in the past by copying what you've done before or embracing your regrets. Don't try to secure your future by following someone else's programs or their model. That only offers false security.

Lay down even your dreams for ministry. You have confused your dreams with mine and trying to fulfill either in your own effort will only frustrate you. Most of what you call ministry has more to do with human aspiration than it does the life of my kingdom. Your pursuit of ministry instead of me will be a barrier, not a blessing.

Let me teach you all over again, how much I love the broken-hearted, the wounded, and the oppressed, and how I set them free. When you see what I am doing, you'll know what you are to do.

> *When you see the ark of the covenant of the LORD your God, and the Levitical priests carrying it, you are to move out from your positions and follow it. Then you will know which way to go, since you have never been this way before...*
>
> JOSHUA 3:3-4 (NIV)

JUN 29 — The Call of the Shepherd, Part 14

You have a choice, you know. I can keep following you and rescuing you out of all the places you get stuck, or you can turn around and follow me and I will lead you to the heights of my glory.

I am the way to Father's fullness, and I want nothing more than to take you there.

Let me scoop you up in my arms and carry you along as I show you the wonders of my Father's kingdom. Tune your ears to my voice and look to me in all that happens to see what I might be showing you.

There is no situation that I can't lead you through, and there is no promise that I cannot fulfill in you. Trust my voice more than your own and yield to my hand as I shape you into the person I created you to be.

There is nothing you can do to earn this—it is beyond your ability. But it is not beyond mine. I am able to make you stand and establish you in my gospel. I am able to make all grace abound to you so that in all things at all times you will have all that you need.

Praise be to the LORD my Rock, who trains my hands for war, my fingers for battle. He is my loving God and my fortress, my stronghold and my deliverer, my shield, in whom I take refuge, who subdues peoples under me.

PSALM 144:1-2 (NIV)

JUN 30 — The Call of the Shepherd, Part 15

I am...

I am able to help you at your weakest moment.

I am your faithful friend, who empathizes with your pain and has all the mercy and grace you need.

I am able to keep you from falling and present you before God's glorious presence, without fault and with great joy!

I am able to gather my flock from all the places it has been scattered. I will take them to the heights of my glory, where they can delight in the greenest of pastures and drink the purest water. Because I am, you will never need to be afraid again. You are safe in my hands.

Come, my Beloved, your time is now. Take my hand and I will show you all that I hold in my heart for you and you will discover the unmitigated joy of living in my rest.

I myself will search for my sheep and look after them. As a shepherd looks after his scattered flock when he is with them, so will I look after my sheep. I will rescue them from all the places where they were scattered on a day of clouds and darkness. I will bring them out from the nations and gather them from the countries, and I will bring them into their own land.

EZEKIEL 34:11-13 (NIV)

JUL 1 — I'd Rather Do It Myself

A number of years ago, I took my son Andy with me for a TV interview in Nashville. My brother was the director, and Andy wanted to see the inner workings of television production since he was considering that as a career.

For the most part, I'm not as cool in his eyes as I used to be. I have even been known to be an embarrassment to him at times, even when I'm not trying. When I had to go off and do other things at the studio, I'm sure he didn't miss me.

That is a part of growing up: Andy was learning to take responsibility for himself in the world. Unfortunately, growing up to be a responsible adult in the world is different from what it means to mature in Christ. Life in Christ can't be lived alone. It's kind of right there in the description.

We got a taste of that on the flight home. My son hates to fly, and to make matters worse we were in a small commuter plane when we encountered severe turbulence as an El Nino storm invaded California. Suddenly, Dad wasn't so uncool anymore.

He wanted me there so that every few seconds he could ask me about our safety. He also needed someone on whom to vent his firm resolve that he would never fly again. That's the picture Jesus wants us to have of him—in times of need and times of joy. With us, not intrusively, but graciously sharing our life with us.

> *...So that you may be mature and complete, not lacking anything...*
> **JAMES 1:4 (NIV)**

JUL 2 — Missing the Moment

It's been there for quite a while—a sense that Jesus is asking something of you. It doesn't nag you at every moment, but it surfaces periodically when something triggers your memory. Suddenly you're aware of a deeper stirring in your heart and are even excited to understand how it might come to pass.

Maybe you're even reminded of something like that right now, as you're reading this.

But just as quickly, that sense often fades as it gets swallowed up in the daily demands of twenty-first century living. Responsibilities at work, chores at home, family needs, and the busyness of life take hold of our day and send us careening from circumstance to circumstance until fulfilling our obligations takes up almost all of our time.

We find ourselves so exhausted in everyday mundane moments that we can only muster enough energy for some brief amusement before falling into bed and starting the rat race again the next day.

That's how we miss our moments with him and then forget his whispers to us. Take note when he nudges your heart. Follow through as best you see, and you'll find yourself living more abundantly.

> *The LORD came and stood there, calling as at the other times, "Samuel! Samuel!" Then Samuel said, "Speak, for your servant is listening."*
>
> **1 SAMUEL 3:10 (NIV)**

JUL 3 — What Is God Asking of You?

Spiritual stagnation can easily ensnare any of us. Instead of living in the adventure of Jesus's work and purpose in our lives each day, we get sucked into the world's way of thinking and we are focused only on surviving the demands of this day.

When that happens, we become so preoccupied with jobs, homes, and activities that we lose our awareness that we are part of a greater kingdom. Even our spiritual passion is robbed by trading Jesus's ever-present voice for the obligations, traditions, and rituals others tell us we must employ.

Many people think of this as going through a dry time and that God's presence has passed us by when nothing could be further from the truth. He's right where he's always been, deep in your heart using everything he can to invite you alongside him. He wants to share his glory with you—not withhold it.

When you feel stagnated, find some space where you can draw away (even for a moment) and recapture the spirit of adventure pulsing deep within you.

> *If all you want is your own way, flirting with the world every chance you get, you end up enemies of God and his way. And do you suppose God doesn't care? The proverb has it that "he's a fiercely jealous lover." And what he gives in love is far better than anything else you'll find.*
>
> JAMES 4:4 (MSG)

JUL 4 — The Melody in the Wind

Can you hear it?

It's the Song of the Ages, still playing beneath the stresses and strains of this world, fresh from your Father's heart. Regardless of all that's going on around you, it invites you into his reality.

It's not the loudest song in the wind. Fears and anger will scream louder. The rancor of political discord will drown it out, and it can easily be swallowed up by the cacophonous strains of anxiety that dominate these troubled times.

But beneath it all, his song still plays, as certain as the rising sun, more triumphant than the most exquisite symphony.

You won't find it while groping for certainty in your imagined future. You won't be able to focus on it while arguing your politics or putting your hope in yet-to-be-fulfilled prophecies about a coming revival.

You have no idea what is to come, and neither do all those voices. The honest ones will tell you that. Your certainty now has to be in Jesus and him alone. All others are mere illusions, which may comfort for the moment but, when they fail you, how deep will that pain be? Circumstances, both favorable and unfavorable, will come and go.

The only refuge is to abandon yourself to the amazing love of a gracious Father and see his divine purpose unfolding around you. He will never let you down.

> *Surely God is my salvation; I will trust and not be afraid. The LORD, the LORD, is my strength and my song; he has become my salvation.*
>
> **ISAIAH 12:2 (NIV)**

JUL 5 — He Is Enough

Come away, my beloved!

There! Did you hear it?

Maybe it was just a few notes, but even a bit of it will begin to breathe hope into your exhausted heart. You'll recognize it as the soothing melody inviting you beside his quiet waters where peace and tranquility will wash over your fear and grief. Linger there and lean away from anxious thoughts and angry voices, both internal and external.

His song carries a different rhythm. *He is enough. You are deeply loved. All of Creation is still in his hands.*

There's no fear or frustration in his song. Its soft and lilting tones draw you more deeply to his heart, where fear no longer thrives. It allows you to embrace a reality far more consequential than anything you see with your eyes or hear with your ears.

It calms your heart with the confidence that God is big enough for this, too.

They sang the song of Moses the servant of God and the song of the Lamb: "Great and marvelous are your deeds, Lord God Almighty. Just and true are your ways, King of the ages."

REVELATION 15:3 (NIV)

JUL 6 — The Rhythms of Grace

None of what is going on in your life has caught Jesus by surprise.

He has not abandoned you to your own devices. His deliverance does not await some future day. Jesus reassured us that his Father is always working. That includes in you... today.

He has a way through this for you—even if someone you love suffers, even if your business does not survive, even if our culture comes crashing down around us, even if this is your time to join him in a kingdom that knows no end.

He has options you haven't begun to consider.

Come away, my beloved.

His song is an invitation, not a compulsion. You'll find it more clearly in that quiet place in your soul where Jesus makes himself known.

It may take a while to tune your ears again to his melody and hold it in your heart. You'll know you've found it when your heart takes a deep breath and begins to find its rest in the unforced rhythms of his grace.

> "Are you tired? Worn out? Burned out on religion? Come to me. Get away with me and you'll recover your life. I'll show you how to take a real rest. Walk with me and work with me—watch how I do it. Learn the unforced rhythms of grace."
>
> MATTHEW 11:28–29 (MSG)

JUL 7 Keep Your Focus on His Melody

You can't hear his melody coursing through the creation around you? It does take different ears than the ones on the side of your head.

Even more important than hearing the song is seeing the one who composed it. Take his hand and follow his lead however you best sense him today. Wake up tomorrow and find that song again.

Everything else in this world will seek to knock you off his melody, drawing you back into its discordant notes. You don't have to give in to these false tones.

You can keep coming back to him and to his quiet waters and bathe yourself there. That's where you'll have the wisdom to live through each day's challenges without fear of your imagined future. You'll know how to respond prudently to what's going on in the world and find compassion for others around you who are struggling too.

When you're at peace in turmoil, his song will flow through you, amplifying it in your corner of the world. Then others will find it easier to hear and perhaps find their way to his peace as well.

*You are my hiding place; you will protect me from trouble
and surround me with songs of deliverance.*

PSALM 32:7 (NIV)

JUL 8 — What Is He Asking of You?

No matter how much you think you have lost sight of him, remember that he has not lost sight of you.

Jesus will continue to offer you the next step in the journey and will wait for you to follow. There is no life, passion, or joy in this kingdom without Jesus walking alongside us. He wants to be the voice that steers you through every situation, the peace that sets your heart at rest in trouble, and the power that holds you up in the storm.

What is he asking of you right now? It could be as simple as taking a treat to a neighbor and getting acquainted, or as life changing as using a gift God has given you to help advance his kingdom in the world. He might be encouraging you to start a lunch-time discussion group at work or help some brothers and sisters near you to find more intentional ways to share his life together.

He could be asking you to give money to someone in need, open a door to reconcile a broken relationship, or come alongside another person in what he has called him or her to do. Or he could be asking you just to sit back and enjoy his presence.

*Surely God is my salvation; I will trust and not be
afraid. The LORD, the LORD, is my strength and
my song; he has become my salvation.*

ISAIAH 12:2 (NIV)

JUL 9 — A Voice to Follow

The world makes fun of the notion that God still speaks to individuals. Some well-intentioned believers do as well.

And you really can't blame them. You probably know a number of people yourself who have done all manner of selfish or destructive things while claiming God told them. It's enough to give listening to God a bad name.

But just because people pass counterfeit money doesn't stop us from using the real thing. At the heart of our life in Jesus is the freedom to hear him and follow him. Paul told the Romans that this life wasn't about following rules anymore, but about following Jesus.

Learning to think through our day with God is not the upgraded, only-for-special-people option of the life of Christ. This is the basic, stripped down version of the life Jesus purchased for us.

But now that you've found you don't have to listen to sin tell you what to do and have discovered the delight of listening to God telling you, what a surprise! A whole, healed, put-together life right now, with more and more of life on the way!

ROMANS 6:22 (MSG)

JUL 10 — A Voice We've Been Taught to Ignore

I love thinking through every challenge in my day with Jesus. I talk to him about those things I'm facing and lay my questions at his feet, confident that he will show me what I need to know when I need to know it.

The New Testament reminds us again and again that each of us can know him so that no one needs to tell us what to do, and no one needs to decide for us what is truth or error. I don't hear voices. I hear his thoughts inside my own. It's rarely easy to tell the difference between his thoughts and mine, at least initially. But as I find those thoughts that seem bigger than me, meditate on them, and share what I'm seeing with other believers close to me, it gets easier to identify which thoughts are his.

What is he doing in you? What is he asking of you today? Almost everything God has me involved in today resulted from simple actions I sensed God invited me to years ago. Some of them were as small as making a phone call, volunteering at my daughter's school, spending time developing a friendship, or walking away from a conflict with a friend when I would have preferred to fight.

Each of those choices set off a chain reaction that opened doors I did not foresee, but I am amazed at what can unfold from following an impulse when it is his.

> *But you have an anointing from the Holy One,*
> *and all of you know the truth…*
> 1 JOHN 2:20 (NIV)

JUL 11 A Growing Conviction

Having a "conversation" with God is not like sitting down with a friend, where I say something and then he or she responds. My exchanges with Father, Son, and Spirit take days and weeks as I hold things before him and his insights grow in my heart and mind.

My friend Jack is from Scotland and served as a young missionary surgeon in the 1950s in a country known then as the Congo. For more than seventy years he has enjoyed a growing relationship with the living God. I met him while he was in his eighties, living in New Zealand.

"You know how I recognize God's voice?" he asked me one day sitting in his home. "For me, it has been a growing conviction over time."

That expresses it well. Many of my own thoughts will vanish with the next distraction. God's thoughts, however, continue to come back to me at the strangest moments, and each time, I'm a bit more convinced that this may be something God is showing me.

So, unless his thought is not urgent, and most times they are not, live with that thought for a few days. See how time seasons it and whether other conversations affirm it.

I regularly spend time talking with Jesus, seasoning my mind with reading Scripture and listening to insights of other believers. Those things that become increasingly clear are often his impulses that eventually rise over the distractions and distresses of our days.

For the word of God is alive and active...
HEBREWS 4:12 (NIV)

JUL 12 Knowing Which Thoughts Are His

How do I know if the thought I'm having is a God-thought or just one of my own? Discovering that is part of the adventure.

Initially, I measure whatever I'm hearing by the content and spirit of Scripture. I don't look for proof-texts, but because I read Scripture regularly I have a sense of the way God works and the kinds of things he might or might not say.

I'm more suspicious of insights I like than ones I don't. I always like my thoughts; it's God's insights that don't so easily fit in my comfort zone. His way is rarely the easier path.

I never trust the thoughts that rise from my anxieties. Jesus warned us in Matthew 6 that the rising tide of anxiety will blind us to his kingdom. He is easiest to recognize when I'm at rest in his love, not worried about the future.

And I don't listen to guilt. Guilt will always lead me away from God's wisdom. Too many think they will only be led by God when they finally stop some temptation or act more disciplined. But they have it backward. We cannot conform our flesh to God's ways, but we can be led by him until our flesh is displaced by his presence and insight.

Therefore I tell you, do not worry about your life, what you will eat or drink; or about your body, what you will wear. Is not life more than food, and the body more than clothes? Look at the birds of the air; they do not sow or reap or store away in barns, and yet your heavenly Father feeds them. Are you not much more valuable than they?

MATTHEW 6:25–26 (NIV)

JUL 13 — Trusting the Shepherd

"Do you really think you're good enough to hear God every day?"

The question came from a young mother in Atlanta. "Of course not," is the only answer I could think of until I changed the question.

What if the question is not whether I'm good enough, but whether God is big enough to get through to me every day? That gets a resounding yes. He's bigger than my doubts, fears, failures, and shame. He knows where I'm thick-headed and where I prefer to feed my illusions; but he is bigger still.

Don't let feelings of incompetence keep you from

listening to him. One thing religious leaders have done well over centuries is convince most people that they aren't educated, anointed, or knowledgeable enough to hear from God. Or that God doesn't speak today at all. They would rather you trust their interpretations of Scripture than learn to follow Jesus on your own.

Don't fall for it. He is able to make the way clear for you.

He calls his own sheep by name and leads them out. When he has brought out all his own, he goes on ahead of them, and his sheep follow him because they know his voice. But they will never follow a stranger; in fact, they will run away from him because they do not recognize a stranger's voice.

JOHN 10:3–5

JUL 14 — Who Is Competent for These Things?

Don't discount his whispers in your heart because you feel you aren't enough to do what he might ask of you. The one who calls you is also the one who will go with you and empower you.

He has spoken some of the most exquisite things into my heart. I rarely feel up to the task, nor do I always wrap my mind around why he would be nudging me in a given direction.

You are going to feel unqualified for most of what he asks of you. Go anyway. You will find him there if you follow him far enough to see his hand at work through you.

And yes, you'll make mistakes at times; no one who walks this way avoids them. I certainly made my share. But learning to follow him comes as much from our getting it wrong as it does from getting it right.

That's why when God asks you to follow him, you'll be the one to take the risk and pay the price when you get it wrong. Too many people trick themselves into thinking that God is telling them to do something that will put others at risk, either a spouse, friend, or business colleague.

> *The Sovereign LORD is my strength; he makes my feet like the feet of a deer, he enables me to tread on the heights.*
> **HABAKKUK 3:19 (NIV)**

JUL 15 — Can You Imagine?

When Jesus told Peter that the day would come when he would be led to his death for the Gospel, Peter wanted to know about John. "What about him?"

If tradition is accurate, John was executed by being boiled alive in a vat of oil some twenty or thirty years after Peter was crucified upside down on a cross. Jesus already knew John's death would be at least as bad as Peter's, but he didn't tell him so. Peter wanted proof of God's fairness by comparing himself to others. Jesus could have responded, "Yes, him too!" but he didn't. He refused to play Peter's game.

Instead, he took a surprising tack. He pointed to John. "Him? If I want him to remain again until I come, what is that to you? You follow me."

Jesus expanded Peter's dilemma to encompass his worst fear. "What if he never dies, Peter. How does that affect you?"

We can't follow Jesus if we are worried about what God has in mind for others. The same thing he said to Peter, he speaks to us. Don't worry about others. "You—follow me."

> *Jesus said, "If I want him to live until I come again, what's that to you? You—follow me."*
> **JOHN 20:22 (MSG)**

JUL 16 — Keep Your Focus on Him

I was a sophomore in college and had been turned down for a student leadership job that I desperately wanted because someone spread a rumor about me. Intensely disappointed and angry, I stood on a hill in Oklahoma in a lightning storm and raged at God's unfairness that let some people be chosen who I thought were less qualified.

I don't know about you, but God has never responded to my angriest accusations, not even with a lightning bolt. It appears he does not want to encourage the perspective that will keep my eyes focused in the wrong place.

When we compare our path to others our eyes are on ourselves and them. And that is as dangerous as trying to drive while staring at people in the back seat through the rearview mirror. Keep your eyes on the road and follow him as best you see him.

He has doors we cannot see, and though that rumor cost me the position I thought I wanted, he opened a door far better suited for what he had in mind for me.

> ...*You do not have in mind the concerns of God,*
> *but merely human concerns.*
> **MATTHEW 16:23 (NIV)**

JUL 17 — Do You Really Need the Big Picture?

Wouldn't it have been nice if Jesus would have left us a discipleship manual with a list of frequently asked questions and their answers, or even a troubleshooting chart to give us options when things don't work out the way we hoped?

Why didn't he? Because he wanted us to follow *him*, not a process.

I often watch people wrestle with a tough decision, weighing all the possible permutations of their choices while trying to figure out what is best. "I just can't wrap my head around it," they will say. Their frustration stagnates them.

If you're following him, however, you don't have to understand the big picture to figure out what you are supposed to do. You only need to focus your eyes on Jesus and see what he seems to be doing around you. It may sound crazy, but whenever I do that, I have greater clarity about the decision he wants me to make.

> *But one thing I do: Forgetting what is behind and straining toward what is ahead, I press on toward the goal to win the prize for which God has called me heavenward in Christ Jesus...*
>
> **PHILIPPIANS 3:13-14 (NIV)**

JUL 18 — The Sin of Assumption

Jesus refused to use God's power to accomplish his own desires.

He didn't call fire down from heaven as the Pharisees plotted against him. He didn't use the truth to give Pilate an out. He didn't cry out for the angels who stood ready to rescue him from the cross.

That's quite a contrast to some of our spiritual leaders who use whatever power they have to destroy people who won't do what they want, or who dare to expose their indiscretions.

How do people who think they love God end up damaging others? Because they convince themselves that their interests are aligned with God's. Doing so allows us to act in God's name when, in fact, we are doing things that harm his work in us and in others.

The only way for us to overcome such temptation is to live the same way Jesus did—stop doing something only because we have the power to do so. Just because it sounds good, meets our needs, is biblically justifiable, or someone is pressuring us doesn't mean we're acting in his name or with his interests at heart.

The only question we need to ask is whether or not this is God's desire.

> *And if on some point you think differently, that too God will make clear to you. Only let us live up to what we have already attained.*
> **PHILIPPIANS 3:15-16 (NIV)**

JUL 19 Trusting Ourselves

In John 15, Jesus said that his Father gathers up unfruitful branches and burns them. Church leaders in Rome thought it their responsibility to act on God's behalf by torturing and killing those who would not conform to their practice or teaching. That's how Rome justified burning at the stake so-called heretics in the Middle Ages. They mistakenly thought they were supposed to do God's work for him.

Of course, that's an extreme example, but we do the same thing whenever we act destructively toward others and justify it as God's will.

It is precisely in those moments when we feel least connected with God that we are most tempted to think our ideas are his ideas. In doing so, however, we not only do great harm to others, but we also miss out on the exceedingly more abundant solution God is offering us.

> *Those who trust in themselves are fools...*
> **PROVERBS 28:26 (NIV)**

JUL 20 — Ever-Present

Jesus has not asked us to live a Christian life without him. It isn't even possible.

Christianity was never meant to be a list of principles to which we conform our behavior. The life of Christ can only be found in living reconciled to God in active communion with him every day.

Many believers, however, miss this incredible facet of our relationship with him. They think God has given us doctrine only for guiding principles to live by. For days or weeks they grow accustomed to living as if he isn't with them and they have to do the best they can on their own.

We make decisions by listing pros and cons instead of asking him to show us the way. We struggle against temptation by our own strength of will, and plan as if we are our only resource.

Without growing in our awareness of him and our ability to recognize how God speaks to us, we will miss the freedom and joy God has for us. The greatest joy of receiving Jesus into our lives is that he's always there. He doesn't come and go at a whim or leave us on our own even when we ignore him.

And surely I am with you always, to the very end of the age...
MATTHEW 28:20 (NIV)

JUL 21 — Making Decisions without Him

Without an ear trained to listen to God, what we call faith is nothing more than presumption and what we call obedience is nothing more than legalism.

We need him every day. He wants to be actively engaged with us as we move through life. Left to our own devices or our own best wisdom will bring certain pain and failure.

No, that doesn't mean we have to ask him permission to brush our teeth or see what his will is for dinner. He wants to live our life with us, and he leaves many decisions in our hands. He often has options, however, to draw us away from our destructive thoughts, or to show us a better solution than the one we're plotting.

> *To you, LORD, I call; you are my Rock, do not turn a deaf ear to me. For if you remain silent, I will be like those who go down to the pit.*
> **PSALM 28:1 (MSG)**

JUL 22 Learning to Listen

I realize that nothing can be more frustrating than trying to hear God's voice and feeling he is giving you the silent treatment. I meet many who genuinely believe that God never speaks to them.

I have seasons like that too. I am convinced, however, that God is always speaking to each of us; it's just that we don't always hear him. There are lots of reasons for that. Sometimes he gets drowned out by the noise of the world or our own fears and anxieties. Sometimes our expectations get in the way, either at what his voice will sound like or what we want him to say.

Some of us have been taught that God is the accusing voice in our lives, when he is not. Most times, he is simply showing us how loved we are and what's true about the circumstances we're in. He rarely tells us what to do, but instead he shows us what we need to know so that we'll know what to do.

Learning to listen takes some time and none of us will ever do it perfectly. Ask him to keep tuning your heart to his frequency so you'll hear him better.

God wants you to live the same way Jesus did—by every word that comes from his mouth.

> *Man shall not live on bread alone, but on every word that comes from the mouth of God.*
> **MATTHEW 4:4 (NIV)**

JUL 23 — The Important Pause

For thousands of years Jesus has been making his voice known to men and women who want to hear it. I can tell you that he wants you to know his voice more than you want to know it.

For me, it simply means that I take an extra beat before rushing headlong into my next, best idea and pause for some time with Father. I ask, "What do you want, Lord? What will bring the most glory to you and fulfill your heart in these things?"

Then stop and just listen. Do it when you're in the car, waiting in line at the store, or doing yard work. Rarely does he answer right away, but over the next few hours or days clarity begins to emerge.

It's best to wait until you have a sense of what he wants to show you, rather than rushing off thinking you got this on your own.

> *No longer will they teach their neighbor, or say to one another, "Know the Lord," because they will all know me, from the least of them to the greatest.*
> **HEBREWS 8:11**

JUL 24 — How He Speaks

Learning to live by every word that comes from God was never meant to be a test of spirituality or a merit badge for maturity...it's just the way Father wanted his kids to live. If you realize you're accommodating yourself to living without that, maybe now is a good time to remind yourself how involved he wants to be with you.

Jesus will show you what he is saying through a conviction in your heart, something you read in Scripture, a comment from a friend or even a stranger, by the way circumstances sort out, or by a combination of all these things.

There's very little certainty in listening to God. Paul compared it to looking through a darkened mirror. We catch glimpses and in following those we'll see more glimpses.

That's why the men and women I know who listen to God the best are also the most humble people I know. Instead of saying, "God has told me such and such," they are more likely to say, "I had a thought come to mind as I was praying the other day."

Teach me your way, LORD, that I may rely on your faithfulness; give me an undivided heart, that I may fear your name...
PSALM 86:11 (NIV)

JUL 25 — The Sweeping Yes

John Beaumont, a teacher from New Zealand, made this observation while we were talking...

"Once you've said 'Yes' to Jesus, it needs to count for the whole of our lives. We need not ever wrestle again with whether or not we'll do what he wants. Once that is decided the only question that remains in everything we consider is simply this, 'What does he want?'"

And if he wants it, why would we want anything else?

We clutter our journey in Christ with way too many considerations. Does this make sense to me? What would be the ramifications? What will other people think? Does it make financial sense? What principle should guide me here? Answering all of those questions can be cumbersome indeed, and many of them will lead me opposite of the way he would want me to go.

> ...the one who is victorious and does my will to the end...
> REVELATION 2:26 (NIV)

JUL 26 Not What We'd First Choose

We are loved by a Father whose ways are much higher than ours; his thoughts are way beyond anything we could ever ask or imagine. So, why would we ever think we could reason out his ways? Often we're just trying to find a justification for what we want to do anyway.

His wisdom often discomforts me at first. His thoughts run counter to my first inclinations and my self-protective strategies almost every time. Why should that surprise us? He's offering his wisdom because ours is not going to be helpful.

That's why when I find myself caught up in an internal argument, I wonder if one of his thoughts has gotten in and my natural mind is fighting it off. I like all my thoughts, so if I'm arguing with myself, it is usually him I'm resisting.

Surely his truth will set us free, but it often messes with me first. If I'm not careful, I can talk myself out of following him without even knowing it.

> *As the heavens are higher than the earth, so are my ways higher than your ways and my thoughts than your thoughts.*
> ISAIAH 55:9 (NIV)

JUL 27 — Our Fellowship Is with Him

The first disciples actually got to see him, touch him, and hear his words. Though they didn't yet know this was God himself clothed in human flesh, they knew he was someone special and took in the things he said and did.

And when he ascended to his Father and they could no longer see him, they didn't pine away for the good old days, when Jesus was with them. He still was and they knew it.

And they wanted their followers to know it as well. For too much of my life, however, I thought following him meant that I subscribed to the principles and rituals of Christianity. Sure, I had moments of knowing him even there, but they always faded away in the busyness of religious obligation and activity, which did more to wear me out than teach me how to live in him.

As I read the New Testament, I'm amazed by how much the apostles reminded the early followers that they were inviting people into a living relationship with Jesus that would allow them to know Father and participate in his unfolding grace in the world.

We proclaim to you what we have seen and heard, so that you also may have fellowship with us. And our fellowship is with the Father and with his Son, Jesus Christ.

I JOHN 1:3

JUL 28 — Why Don't We Want People to Follow?

I regularly meet people who have been faithful elders, pastors, and participants in good, religious institutions who do not yet have a clue how God can speak to them and how his love will transform them.

I look back now at my pastoral days and see how I discouraged people from thinking they could follow Jesus without me. I didn't mean to. I thought I was teaching them to follow him, but in the end, they only learned to listen to me. And that worked only as long as they liked what I said. When they didn't, they just found someone else to tell them what they wanted to hear.

I was talking to a group of elders one day about equipping people to follow Jesus, rather than letting the institutions be his substitute, and one asked me with an incredulous look on his face, "You mean I'm going to have to learn to follow him myself?"

He had no idea how to enjoy a relationship with a Father and his Son that gives hope and direction in his darkest days and teaches him how live in his power instead of his own efforts. To his credit, however, he was excited to learn.

The New Testament is replete with the invitation to follow him, not to follow the dictates of a religious program. Why would we rob people of that by substituting our own programs?

> *...Jesus Christ, our only Sovereign and Lord.*
> **JUDE 1:4 (NIV)**

JUL 29 — The Voice of a Stranger

Jesus knows each of his sheep by name and leads them with his voice. That doesn't seem too complicated. He connects with us; we follow him. He said that when they became familiar with his voice, they wouldn't follow a stranger.

His sheep really do hear his voice; it's just that they've been taught not to trust it. When they hear the voice of a stranger, it sounds wrong to them even if they can't put their finger on exactly why. But that's when they often get talked into ignoring what they know to be true inside. They are accused of independence, arrogance, and rebellion to make sure they get back in line and don't cause any trouble.

"Who are you to think you can know God? You don't have the training we have, or the anointing. Do you read Greek? Are you going to argue with the 'wisdom passed down through the ages'?"

As well-meaning as some of that might be, its effect is to destroy people's trust in Jesus as the one who wants to lead them, teach them, protect them, and free them to live powerfully in his life.

And don't let people maneuver you into taking charge of them. There is only one Life-Leader for you and them—Christ.
MATTHEW 23:10 (MSG)

JUL 30 — One Flock, One Shepherd

Leadership in the early church helped people learn how to walk with the living Jesus, not subvert that relationship by inserting themselves in its place. Doing so not only undermines spiritual growth, but also divides the body over the differing views of those who think they are leading his flock.

I love it when people tell me that something I wrote or said touched them deeply—not because it was new to them, but because it gave voice to something the Spirit had already been showing them for some time. Maybe they were just afraid to believe it was true with all the religious voices telling them otherwise.

The language of real fellowship will always make us more aware of his voice and less influenced by our desire to please people, especially those who lead in his name without sharing his priorities.

That's why Jesus said we could be one flock when we have one shepherd.

> *Don't set people up as experts over your life, letting them tell you what to do. Save that authority for God; let him tell you what to do.*
> **MATTHEW 23:10 (MSG)**

JUL 31 — All over the World

As long as we continue to have hundreds of thousands of people claiming to lead the body of Christ, his family will continue to be fragmented.

Fortunately, that has been changing in recent years as an increasing number of people are simultaneously and spontaneously seeing through Christianity as the religion it has become and is learning how to simply follow Jesus again, even when it goes against the grain of other people's religious expectations.

I've been blessed to meet thousands of these people all over the world. They seem to be on the same adventure I'm on and when we connect our fellowship is immediate, deep, and filled with life. And even though many of these people don't fit into the traditional structures we've inherited, they are not independent or rebellious, as others want to characterize them.

Those learning to follow the Lamb have a deep desire for authentic fellowship with others, a better understanding of leadership that equips instead of commands, and a desire to see the church emerge in our day as a true reflection of God's glory in the world.

> *No one else should carry the title of 'Father'; you have only one Father, and he's in heaven…*
> **MATTHEW 23:10 (MSG)**

AUG 1 — Spiritual Couch Potatoes?

Many people have found meaningful community inside some of our religious institutions. I'm grateful that his life is reflected there.

Others, however, found that environment stifling to their faith and have found a more vibrant journey outside of the institution. It makes no sense to me why some belittle those who no longer attend a religious institution, calling them independent spiritual couch potatoes. They say that without accountability to gifted leaders to keep them from error and to coordinate their efforts, the church of Jesus Christ will end up weak and ineffective.

Really? What does that say about Jesus's ability (or should we say inability?) to raise up a flock after his own heart and release them to live and work together however he might desire? And why would we listen to those who have no trust in Jesus's ability to do that?

Those who judge them have not seen the body of Christ that I have seen taking shape all over the world. They are growing in dependence on Jesus rather than following programs crafted by a human leader or denomination, and they are being powerfully transformed by his life and are making an incredible impact in the world.

And while individual actions may not warrant magazine coverage, the sum total of the simple obedience of those believers allows God's kingdom to be known in the world in ways that more institutional forms can't express.

Why can't we celebrate all the ways Jesus makes himself known in the world?

Don't let people do that to you, put you on a pedestal like that.

You all have a single Teacher, and you are all classmates.
MATTHEW 23:10 (MSG)

AUG 2 — The Submitted Flock

Thomas Friedman, the *New York Times* political columnist, wrote a book a number of years ago called *The Lexus and the Olive Tree*. In it he describes a fundamental shift in power from the political leaders of nation-states to what he called the electronic herd—the millions of individual investors who wake up every morning, turn on their computers, and trade in stocks and currencies for their own financial gain.

Friedman asserted that this trend was so profound that power had already begun to shift away from governments and political leaders. In time, nations will no longer be able to successfully manipulate their currency or economies because when the electronic herd gets wind of it, they will flee overnight to better investments.

Their power is derived from the sum total of their actions, not from any coordination between them, and yet they are economically restructuring our world. Lately that book has come back to mind as a parable of what is happening spiritually in the Father's family.

Jesus is raising up his own submitted flock—those who will simply respond to the Shepherd one action at a time, one person at a time, and in each situation as it comes.

> *Who here qualifies for the job of overseeing the kitchen? A person the Master can depend on to feed the workers on time each day. Someone the Master can drop in on unannounced and always find him doing his job. A God-blessed man or woman, I tell you. It won't be long before the Master will put this person in charge of the whole operation.*
>
> MATTHEW 24:45–47 (MSG)

AUG 3 — A Vibrant Flock

Can you imagine the power of millions of individual believers from all over the world simply following the inclinations that Jesus would allow to grow in their hearts? I get a glimpse of that reality every day just from the folks I know. I hear incredible stories of lives being changed. I see Jesus's hand as he connects people with a task for them to do together.

I see an increasing number of people more focused on doing what Jesus asks of them rather than building large programs or ministries to try to catch the attention of the world. They will go wherever he asks them to, link arms with other believers he invites to the same task, and do it all without the need for power, self-glory, or vocational provision.

This is the picture Scripture paints, and those who aspire to work with him in this venture will not seek to replace him in people's lives but equip them to live it too.

I sit here today overwhelmed by what Jesus is doing in our world and almost laugh, thinking, of course it would be this way. He said it would. He would be the Shepherd, and all would follow him with his laws written in their hearts.

He never wanted us to follow the programs of men but to learn to live in a growing trust in his ability to coordinate his body and love the world through us.

> *I will remain in the world no longer, but they are still in the world, and I am coming to you. Holy Father, protect them by the power of your name, the name you gave me, so that they may be one as we are one.*
>
> **JOHN 17:11 (NIV)**

AUG 4 — She's Not a Model

I'm not on any bandwagon with those who claim they have God's proven model for church life. The church isn't a model; it's a living, breathing family living on the earth with the Father's heartbeat at her core.

When our focus is on following a model (even a good one) rather than following him, we'll still miss out on how he is knitting this family together. If you're pursuing house church, cell church, seeker-sensitive or purpose-driven church instead of following him, you will miss those he might ask you to walk beside who are in more traditional congregations or in no formalized group at all.

The important question is what he's asking of you, and who he is asking you to walk alongside in this season of your life. Believe the growing convictions Jesus puts on your heart and follow them as best as you can. Be gracious to others as he shapes his image in you.

Don't worry about the mistakes you might make and don't condemn others for making theirs. Celebrate the friendships God has given you in this family in whatever environment he is helping them grow.

> *Because there is one loaf, our many-ness becomes one-ness—Christ doesn't become fragmented in us. Rather, we become unified in him.*
> **1 CORINTHIANS 10:17 (MSG)**

AUG 5 — A People Like No Other

The glory of life in Jesus is not found in finding the best formula to follow, the right principles to believe, or even the most emotional rituals to observe.

It is about knowing Jesus as our older brother, faithful

high priest, and friend. Live inside that relationship and live with joy wherever he happens to lead you.

Without that freedom, we'll just be a bunch of Christians caught up in the boring and powerless religious activities that cannot bring life, much less help us touch the world around us.

Jesus can do anything he wants with us in any given day and cause anyone to cross our path that he desires. Isn't that something worth waking up to every morning?

> *We don't reduce Christ to what we are; he raises us to what he is.*
> **1 CORINTHIANS 10:17 (MSG)**

AUG 6 Following Your Passion

Many who claim to be following Jesus are only indulging their own self-interest.

Instead of increasingly demonstrating his grace and truth, they become arrogant, isolated, and so filled with their own agenda they suffocate anyone near them. These are not those who are growing to know him, however. They are those who have reacted to religion by falling back into their own selfishness. God can rescue them, too, when they get weary enough of living that way.

The fact that people can abuse the truth does not negate that truth. My words are not designed for those who want to use his freedom as an excuse to do whatever they feel like doing. I write to encourage those who passionately want to know Jesus and be transformed by his life.

Many of those who take their freedom from religious activity find themselves stirred by a deeper passion and challenged to a more resilient faith. As he grows more real in them with each passing day, they also have an irresistible desire to connect with others who share the same hunger. They may not find them easily or quickly, but in time Jesus will connect them to others.

Exercise your freedom by serving God, not by breaking the rules. Treat everyone you meet with dignity. Love your spiritual family.
1 PETER 2:16 (MSG)

AUG 7 — Marks of Transformation

I see a vast number of people around the world learning to depend on him more each day. I have recognized at least seven attributes that increase in them as they learn how to follow the Lamb wherever he goes:

- They live by the reality of love, not by expectations.
- They live with a growing trust in Father's purpose and power, not out of fear.
- They live at the Father's pleasure, not in the tyranny of fulfilling their agendas.
- They trust in his ability, not their own efforts.
- They live in the moment, not in the anxiety of their imagined futures.
- They live in authentic expressions of community, not in isolated independence or prefabricated programs
- They live generously and graciously in the world, not seeking to exploit others with their own agenda.

When those passions stir in you, lean in to that space.

But you are the ones chosen by God, chosen for the high calling of priestly work, chosen to be a holy people, God's instruments to do his work and speak out for him, to tell others of the night-and-day difference he made for you—from nothing to something, from rejected to accepted.

1 PETER 2:9–10 (MSG)

AUG 8 — The Radically, Unprotected Heart

I loved this insight from Ian M. Cron's book, *Chasing Francis*. How can you tell if your heart is being shaped by embracing the reality of Jesus, or by religion?

He wrote that a follower of Jesus has a radically unprotected heart: *"It's to live dangerously open, revealing all that we genuinely are, and receiving all the pain and sorrow the world will give back in return."*

The religious person has a well-defended heart: *"It's a guarded and suspicious spirit that's closed to the world. It sees everything and everyone as a potential threat, an enemy waiting to attack. It shields itself from the world."*

I have found that to be true in my own journey. For many years I lived with a defended heart; it's only more recently that I have experienced the power and joy of an increasingly undefended one. Jesus wants to transform us so that we have a radically, unprotected heart so that we can live authentically and freely in the world.

I am Light that has come into the world so that all who believe in me won't have to stay any longer in the dark.

JOHN 12:44 (MSG)

AUG 9 — The Grace of a Vulnerable Heart

Roman leaders and Pharisees alike demonstrated the bondage of a well-defended heart. It appears that both our flesh and rote, religious activity produce a heart that protects itself at all costs. You can see it in your own rigidity, in a judgmental attitude toward yourself and others, and in an arrogance that despises those who do not share your faith.

But as you become more transformed in your relationship with Jesus your heart begins to soften, both toward yourself and others. The radically, unprotected heart emerges over time with a grace and beauty that will change the way you talk to yourself and how you treat others in the world.

It is the fruit of Jesus changing you on the inside that will free you to live more like him on the outside. As we know with increasing certainty that we are safer in him than we are protecting ourselves, we won't need to defend ourselves any longer.

More and more, I want to know the dangerous beauty of living in the world with a vulnerability to his grace and to the needs of others around me.

> *We wait in hope for the LORD; he is our help and our shield. In him our hearts rejoice, for we trust in his holy name. May your unfailing love be with us, LORD, even as we put our hope in you.*
>
> **PSALM 33:20–22 (NIV)**

UG 10 — A Peace that Makes No Sense

On the way to the airport for my recent trip to Dallas, I got a call from a friend who had a number of circumstances crashing in on him at the same time. As he described the events playing out in his life, he told me he had never been more circumstantially confused and personally unsettled about all that was going on around him.

None of his old boxes or definitions seemed to help

him understand better what was going on. "Yet," he said, "I've never known such peace and confidence with my life in such disarray."

He was a bit unsettled with that reality and wanted to know if I thought this sounded like God.

Peace in the midst of crisis? Confidence in the face of uncertainty?

Absolutely. It has God's fingerprints all over it.

And the peace of God, which transcends all understanding, will guard your hearts and your minds in Christ Jesus.
PHILIPPIANS 4:7 (NIV)

AUG 11 Where Peace Really Resides

When you live out of your natural mind, you will only feel secure when you have every detail nailed down or are confident that you have the future figured out.

The only problem with that is that most of what we think we've figured out is based on human wisdom and false assumptions. When those fail us, what do we have left?

Our natural mind feeds off the illusion that we are in control of our lives. That's why when all is well our mind will be at peace and in times of calamity, turmoil. When things unravel, we get thrown into confusion and doubt about either God's love for us, or whether we've been good enough to earn it.

Paul wrote about the peace that passes all understanding—the security God gives us in himself when the storms rage about us. We can know that we are safe in him even if we don't have the foggiest idea how circumstances will turn out.

> *Peace I leave with you; my peace I give you. I do not give to you as the world gives. Do not let your hearts be troubled and do not be afraid.*
> **JOHN 14:27 (NIV)**

AUG 12 — Embracing Him in the Moment

Sheba is a lop-eared shepherd/Lab cross with an exuberant spirit...sometimes too exuberant. Even though she has severe dysplasia in her hips and pain from time to time, she is the happiest dog we have ever owned. She's not real bright, but she is always smiling, always ready to do something fun, and a joy to be around. Well, most of the time.

The thing I hate most to do with this dog is taking her for a walk. We are trying to teach her not to pull on the lead, but to simply walk alongside us. Even though we have one of those sixteen-foot retractable leashes, she constantly strains to get beyond it. It's as if she can't wait to get to the next place. But when she gets there, she is already trying to get to the next one. It's nuts, really. She can't enjoy any place in the moment because she's always trying to get somewhere else.

As I grew impatient with Sheba one night on a long walk, calling her back again and again and again from pulling on the lead, I realized she is more like me than I care to admit. Though Jesus is patient with our impatience, I have no doubt he is overjoyed when we trust him enough not to pull him where we want to go.

> *So watch your step. Use your head.*
> *Make the most of every chance you get…*
> **EPHESIANS 5:15–16 (MSG)**

AUG 13 — Contentment Is not Complacency

Only in the last few years have I begun to live contentedly in Father's work in me and around me. Most of my spiritual life I have strained against Jesus's presence in my life. I have always tried to push him on to something else instead of staying in the moment with him, knowing that he is taking me on in his time, not mine.

It made me think how much more fun it would be to walk with Sheba if she stayed alongside me. Her constant straining against the lead and pulling at my arm gets tiresome and frustrating. I wonder if that's been true for Jesus in my walk with him.

Contentedness is a great gift in this kingdom. I would love to come to the place where he needs no leash with me because I'm never further than a few feet from where he is.

> *Do not be like the horse or the mule, which have no understanding but must be controlled by bit and bridle or they will not come to you.*
> **PSALM 32:9 (NIV)**

AUG 14 — The God Who Sneaks Up on You

You would probably have had to grow up in the sixties and seventies to understand the title. Back then, it was big-time preaching to take the names of God from the Old Testament that used the word "Jehovah" as a prefix. For instance, Jehovah-Jireh (the God Who Provides), Jehovah-Rapha (the God Who Heals You), and Jehovah-Tsidkenu (God Our Righteousness). Since then translators have used the more accurate "Yaweh," and have left out the Hebrew suffixes.

So, that sermon doesn't preach as well today though it was an interesting study in the redemptive attributes of God throughout the Old Testament.

A college student from California recently uncovered another one. This one isn't in the Bible, but she swears it's true, nonetheless. She talks about Jehovah Tsnikki. You'll have to read that out loud to make sense of it—Jehovah Tsnikki, The God Who Sneaks Up on You.

How many times have you followed the Lord's leading into a situation, certain just how it would turn out, and are absolutely shocked when you realize that God had an entirely different outcome in mind?

Sometimes, that has led to a challenge I never saw coming. At other times, however, I've found him sneaking up on me right in the midst of some mess I've made, making himself known and accomplishing his purpose anyway.

> *God's voice thunders in marvelous ways;*
> *he does great things beyond our understanding.*
>
> JOB 37:5 (NIV)

AUG 15 Jehovah Tsnikki

There is lots of evidence of Jehova Tsnikki (the God Who Sneaks Up on You) throughout the Bible. God told Paul he would be going to Rome. At the time, I'm sure Paul had no idea it would be as a prisoner.

God sent Peter to Cornelius's house before he had any idea God was going to allow those pesky Gentiles to get saved! And who can forget Joseph's dream that he would rule over his brothers? Little did he know it would be only after they kidnapped and sold him into slavery.

I have no doubt God seems sneaky to us because we are oblivious to what he's really doing in our lives, but

I love the playfulness of Jehovah Tsnikki! What a great name for an incredible Father who dazzles us again and again with the sheer wonder of his character and an unfolding purpose that isn't even thwarted by our own ignorance or misguided efforts.

Would you expect anything less from someone who's ways are far higher than ours?

> *You will go out in joy and be led forth in peace; the mountains and hills will burst into song before you, and all the trees of the field will clap their hands.*
>
> **ISAIAH 55:12 (NIV)**

AUG 16 — Finding out What We Really Want

I was in Florida having lunch with a man I'd met a few years before. He had moved to Florida to plant house churches and ended up discovering that the church was wilder and more wonderful than he yet knew.

We were sitting in a restaurant called Ford's Garage, and a quote by Henry Ford was emblazoned on the wall in front of me: "If I had asked people what they wanted, they would have said faster horses." He had dreamed up something so much better than what people thought they wanted, and his automobile took over the world.

I wonder how many of our prayers sound like that to God. We are asking him for the thing we want, unaware that he has plans for us that are beyond our comprehension. Most of my prayers used to center around my own comfort or happiness, when he had things in mind that would radically change the way I think and live in the world. His ideas have always proved to be so much better than mine.

It made me think of my favorite line from the movie *Bruce Almighty*. The God-character asks, "Since when does anyone have a clue about what they want?" So true! We think we do, but then God takes us on adventures we had never contemplated, and we discover that what we really wanted is very different from what we thought we wanted.

Now to Him who is able to do far more abundantly beyond all that we ask or think, according to the power that works within us, to Him be the glory in the church and in Christ Jesus to all generations forever and ever. Amen.

EPHESIANS 3:20-21

AUG 17 — An Unfortunate Overestimation

Oh, for the grace each day to recognize the difference between God's work and mine—to simply do what he guides me to do and watch his greater purpose unfold!

I was in Tulsa one evening meeting with the leadership of a congregation who had taken over a country and western bar for their gatherings. In the middle of a question and answer session with some of their leaders, I was asked, "What do you think is the greatest deterrent to following Jesus every day?"

Immediately, I heard my own voice answer the question before I even had a chance to gather my thoughts, "The overestimation of our own capabilities."

I had to pause and think about that myself. I wouldn't change that answer today. We've all been seduced by Ben Franklin's dictum, that "God helps those who help themselves." Most Christians actually think that phrase is in the Bible.

I'm always surprised by how easily God lets me take over something he begins. And like a young child with a new gadget he thinks he already knows how to use, I usually end up breaking it. And like a tender Father, he finds a way to mend my mess and give me a fresh start.

> *For it is we who are the circumcision, we who serve God by his Spirit, who boast in Christ Jesus, and who put no confidence in the flesh.*
> **PHILIPPIANS 3:3 (NIV)**

AUG 18 — Letting God's Voice Sink In

Have you ever skipped stones across a lake? You know, the nice flat ones that take two, three, or sometimes four bounces before they sink? Sometimes I think listening to the Lord is like that. It takes a couple of tries before it finally "sinks in." Maybe that's what God is doing with me. It seems he is always speaking but I'm not really listening.

This thought came in an email from someone going through a painful season. I love that description. It often works that way with me.

I get a glimpse of a thought, but not really enough to grasp it. Then, in a conversation or something I am reading the thought appears again. Eventually, the stone drops, and the thought clarifies with the fragrance of Father about it.

Maybe it's part of us looking through a darkened mirror to discern the voice of Jesus. It takes a few looks for us to get the idea of what's there. Maybe that's part of what Paul meant when he talked about letting God's voice be confirmed by two or three witnesses.

When God wants you to know something, he'll circle back again and again to help you recognize him. Many will say that's when God finally spoke to them, but in reality, he was speaking all along.

> *God always answers, one way or another,*
> *even when people don't recognize his presence.*
>
> JOB 33:14 (MSG)

AUG 19 — To Trust or Not to Trust

"How do you teach believers to trust each other?" my wife asked.

By the facial reactions around the room, you might have thought Sara asked if they sacrificed animals. I was taken aback. We had spent the last few days with a group of people in the bush an hour outside of Melbourne, Australia, and were touched by their sense of community. We had witnessed their honesty, their openness, and their service to one another. Surely they worked on trust.

One finally spoke, "Where does Scripture teach us to trust each other?"

I started probing the deep recesses of my memory, whirling through every Scripture I could recall. I couldn't find any.

How could this be? Much of what I taught about the power of Christian community focused on helping people see how much they need one another and to assist them in building the kind of trusting relationships that would allow them to work together.

No matter what we did, however, it didn't last. Trust would always break down as people abandoned their commitments whenever it suited them. We are imperfect people after all, who will make mistakes and fail each other especially at critical moments—which is why many church conflicts often leave a wake of broken friendships.

Scripture encourages us to place our trust in God

alone. That's why when we trust other people or the church, our expectations fail us. Humanity cannot be trusted but they can learn to love. Jesus is the only person worthy of our trust.

> *Jesus didn't entrust his life to them. He knew them inside and out, knew how untrustworthy they were. He didn't need any help in seeing right through them.*
>
> JOHN 2:24 (MSG)

AUG 20 Learn to Love Instead

In most teaching, three words often crop up regarding the importance of church life—commitment, accountability, and trust. I used them often to help people understand how to participate in church life. It's only more recently that I've come to realize how mistaken I was.

"Commitment" is not used at all in the New Testament, though its root, "commit," is. Interestingly enough, it is overwhelmingly used to talk about committing sin, as in committing adultery. In the Old Testament, we can find references about committing our ways to the Lord, and twice the New Testament talks about committing people to the grace of God. All of these, however, are clearly directed at the Father and his work, nothing is spoken of being committed to one another or to the church.

Likewise, "accountability" in Scripture is only directed at God. We are not told to be accountable to each other.

We are not encouraged to "trust" each other either, as a practice. Trust can develop between people as they demonstrate the trustworthiness of their love over the long haul.

We are told to love each other, pray for each other, bear each other's burdens, be honest about each other's sins, forgive each other, serve each other, stimulate each other to love and good deeds, be kind to each other, and many other such things, but we are never told to be committed, to be accountable, or to trust another person. To do so only sets us up for abuse.

Love one another, for love comes from God.
Everyone who loves has been born of God and knows God.
1 JOHN 4:7 (NIV)

AUG 21 Turning to the Word

All references to trust and belief in Scripture are firmly and exclusively directed to God. If he is the one in whom all of our trust is invested, what do we have leftover to give to another believer?

Interesting, isn't it? Words we consider critical building blocks to body life—such as trust, commitment, and accountability—are not even part of the foundation that Jesus laid for the church. Why are they so important to us?

For centuries, religious leaders have used them to bind people to its programs and agendas: "Don't you trust the leadership here?" "If you're going to grow you need to be committed to what God is doing among us." "You've got to be plugged in somewhere so you can be accountable."

The New Testament community doesn't thrive on our trust in one another, but our faith in the Father. Jesus gave us two directives: Love God and love one another. In doing that, we will fulfill all his ambitions for our lives and be foundation enough for the most endearing community humans can share together.

This is my command: Love each other.
JOHN 15:17 (NIV)

AUG 22 — Beware Any Who Demand Your Trust

No one who demands your trust is out to help you. People out to con you out of money, politicians, and abusive uncles tell you to trust them. Even well-intentioned people who think trusting them will help you, will eventually fail you and leave you hurt.

Personal hurt is a painful reminder of misplaced trust and hopefully a warning not to do it again. That doesn't mean you won't cross paths with untrustworthy people in your life, but they will earn your trust by their constant willingness to lay down their life for you. They will never demand it of you, knowing that you'll come to recognize it soon enough.

So, what do healthy relationships with others look like?

A man in Australia expressed it best: "It looks like this, Wayne. In my relationship with you I don't want you to trust me more, I want to help you trust the Father like you never have before. If you're doing the same thing with me, then we're sharing fellowship. If I am encouraging you and you're not encouraging me, then I get to serve you, which is also joy. Either way, I'm not being cheated because I'm trusting the Father for everything I need."

That's a man I grew to trust.

Woe to those who go down to Egypt for help, who rely on horses, who trust in the multitude of their chariots and in the great strength of their horsemen, but do not look to the Holy One of Israel, or seek help from the LORD.

ISAIAH 31:1 (NIV)

AUG 23 — The Most Beautiful Girl in the World

Commitment, accountability, and trust are institutional words, and they are necessary for the survival of any institution because people have to conform to cooperate effectively.

The church of Jesus Christ, however, is not a conformity-based institution. It is a transformation community where people are free to grow, discover, and find just how much love can change the way people relate to one another.

Regretfully many people don't have an accurate distinction in their minds between the church as God sees it and the institutions that have sprung up around it. They are not the same thing.

God sees one church as the world that encompasses all the people who belong to him. He sees this not in institutional failures or the weaknesses of its leaders or adherents, but as the bride he is preparing for his son. He views the church with great affection, desire, and adoration.

Gene Edwards, a well-known author, has called the church "The Most Beautiful Girl in the World." I love that description; understanding the church from that perspective will keep us from growing cynical and sarcastic about that which God loves so much.

...as Christ loved the church and gave himself up for her...
EPHESIANS 5:25 (NIV)

AUG 24 — The Father's Community

Jesus talked about God as a community—Father, Son, and Spirit, completely unified, sharing together their love, wisdom, and work in the Creation.

On his final night with the disciples, Jesus invited his followers into that same community. "On that day, you will realize that I am in my Father, and you are in me, and I am in you." He wanted to transfer the friendship he had with them to the Father and the Spirit, and with himself on the other side of the Resurrection.

Imagine participating in the community that exists among the Trinity—not just with them, but with other fellow travelers who are learning to follow him as well. That's the hunger that beats in the hearts of his followers. They don't necessarily want or need all the trappings of our church institutions or the political drama that also comes with it.

Whether you attend a congregation or not, look for those people around you who lean into authenticity, graciousness, and a focus on Jesus that beats with your heart. That's how to identify the church Jesus is building.

Spend time with people because that's the community in which believers will find their unity and be able to demonstrate his glory to the world.

> *I have made you known to them and will continue to make you known in order that the love you have for me may be in them and that I myself may be in them.*
> JOHN 17:26 (NIV)

AUG 25 Body Life, Father Style

As you learn to dwell in the community of the Father, Son, and Spirit and embrace others around you who are doing so as well, the Father's love in you will spill out—almost without trying—causing you to "one another" believers with love, prayer, forgiveness, insight, money, help, and anything else others might need that we have.

Only out of that fullness and trust in God to fill our needs will we be able to share without any expectation for others to reciprocate, or any desire to manipulate their response.

This is the essence of fellowship: believers freely loving one another and assisting however they can, without any compulsion to get others to do it our way.

> *If anyone has material possessions and sees a brother or sister in need but has no pity on them, how can the love of God be in that person?*
> 1 JOHN 3:17 (NIV)

AUG 26 — A Different Set of Signs

One of the most shocking lessons I've had to face in the early days was how many of the signs I had been taught to use to affirm God's will, were actually marking the path leading me away from him.

Like a traveler on a road, I would hear him calling me; but when I looked in the direction I thought it came from, I saw signs warning of danger, risk, and potential conflict. When I turned to look elsewhere, I would see signs pointing to convenience, gratification, and security.

How easy it was to convince myself that his voice had come down the more appealing path. However, when I set out in that direction, I would find God's voice growing quieter and my spiritual life drier and emptier.

One does not have to twist Scripture far to think that following Jesus will lead down a path that leads to comfort, popularity, financial rewards, or security.

I never even considered how often those who don't know how much their Father loves them seek those same things. So, like them, I pursued my self-interest thinking it must be God's too. For the longest time, I couldn't figure out how I was being drawn off the mark.

> *But small is the gate and narrow the road that
> leads to life, and only a few find it.*
> **MATTHEW 7:14 (NIV)**

AUG 27 The Markers We Use

Obviously, I needed better markers to help me recognize his leading.

If we only obey God's voice when it is easy, brings us the applause of others, or benefits us financially, we will find our spiritual life dry, empty, and boring.

While it offers the illusion of joy, it cannot bring us the reality that only comes from living in the confidence that we are loved and cared for by him, not our own efforts.

Jesus warned us that the life of the kingdom awaited those who walked a narrower road, away from their own self-interest. In this kingdom, everything seems to work backward. If you want to save your life, you lose it. If you want to be first, you have to choose to be last.

When you confirm his leading off the wrong markers, you will be confused when he speaks to you and try to talk yourself out of following him. So, every once in awhile, it wouldn't hurt to take a look at the signposts along the path. They will tell you whether your journey is drawing you to him along the narrow road, or back to a broader road of personal comfort and ease.

> *Then Jesus said to his disciples, "Truly I tell you, it is hard for
> someone who is rich to enter the kingdom of heaven."*
> **MATTHEW 19:23 (NIV)**

AUG 28 — Resisting the Urge for Busyness

I used to think being busy for God was a merit badge to wear proudly. There was no end to the good things I could do in God's name. Everywhere people beg for money and volunteers and it was easy to get caught up in a whirlwind of activities and miss out on what it means to build a deepening relationship with him.

In fact, the more insecure I was in my relationship with him, the greater workload I took on in a failed attempt to prove otherwise. It's often true that the people busiest with religion are often the most unfulfilled spiritually. Rather than being changed by his life, they are often short-tempered, demanding, and unaware of people around them. They fail to understand how religious activity can dull our hunger and distract our passion to know him. They pursue the latest program, observe demanding disciplines, seek out being "fed" by teachers they enjoy...but they never grow closer to the one who loves them so deeply.

The surest sign that you are walking the road God has for you is an ever-deepening friendship with him where you are increasingly at rest in his love. You grow to know his heart better and are increasingly transformed into his image.

Now I pause regularly in my journey and ask whether or not I know him better today than I did a few months ago. If the answer is no, or I'm uncertain, then I look for something to change. He wants nothing more than for you to learn to abide in him every day. By doing that, everything else concerning you on God's heart will be fulfilled.

And we all, who with unveiled faces contemplate the Lord's glory, are being transformed into his image with ever-increasing glory, which comes from the Lord, who is the Spirit.

2 CORINTHIANS 3:18 (NIV)

AUG 29 — Blind Guides

No one gave Jesus more trouble than the elders and Pharisees in Jerusalem. Their only priority seemed to be protecting their position of importance and that complicated how they could deal with the miracle-working teacher from Galilee.

To say they were the most disingenuous people he dealt with would be an understatement. They constantly covered up their real motives and actions, afraid of the people who supported him.

In his final words to the city of Jerusalem, only days before his death, he exposes them for what they really are—hypocrites who turned the work of the loving God into a religion they manipulated for their own gain and sense of self-importance.

He called them blind guides, and he exposed them for keeping people from the reality of the kingdom: for loving the honor of people, for making converts they only lured into greater bondage; for skewed priorities; for pretending to be righteous on the outside when evil raged within, and for glorifying the prophets of the past and rejecting the prophets of their day.

That's a road not to go down.

Woe to you, teachers of the law and Pharisees, you hypocrites! You travel over land and sea to win a single convert, and when you have succeeded, you make them twice as much a child of hell as you are.

MATTHEW 23:15 (NIV)

AUG 30 — The Worst Curse

"You brood of vipers," Jesus called the Pharisees, "how do you think you will escape the sentence of hell?" They honored the prophets of old but would soon be killing the ones God was sending to them. Jesus warned them that because of this "the guilt of all the righteous blood that has been shed on earth" would come upon them.

What a curse! He made them responsible for the murder of every righteous person since the day Cain slew his own brother Abel. He could already see the consequences bearing down on them like a firestorm of wrath that would consume them.

Such a curse seems so completely out of character for Jesus. His message of love and forgiveness had captured the land, inviting to himself some of the most sinful people of his day.

Yet, he condemned these religious leaders in the cruelest of terms. Had he utterly rejected them? That's how it appears on the surface, but look closer. Rather than taking delight in their coming devastation, he exposed his love for them.

If they would just come to him, he would take all that guilt for them.

As he approached Jerusalem and saw the city, he wept over it and said, "If you, even you, had only known on this day what would bring you peace—but now it is hidden from your eyes..."

LUKE 19:41-42 (NIV)

AUG 31 *Under His Wings*

Jesus knew the firestorm was coming. Evil was already deploying its forces to destroy their temple and devastate their children. Jesus had come to rescue them, but they could not see it. They saw him as a threat, not a Savior.

They rejected his visitation, and now plotted to kill him. They would reject the messengers God was sending to invite them back to himself. Even though many in that crowd would cry for his crucifixion only a few days later, he was still trying to save them. He had invited them under his own wings like a hen gathering her chicks, so he would bear the fire on their behalf.

"But you were not willing." The story's end was tragic for those who stood around Jesus that day. Unwilling to come to him, they would have to endure the fire themselves to its tragic end.

What does it take for chicks to come under the wing of their mother when panic sets in and it doesn't look very safe? What must it take for a bird to stay over her babies as the wildfire draws ever closer, then begins to sear her head and back? What must it have taken for God himself to endure the fury of the wrath our sins deserved and stay through it to the end so that those under his wing might be saved?

He did, but they were unwilling. Sad, sad words! Always be willing. No matter how much you think you know best, when God comes to rescue you, run to him.

What will you do on the day of reckoning, when disaster comes from afar? To whom will you run for help??

ISAIAH 10:3 (NIV)

SEP 1 Love that Exposes the Lie

Look how closely our choice in Christ parallels Adam and Eve's in the Garden.

If they had trusted their Creator's love for them, they would not have fallen for Satan's lie. God wasn't holding out on them but warning them against a real danger that sought to destroy them. Once they doubted his love for them, though, they could only fall back on their best wisdom, which proved woefully inadequate.

The leaders in Jerusalem faced the same choice. Would they trust their own religious ways to save themselves, or would they trust God's work in Jesus? Remember these were not self-indulgent men fulfilling their passions by outwardly sinful acts. No, the deception for them was much like it was for Adam and Eve. These men were trying to be godly, or so they thought. They observed cumbersome rituals and traditions, thinking that would make them like God. They spurned the pleasures of the world in an effort to earn his approval—but being good was never going to be good enough.

If they trusted God's love for them, they would not have needed to kill Christ, Stephen, or James.

We, too, face the same choice. If we're not confident in Father's love for us, we'll have to resort to the best thing we can do to try to save ourselves. No matter how righteous we can be on the outside, it will bring us no closer to God. Trusting ourselves instead of him will still leave us outside of his garden having to fend for ourselves.

> *So we, too, have put our faith in Christ Jesus that we may be justified by faith in Christ and not by the works of the law, because by the works of the law no one will be justified...*
> **GALATIANS 2:16 (NIV)**

SEP 2 — The Worst of Sinners

Paul, formerly called Saul, grew up training to be a Pharisee. Everything about his life conformed to their code. Paul could later say that no one was his equal in zeal for God or his faultless performance under the law.

Garbage!

That's what Paul called his performance-driven life under the law. It was boasting in the flesh, he said, and that flesh had not saved him. It had only driven his sin ever deeper underground. Though he appeared to be one of the most righteous men in his day, in reality he was the worst sinner of them all—a blasphemer, persecutor, and violent man.

Don't mistake his assessment here as the mere humility of a gracious man. Paul wanted us to know the only thing worse than unrighteousness is self-righteousness. The problem with legalism is not the horror of failing at it, but the arrogance that comes when you think you're good at it.

> *What is more, I consider everything a loss because of the surpassing worth of knowing Christ Jesus my Lord, for whose sake I have lost all things. I consider them garbage, that I may gain Christ,*
> I CORINTHIANS 3:8-9 (NIV)

SEP 3 — His Unlimited Patience

I've sat with people who were convinced they had made far too many mistakes for God to want them. In their mind, they were damaged goods, beyond redemption.

I have one simple question for them: "Have you done worse things than Paul did before he knew Christ?" He called himself the worst of sinners because he killed God's people thinking God wanted him to.

But even in that state, God poured out his grace on Paul and came to him to reveal how much he was loved by the God he was working against. God did this, according to Paul, so that he could demonstrate to everyone else his unlimited patience.

If he could rescue the one most lost, we could all rest assured we are not beyond his reach. No matter how damaged you think you are, the Father's open arms are still extended to you.

But for that very reason I was shown mercy so that in me, the worst of sinners, Christ Jesus might display his immense patience as an example for those who would believe in him and receive eternal life.

1 TIMOTHY 1:16 (NIV)

SEP 4 — A Real Covering

Shame craves to be covered up.

Almost everybody tries to hide their failures in an attempt to protect themselves. We make excuses for ourselves while we shift the blame to others. We gossip about other people in an attempt to feel better about ourselves. We push to achieve beyond our peers so we can feel superior to them.

We even look for religious institutions to affirm us so that we can ignore the doubts that assail us. That's why relationships in religious environments can turn so painful: people have to tear others down to make themselves look better.

After the fall, Adam and Even tried to cover up, too. They did a bit of blame-shifting to the serpent ("he deceived me"), each other ("it was the woman"), and even to God ("the woman *you* gave me). Still, their shame was so overwhelming they put on clothing for the first time, no longer feeling safe with each other.

Unfortunately, they chose their underwear from the Fig Leaf Collection. Taking pity, God made them more practical and comfortable alternatives from animal skins. It was not only an act of mercy, but also prophetic demonstration. The blood shed to cover them that day foreshadowed a future day when Jesus's death for us would provide all the covering we really need.

Now we don't have to hide our shame anymore.

*Do not be afraid; you will not be put to shame.
Do not fear disgrace; you will not be humiliated.
You will forget the shame of your youth...*

ISAIAH 54:4 (NIV)

SEP 5 — The Fig Leaf Collection

When you find your covering in the work of Christ, the debilitating effects of shame vanish.

You'll find yourself free to own your mistakes, quick to apologize, and able to forgive yourself and others more easily. Friends I have like that are such a pleasure to be around. They are not always maneuvering to protect themselves. They don't take any joy in gossip, and you won't blame others to take the heat off of you.

Being free from condemnation, shame, and the fear of what others might think of you are great freedoms. They are the fruit of growing to trust his work in you, and yes, that takes time for us to embrace.

When difficulties press in around me, it's easier to believe that God's not for me. But that is only the voice of the serpent whispering in your ears, "If God's not going to give you what you think you need, maybe you should go get it yourself."

Trusting our own wisdom is easy, so we often find ourselves doing it before we ever realize it. When you realize you are scurrying to try to save yourself, that would be a great time to lean back into his covering.

*Seek the LORD while he may be found;
call on him while he is near.*

ISAIAH 55:6 (NIV)

For the next few days, let's look at the time Jesus calmed the storm in the Sea of Galilee for his terrified disciples. (Matthew 8:23–27). There is so much treasure in this little story.

SEP 6 — Why Are You So Afraid?

Jesus looked in their panicked eyes and asked them one simple question. "Why are you so afraid?"

Why?

Because.

Because they were a long way from the shore. Because their boat was at one moment tossed into the air by an angry wave, and in the next it would slam into the bottom of a trough where more waves washed over the side, threatening to rip them out of the boat. Because they were about to capsize and die in the maelstrom.

Sure, these fears might seem silly now that the sky was clear, the wind barely a whisper, and only the tiniest of ripples lapped against the side of the boat, but how were they to know he could or would command the storm to silence? How were they to know that they would be safe after all?

Certainly, the circumstances were such that any rational person would be afraid.

Unless…

Unless they were looking at someone more certain than the wind, more powerful than the waves, more loving toward them than any of them yet knew.

> *Be strong and courageous. Do not be afraid or terrified because of them, for the LORD your God goes with you; he will never leave you nor forsake you.*
>
> **DEUTERONOMY 31:6 (NIV)**

SEP 7 — You of Little Faith

While they were terrified in the storm, Jesus called them, "You of little faith."

I would love to have seen the look on his face when he did so. I don't think it was the angry rebuke our movie versions make of it. Couldn't he have said it with a chuckle in his voice as he roughed up Matthew's hair?

That's what I suspect, because this was a lesson—not a test. There was something he wanted them to grasp here.

Having "little faith" is not a measurement of quantity. On another occasion when Jesus pointed out how little their faith was, the disciples asked him to increase their faith. He responded that faith as small as a mustard seed could move mountains.

So, if quantity was not his concern, then it must have been something else.

If your faith is in a boat to hold you up, you will only feel safe when it quietly rests in the water. When you learn to vest your trust in Father's love and care for you, then it matters little what wind and sea can hurl at you.

> *"You of little faith, why are you so afraid?" Then he got up and rebuked the winds and the waves, and it was completely calm.*
>
> **MATTHEW 8:26 (NIV)**

SEP 8 — Learning to Trust

For us to be free to trust God, we have to put more faith in what we cannot see than what we do. Nothing is more difficult for us to learn. We are physical creatures who find it easier to trust the tangibles in time and space more than we trust Father's love for us.

Ultimately, isn't our trust in circumstances really trusting in ourselves?

Before the storm hit, the disciples trusted the skills of the fishermen among them. They were certain of their abilities to sail that sea in most kinds of weather. They'd been doing it all their lives. They had no fear because they were certain of themselves. But when the storm reached its full fury, they knew they were in over their heads.

We do the same thing, don't we? We take care of ourselves the best we can. As long as everything works the way we want it to, we are content. But when crisis hits, our misdirected faith is unmasked. We are not as well equipped as we thought.

Not only do our eyes fix on the circumstances that rage around us, but also on our own inability to deal with them. That's the perfect place to ask God to teach you how to trust him and for what's unseen to become more real than what is.

> *Now faith is confidence in what we hope for and assurance about what we do not see.*
> **PROVERBS 3:5 (NIV)**

SEP 9 — Bigger than Our Failures?

I wonder if the disciples were a lot like people I've been with in crisis. When people feel insecure, they look for someone to blame: "We should have stayed closer to land." "Why didn't we take a bigger boat?" "Whose idea was it to go sailing today anyway?"

Once you start looking for someone to blame in crisis, you'll lose all hope. How can I trust God with something when it's my own fault to begin with? We can rattle off a hundred things we could have done differently, and all of them are just excuses for why we can't trust him now.

Trust in God based on our own performance is still

trust in ourselves. If God only helps the perfect, what hope have any of us? If we must earn the right to trust in Father, then we still end up only believing in ourselves. It will work as long as the weather cooperates, but when the storm crashes down, we are lost.

Thank God we are loved by a God who is bigger than our own failures.

> When hard pressed, I cried to the LORD; he brought me into a spacious place. The LORD is with me; I will not be afraid. What can mere mortals do to me? The LORD is with me; he is my helper...
>
> PSALM 118:5–7 (NIV)

SEP 10 Put Your Faith in Something Big

Jesus wanted his closest friends to come to the end of themselves so that they might trust in Father alone.

No matter how hard they tried, they always came up short. Even on the night Jesus was arrested, Peter was certain his love for his friend would overcome any temptation to deny Jesus. But it wasn't so. As soon as the heat was turned up, he caved in, his fears overwhelming his faith.

You know what that is like, don't you? If you're like me you probably have plenty of stories where you really needed to entrust yourself to his care, but instead reacted to your fears. Like Peter, we look back at our faithlessness and weep. Blame and accusation swallow up any confidence we have that God will work in our lives.

But our self-focused faith lets every trial and difficulty prove that either we're not good enough, or that God doesn't care enough about us. Both will make us afraid. And both make us people of little faith, because that faith is vested in something so little—ourselves!

Surely God is my salvation; I will trust and not be afraid.
The LORD, the LORD himself, is my strength and my
defense; he has become my salvation."

ISAIAH 12:2 (NIV)

SEP 11 — Why Are You So Afraid?

God invites us into a relationship with him that becomes far more real than any circumstance we encounter.

Instead of seeing wind and waves, or our inability to deal with them, we see him in the midst of it all. We may not know how he is going to deal with our circumstances, but we can rest secure that no one loves us more. And as his work unfolds in our lives, no circumstance is a cause for fear.

How can we get to that place?

Wrong question…in asking it we only prove our eyes are still on ourselves.

Like the storm on Galilee, it matters little what we can do. What matters is what he will do. In times of anxiety I have one simple prayer: "Father what is it about your love I don't know that if I know it, I wouldn't be anxious here."

It's a prayer he always answers, though rarely immediately, nor does he even tell me what it is I need to know. But as I keep looking to him in the face of my circumstance my trust grows until I'm at rest in his love. No matter what I might encounter in this life, when I see what he is doing in me and around me even in the most painful circumstances, it absolutely astounds me.

The Sovereign LORD is my strength; he makes my feet like the feet of a deer, he enables me to tread on the heights.

HABAKKUK 3:19 (NIV)

SEP 12 — Sometimes You Just Have to Start Over

Nicodemus was a religious leader who sought Jesus out in the dark of night. He knew Jesus's miracles were proof that God was with him, and Nicodemus wanted to be part of his kingdom. But he had no idea what it would demand from him.

Perhaps Nicodemus wanted some instructions to follow, new rules that would let him in on how Jesus lived. But Jesus didn't offer any. He simply told Nicodemus that he needed to be born all over again. The idea sent Nicodemus's head spinning as he tried to conceive how he, an old man, could be born a second time.

It was not a physical rebirth that Nicodemus needed, but a spiritual one.

He thought he had God all figured out, and he had risen to the heights of religious leadership in his time. Obviously, he knew a lot. But what he knew wasn't going to help him because he had the wrong center from which to understand it all.

If he was going to see into the reality of this coming kingdom, he needed a rebirth of the Spirit. He would have to put aside all he thought he knew to start over as a little child, dependent on Jesus.

Nothing in this kingdom can be seen, embraced, or pursued by the flesh no matter how well-intentioned. It runs contrary to every way our flesh wants to respond.

> Flesh gives birth to flesh, but the Spirit gives birth to spirit. You should not be surprised at my saying, "You must be born again."
>
> JOHN 3:6–7 (NIV)

SEP 13 Windblown

Jesus offered Nicodemus a completely different way of living, not another performance standard. He found he would need a rebirth of the Spirit that would open his spiritual senses to discern the reality of God's Spirit.

Jesus said this Spirit is like the wind, blowing wherever it wills, but it is difficult for us to see where it came from and where it is going. Then he added, "So it is with everyone born of my Spirit."

I remember the first time I heard these words in my childhood. I understood the Spirit could be like the wind we can't define or control. But what was he saying about us? If we were truly born on the wind of the Spirit, would it be just as difficult for people to appreciate why we do what we do?

I didn't even know what that meant when I first heard those words as a young teenager. Yet, they filled my heart with an irresistible call of mystery and adventure that I still follow to this day.

The wind blows wherever it pleases. You hear its sound, but you cannot tell where it comes from or where it is going. So it is with everyone born of the Spirit.

JOHN 3:8 (NIV)

SEP 14 The Label Is Not the Reality

The term "born again" is often synonymously used today with the term "evangelical" to validate a conservative brand of Christianity and to question the faith of others who don't use the same label.

We have turned a term Jesus used to invite people into his kingdom into the most divisive term in Christendom, proving that we missed his point entirely.

If Jesus were going to define his kingdom by a creed, this was his time to say it. If we could see the kingdom by participating in certain rituals or sacraments or ascribing to the ethics of a Godly life, Jesus would have told us.

Jesus was not refining the religion of the Old Covenant; he was offering a new way of living that was indefinable and incomprehensible to the natural mind. Just because we use the label, doesn't mean we've embraced his reality.

> Jesus replied, "Very truly I tell you, no one can see the kingdom of God unless they are born again."
> JOHN 3:3 (NIV)

SEP 15 · On Being Born Again

The religion Nicodemus knew so well would never evolve into the life-transforming faith he sought.

Being born again meant that in spiritual things he needed to lay down everything he thought he knew and learn how to live by the breath of the Spirit. Jesus knew that would be difficult for a man so steeped in religion, and Nicodemus's ensuing struggle over Jesus's words demonstrated how right he was.

And so it is with us. The more we have been schooled in religious activity, the more difficult it is to see this kingdom for what it really is. Millions of people on the planet today are claiming to be born again, but they don't have the foggiest idea who Jesus is or how to live in his reality.

They may subscribe to Christian beliefs, follow Christian ethics, and practice Christian rituals, but they do not know how to ride the wind of his Spirit and be transformed by him.

Being born again is a real process that opens our eyes and heart to a different world that supersedes the material world to which we are accustomed.

I have spoken to you of earthly things and you do not believe; how then will you believe if I speak of heavenly things?
JOHN 3:12 (NIV)

SEP 16 You Are Not in Control

The Spirit blows where he wills.

No one controls the wind, even with our increased technologies. It is controlled by forces much larger than humanity can influence. There are times we might like for it to stop or blow a different direction, but there isn't a thing we can do about it.

While the wind is invisible, you can still hear it, feel it on your skin, and see its effects on the world around you.

Haven't you ever wondered where all that wind comes from and where it ends up? What an excellent metaphor to describe the working of the Spirit.

He is like the wind, uncontrolled by human convention. The current of God's reality swirls in and through every experience you have. You cannot force him to do what you want, but you can learn to ride with him and become a significant part of what he is doing in the world.

As you do not know the path of the wind, or how the body is formed in a mother's womb, so you cannot understand the work of God, the Maker of all things.
ECCLESIASTES 11:5 (NIV)

SEP 17 — A Different Motivation

Why do his followers become like the wind?

They live out of different motivations than the world around them. While everyone else is acting in their own self-interest, they are living up to different motivations.

People like that used to drive me nuts. When I was a pastor, it bothered me that some of the most spiritual men and women I came across wouldn't fit into our programs the way I wanted. They were uninterested in staff positions I dangled before them, and they declined invitations to ministry I thought would bless them. I was constantly befuddled by the decisions they made.

Maybe they weren't as spiritual as I thought.

I came to find out, however, that they were tuned to a higher frequency. When I expressed my frustration to one of them, he answered, "I don't know that I can explain it, but one day you'll know." I didn't like his answer at all until five years later when I heard myself saying almost the exact same words to a group of elders courting me to become their next pastor.

I've now come to really appreciate those who don't fit into the normal choices people would make because something deep inside calls them to a higher good. They are the most intriguing people I know and have incredible impact on people around them.

> *Come, breath, from the four winds and breathe into these slain, that they may live…*
> **EZEKIEL 37:9 (NIV)**

SEP 18 — Just Enough to Be Miserable

When I was growing up, my father often said that most people get just enough of Christianity to be miserable. By that, he meant they learned the doctrine, ethics, and rituals without ever knowing him. They miss the beauty of what life in Jesus can be and hunker down to the drudgery of meeting what they perceive to be his expectations.

My father spent almost thirty years in that misery before discovering how fulfilling a relationship with Jesus could be.

Following Jesus is a life of love, not a life of obligation. Having embraced his love for us we get to live out of endearment, not drudgery.

It is not what we know about God that matters nearly as much as knowing his affection for us, and loving others in the same way. Paul told Timothy to keep that in mind especially when believers become more enamored with controversies of doctrine, rather than living in love.

Learning to be loved abundantly and to love others extravagantly will help you discover how to ride the wind.

> *The whole point of what we're urging is simply love—love uncontaminated by self-interest and counterfeit faith, a life open to God.*
> 1 TIMOTHY 1:5 (MSG)

SEP 19 — Living Well Loved

We all recognize living to our own self-interest, looking to maximize our benefit or to minimize our pain in the circumstances we face. We have learned to survive that way in the world. The wind Jesus revealed to Nicodemus doesn't operate on self-interest, but rather on love that lays down its life for the good of another.

That's what will mark his people in the world. We understand when people do whatever is best for them, seeking power and pleasure often at the expense of others. People can even use their religion to selfish ends. Jesus exposed the Pharisees for doing so when they declared some of their possessions "devoted to God" and therefore didn't have to share them with others in need.

Love displaces the power of self-interest and the quest for power over others. How can you live selfishly when doing so will negatively affect someone you care about? Love offers us a host of better options that will spread his wonder in the world.

People who know Father's love will live graciously, generously, and kindly in the world.

Those who are well loved will love well.

> *Flee the evil desires of youth and pursue righteousness,*
> *faith, love and peace, along with those who call*
> *on the Lord out of a pure heart.*
>
> 2 TIMOTHY 2:22 (NIV)

SEP 20 · The Spirit of Truth

I used to think that Christian growth came by learning new truths and putting them into practice. I was taught to structure my sermons that way, with a powerful application at the end.

It took me a long time to realize that doesn't work. How many of us have heard a powerful sermon or read an inspired book and attempted to embrace its message and committed to living it out, and then failed to follow through? We blame ourselves for not trying hard enough and only end up with another expectation by which to measure our failure.

That's why Jesus left his Spirit to guide his followers into all truth. Change rarely comes in learning a principle and applying it; it comes in real moments of choice as the Spirit leads us to choices that honor his work in us.

This is not something we can do on our own, like studying algebra or Latin. Jesus challenged Nicodemus not to think of his life as learning a new catalog of information, but to learn to live in love.

That would so change everything about how he lived and confound the people around him.

> *But when the Friend comes, the Spirit of the Truth, he will take you by the hand and guide you into all the truth there is.*
> JOHN 15:13 (MSG)

SEP 21 A Fool's Errand

Every time I think I've figured out the way God works he'll amaze me yet again with how differently he thinks compared to me.

He zigs where I would zag. He asks me to give in where I would prefer to stand my ground. He has often proved himself to be suddenly and conspicuously absent from the plans I hoped would contain him.

This used to frustrate me. It doesn't anymore. I am finally settled in the reality that he wouldn't do anything the way I would. I'm convinced of the fact that he does all things well, even if he doesn't do them for my comfort or convenience. And I am convinced that following him is the only real way to live.

The pursuit to find any formula that can be applied to produce his righteousness, provide New Testament church life to me, or to even grow my trust, is a fool's errand. It will fail time and time again until in the end I come to realize that this reality only comes through a growing friendship with him.

The more I know him and the more I recognize his hand at work around me, the freer I will be to trust him and live in his kingdom.

> But I am afraid that, as the serpent deceived Eve by his craftiness, your minds will be led astray from the simplicity and purity of devotion to Christ.
>
> 2 CORINTHIANS 11:3

SEP 22 When Others Don't Understand

I am convinced that my need to follow his Spirit and be born again is not a one-time experience but a daily choice to shed my expectations about the way things should be, to mistrust my own desires and agenda, and to tune my mind to the breath of his Spirit and the truth of his word.

Where I live in the newness of his Spirit today, I will ride that wind with increasing joy and freedom. I will see his fingerprints in the jagged places of life and be able to cooperate with his purpose in me.

When I live out of my own selfish ambition, religious performance, or natural wisdom, I will struggle with unanswerable questions and act in ways that are hurtful to others. I'm so tired of that.

Though I'm a long way from living it perfectly today, I want to live no other way—more today than yesterday and more tomorrow than today. And the only way I can do that is to continue to lean more deeply in him, watching which direction the wind is blowing, and riding it.

I do find that some of the most significant people in my life can't understand what I'm doing or why. But now I'm at rest knowing Jesus warned us it would be that way.

When God lives and breathes in you (and he does, as surely as he did in Jesus), you are delivered from that dead life.
ROMANS 8:11 (MSG)

SEP 23 — Following Him, Not It

Any time we choose to follow a model of spirituality, someone else's formula for success, or an agenda no matter how well-intentioned, we will end up walking by our own limited wisdom.

The invitation to this kingdom is to follow a person. Jesus doesn't give us the way; he is The Way. He doesn't have life; he is The Life. He doesn't just speak the truth; he is The Truth itself. Everything about his kingdom begins and ends in him and we experience that through a growing friendship with him.

That's often the hardest thing for people to see when they have been disillusioned by their religious experience. Immediately they begin to look for another way of doing church or another guru to follow.

They jump right back into a different form of religious performance, rather than learning how to simply know him.

Jesus answered, "I am the way and the truth and the life. No one comes to the Father except through me..."
JOHN 14:6 (NIV)

SEP 24 — Putting Wind in a Box

Have you ever tried to stuff the wind into a box? Absurd, isn't it? You wouldn't even try. You can get the air in a box, but once it's there it ceases to be wind.

Hopefully we'll come to see our attempts to control

God's working to be as absurd. Then we might stop wasting our efforts to try to get God to work in the boxes we prefer or trying to control the outcomes we want from him.

He blows where he wills, our only choice is to follow or not. That's why when we try to get God to bless what we want him to do he will seem more distant, like a concept rather than a presence with us.

The person who is born of the Spirit loses his moorings in the temporal world where the cravings of safety, security, and stability must be satisfied. When we do that, we too become like the wind, available to him at each moment to do what he would ask of us.

Part of what Jesus was encouraging Nicodemus to do when he told him to be born again was to stop trying to put boxes around the work of the Spirit, because his Spirit can never be contained.

> *Don't suppress the Spirit, and don't stifle those who have a word from the Master.*
> **1 THESSALONIANS 5:19 (MSG)**

SEP 25 — Obeying the Nudges

Faith doesn't flow from theology; it flows from relationship.

That's not to say theology is unimportant, just that learning about God and knowing him are two different things. If we only learn theology, then our trust will be in our theology, which is not what God has in mind.

Even from our earliest days, he shows us how to embrace his unfolding revelation to us and he teaches us how to follow him. I don't know any other way to describe it than simply following those nudges he puts in your mind and heart. He might be revealing something about himself, inviting you to some time with him, drawing you to read the Bible, or leading you to serve or encourage someone else.

Learning to recognize those nudges and respond to them will help us distinguish between our desires and his. Those nudges almost always begin not by calling us to grandiose ministries, but by teaching us to live outside our self-interest in mundane ways in which we can serve others around us.

To many people this may sound like emotion-driven, touchy-feely nonsense. I hear those objections often by those threatened with a life in God they won't be able to control by their disciplines and doctrines. But they couldn't be more wrong. This is a dance of head and heart together, discerning God and his ways.

The heart without the head can lead to well-intentioned disaster; the head without the heart will exalt doctrine over love and destroy others with its arrogance.

> *Be assured that from the first day we heard of you, we haven't stopped praying for you, asking God to give you wise minds and spirits attuned to his will, and so acquire a thorough understanding of the ways in which God works.*
>
> **COLOSSIANS 1:9-10 (NIV)**

SEP 26 How Do I Know?

So, how do I sort out his nudges from my own thoughts? Most nudges I get from his Spirit are simple ways of loving and serving people around me. I am not too worried about getting those wrong. There aren't many downsides to serving others.

To have some measure of confidence to step out in a larger action Jesus may be asking of me, I look for four things to come into agreement:

1. An intuitive, growing conviction of his leading over time.

2. Affirmation in the truth and spirit of Scripture about how God works.

3. Confirmation from other brothers and sisters as I discuss it with them or read books from people whose journeys I admire.

4. And the reality of my unfolding circumstances as I follow them.

When those voices are in synch, I have greater confidence that I am following him. But you know what? Sometimes all of these line up and I still get it wrong.

That's why people born of the Spirit rarely use language like, "God told me to..." and will instead talk in terms of what they sense. They've been wrong enough times not to be so presumptuous, even when they're most certain.

I've forged God's name on my agenda a number of times, only to find out later that it was my handwriting all along. But I'm still ready to get up the next day and follow as best I know.

And while I'm willing to pay the consequences for being wrong, I also know he can weave my mistakes into his purposes.

He knows us far better than we know ourselves, knows our pregnant condition, and keeps us present before God. That's why we can be so sure that every detail in our lives of love for God is worked into something good.

ROMANS 8:26–28 (MSG)

SEP 27 — Taking Wing

To be born of the Spirit has nothing to do with a sinner's prayer or speaking in tongues. It means we've taken wing on a breath of wind that comes from the Father himself and are learning to trust his insights over our human reasoning and justifications.

It means we don't have to have everything figured out to take the next step he's put on our hearts, and we no longer have to play for the applause of the crowd. It means we're finally free to surrender our need to think we're in control and know his plans are far better.

It means we lay aside the lies of shame and the demands for performance that drive us from him and find our security in his affection for us. That alone will allow him to keep transforming us.

It means finally realizing how our selfish ambitions work against his purpose in us and others around us and laying them down in our growing trust that he knows better than we do. It means knowing he does all things well.

> *He will swallow up death forever. The Sovereign LORD will wipe away the tears from all faces; he will remove his people's disgrace from all the earth.*
>
> **ISAIAH 25:8 (NIV)**

SEP 28 — The Adventure of Love

What great freedom to realize that I never had the power or wisdom to accomplish God's purposes!

Who would have thought that losing confidence in my flesh would only free me to live more dependent on him and more grateful when I see his hand at work?

What a joy to wake up in the uncertain adventure of

life and not be distressed at what might happen today, because he is with me!

How could human effort ever have produced this? It's a gift from him.

Living this way is not something you have to achieve, oddly enough; trying to achieve it will only leave you frustrated.

God's work in us is a reality you relax into as your trust in him grows.

> *We pray that you'll have the strength to stick it out over the long haul—not the grim strength of gritting your teeth but the glory-strength God gives. It is strength that endures the unendurable and spills over into joy…*
>
> **COLOSSIANS 1:11–12**

SEP 29 — Waiting in the Fog

"When Scripture says something important, it is very clear. When it isn't clear, it's usually not important, at least not for me today."

I learned that from a man in New Zealand who taught Scripture most of his life. I am always reminded of it when someone asks me a question from some of the more obscure Scriptures. I used to think there was a logical explanation for everything, and we should know what it is. We get frustrated at the inexplicable, fear the uncertain, and feel lost when our plans go off track. If that's your passion, you're not going to find it easy to live in Jesus's kingdom.

One person who wrote to me recently said that they felt like they were in a dense fog. "When others ask me to explain myself, I don't have the language to make sense of where I find myself on the journey. My heart gets it, but I just don't have the words. My head swirls with condemnation when people feel I should be 'doing something.' However, I am going to wait for the fog to lift and trust that it will."

He expressed so much of what Sara and I experienced in the early days of this journey. Our hearts were drawing us into his reality, while our minds and often our friends tried to pull us back into human logic and reasoning. More damage has been done to Jesus's kingdom by those who feel the need to explain something they didn't understand, or just do something to fill up the guilt of feeling like we're not doing enough.

Wonderful things happen in the fog. Waiting and trusting seems so futile, but there is no place where we're strengthened to resist the urge to figure out on our own what makes us most comfortable instead of what makes us most alive.

> *Wait for the Lord; be strong and take heart and wait for the Lord.*
> **PSALMS 27:14**

SEP 30 — Comfortable in Uncertainty

Most of our lives are lived in the fog. We have enough light and grace for this day, not for all the uncertainties and inexplicable concerns that lie ahead. The longer I walk this journey, the more comfortable I get not knowing what lies ahead. I don't need an explanation for everything; it is enough that he is in it with me. He will share them with me when I truly need them, not necessarily when I want them.

As you follow Jesus, you'll find yourself more comfortable in uncertain events because your confidence will come simply from the fact that he is with you. You don't owe people an explanation that will make sense to them. You can simply say, "I feel like God is doing something a bit different in me and I'm going to follow him for a little while and see where it leads. I hope you can love me through this time, because my love for you hasn't changed at all."

All our long-term strategic plans were our plans anyway, and they only provided a false sense of security. After all, how often did they pan out the way you thought?

We follow Jesus one day at a time. *What are you giving me today? What are you asking of me? Do I have enough?*

God is in the fog, in those moments when we most feel alone. And it is in the quiet of our inactivity that he draws us into his work. That has been my experience; it has opened me up into a larger world where there is no condemnation and now ever-lessening fears because I am learning to follow him, not my own wisdom and conclusions.

So do not fear, for I am with you; do not be dismayed, for I am your God. I will strengthen you and help you; I will uphold you with my righteous right hand.

ISAIAH 41:10

SECTION 4
Loving Others

OCT 1 The Irresistible Force

A lot of time and energy is spent trying to convince Christians to share their faith with the lost. What a contrast that is to the earliest believers who contained God's love, even when they were being beaten with whips, battered with stones, or threatened with death.

They told their tormentors, "We cannot help speaking about what we've seen and heard."

Having been touched by the greatest force in the universe, they were unable to keep it in, even when they knew it could cost them their lives.

Such is the nature of God's love. Once you experience it you will not be able to hoard it. When it's real, it will find its way to others through us even at the most inconvenient times.

All the effort in the world can't keep it in.

> *As for us, we cannot help speaking about what we have seen and heard.*
> **ACTS 4:20 (NIV)**

OCT 2 — Love Is Not a Command

I grew up viewing love as a command. After all, it's the new command Jesus gave us. I took that to mean I had to be nice to others, even when I didn't feel like it.

So, I tried to act compassionately toward people, even if I didn't have compassion for them. It was one thing to do it for other believers, but we were also told to love our enemies. Most of my attempts to share God's love were driven by my feeling condemned if I didn't, rather than out of genuine concern.

When we are more motivated by our need to obey Christ, rather than their need for him, we aren't really loving them. This is probably more obvious to them than it is to us, but instead of feeling loved, they feel exploited by those who want to put another notch on their belts.

That's the trouble with love as a command. If it isn't in your heart, you can only pretend to love and that is not the same thing. But the story doesn't end there. If we lack love, the only place to find it is in him.

Regarding life together and getting along with each other, you don't need me to tell you what to do. You're God-taught in these matters. Just love one another! …Keep it up; get better and better at it.
1 THESSALONIANS 4:9 (MSG)

OCT 3 Learning to Love

As long as we see love as an obligation, we will fall far short of what Jesus wanted us to experience. Love is not pretending to care; it's actually caring. I'm finding it easier to be honest about that in my relationship with God.

Some people are easy to love, and you find yourself caring about their well-being almost from the first meeting. Others prove more difficult to love because of broken places in their life or ours that rub us the wrong way.

My neighbor met me at my door one Sunday morning, with his three-year-old child, cursing at me for something I hadn't done. He was well known in the neighborhood as a bully who would take advantage of anyone he could. Every time I went past his home, I'd think about him, knowing God wanted me to learn to love him.

"I don't love him," I'd tell God as if he didn't know. "I know you want me to. I know that you love him. Teach me what I don't know, Father, about you or him that would allow me to love him like you do."

That's all I can do. Yes, I could still be kind and gracious to him when we crossed paths but loving him is something more. Unfortunately, he sold his home and moved away before I got to love him from the heart. I was well into the process, however, and my heart had softened considerably.

The unfolding of love in our lives can only begin with the wellspring of love—the Father himself! Once we experience love as God defines it, we will not be able to keep from sharing it with others.

> *In the same way I loved you, you love one another. This is how everyone will recognize that you are my disciples—when they see the love you have for each other.*
>
> JOHN 13:34–35 (MSG)

OCT 4 — The Wellspring of Love

Generosity begets generosity.

Where God is generous with you, you will be generous with others. Where God affirms your worth in him, you won't seek its substitute in others. Where you know God forgives your flaws, you'll forgive them in others.

For most of my life, however, I didn't live with a generous God. It seemed he was very miserly with me. He didn't answer my prayers the way I wanted, and he didn't provide for me the way I thought he should. Most days, it felt like I had barely enough of what I needed to get through the day and if I didn't hold it tightly, I could lose it. Needless to say, I wasn't very generous with others.

Only later did I come to discover that I'd been viewing God wrong. The religious God I was trying to appease didn't appear generous with me because I couldn't get him to serve my agenda. I was asking him to bless my plans and he was inviting me into his love so I could enjoy his plans for me.

When I gave up my agenda and sought to follow his, I discovered just how generous this God is. He always provides what I need as each day unfolds. No, he doesn't give us a six-month supply of grace, but because he is with us, I no longer have to fear not having enough.

And what I give away, strangely, doesn't diminish what I receive from him.

And God is able to bless you abundantly, so that in all things at all times, having all that you need, you will abound in every good work.
2 CORINTHIANS 9:8 (NIV)

OCT 5 — Conformity Is Not Love

Why is it so hard for church organizations to truly love one another? Organized groups almost always slide into conformity as their means of operation.

Someone sets the expectations for the group and people choose to go along or go away. From the outset, conformity presses us to do the same things in the same way and to think alike. This supposedly maintains our identity.

Conformity, however, does not lead to the reality of Christ expressed among his people, unless you give in to the misguided notion that you love me so you make me do the things you think are best for you. Jesus asked us to love, which gives people the space to grow and change, rather than force them into a mold.

Conformity is not love. That's using a false idea of love as a weapon: when you do what I want I will treat you well, and when you don't I'll distance myself from you. Loving someone means caring enough to walk with them as they discover how Jesus takes expression in them.

If the body of Christ is going to demonstrate herself today in the corporate majesty of her collaboration and cooperation, then Jesus will have to be our only focus and loving others our only motivation.

Let me give you a new command: Love one another.
JOHN 13:34 (MSG)

OCT 6 — A Love that Demonstrates His Glory

You don't have to agree with someone to love them. You only have to understand them and care about them.

Too many of us think we have all the wisdom we need and anyone who disagrees with us is a threat to our world. It only takes one person like that to destroy the freedom to live, love, and grow together.

Until we have enough brothers and sisters with a passion for truth that does not outrun their calling to love others, the body of Christ will continue to be fractured and impotent in the world. And until they have enough courage to lovingly stand up to those who are divisive and who demand that everyone think like they do, we won't have a chance for love to thrive.

But where we can differ in conscience and still honor one another, and where we can celebrate the individual being true to their conscience even if we disagree, then we'll discover relationships that will demonstrate his glory in the earth.

This is how everyone will recognize that you are my disciples—when they see the love you have for each other.
JOHN 13:34–35 (MSG)

OCT 7 — No Compulsion to Conform

In my journey, I've noticed that those who are most settled in God's truth feel no compulsion to conform others to it. They know truth has a power all its own and that their generosity of spirit inside truth will allow people to embrace it sooner than they would if they were bashed with others' opinions.

How I yearn for the day that the body of Christ can come together not based on the false unity of human conformity, but on a love that is greater than all our disagreements and with a humility of spirit that allows our differences to be discussed openly without others being hurt.

Then we won't need so-called leaders to police the peace or make us act like we are of one mind because only one mind is allowed to be expressed.

Knowing the truth is critical for all of us, but truth travels best inside of love instead of compulsion. When we live in that reality, the world will see that Jesus was the gift of the Father and that they too can share in his glory.

I appeal to you, brothers and sisters, in the name of our Lord Jesus Christ, that all of you agree with one another in what you say and that there be no divisions among you, but that you be perfectly united in mind and thought.

1 CORINTHIANS 1:10 (NIV)

OCT 8 — The Journey Together

When I was a pastor, one of the great misconceptions I had was the idea that a relationship with God rises out of an effective church program. I've discovered that it is just the opposite.

Embracing a relationship with God is a personal pursuit. People can sit for years in religious services and never explore what it means for them to walk with God. Unless we open our hearts to him and learn how to follow him, we'll never know the power of the life of the church.

Instead, the church will become our substitute for what we're not finding in God, and not only will that continually disappoint us, it will frustrate others in the process. We can share Jesus's life with one another, but we can never be God for one another.

That's why there is a move today of God calling people back to himself. For too long we have looked to groups or gifted "leaders" to provide what Father wanted to give us. That's because he wants to be the center of your life first, and then discover that we'll be able to find the healthy relationships with others that will encourage us to live in his reality.

Truly my soul finds rest in God; my salvation comes from him.
Truly he is my rock and my salvation; he is my fortress,
I will never be shaken.

PSALM 62:1-2 (NIV)

OCT 9 The Joy of Connection

Setting people free to discover their own trajectory in Christ makes religious leaders nervous. They fear that if people find a vital life in God, they will shun gatherings with other believers.

Admittedly, they may find many religious activities to be not so engaging, but God has put in us all a hunger for real community. That hunger may get buried in our defense mechanisms from past hurts and abuse, but you can't know the love of the Father and not have an increasing hunger to share this life with others.

Paul said that each one of us sees a glimpse of who the Father is and a facet or two of what's true in his universe, but the church is "the fullness of him who fills everything in every way."

You can walk in your own limited relationship if you want to, but why would you? I want so much more; I want to know how Jesus is making himself known to others as well. Authentic community may not be easy to find in this day and age, but don't stop looking for others to share the journey with and don't stop asking God whom he wants you to walk alongside in this season of your life.

You may find it easier to find the people God is giving you to love, than to find an organized group that shares your passion.

All the believers were together and had everything in common.
ACTS 2:44 (NIV)

OCT 10 Loving in the Moment

Jesus had the amazing ability to love what he did not condone and forgive without minimizing an offense. He confronted the false spirituality of the Pharisees and he invited prostitutes into his kingdom.

Sometimes we are tempted to think of love as simply making nice at the expense of genuine. We find it easy to smile and feign love in someone's presence, while later we take the liberty of tearing them down with gossip.

Love is a reality. It is putting the care of another person above your own needs and discovering what they need most to find themselves drawn into the orbit of the God who loves them. It doesn't follow a set of principles but responds in the moment to take the situation you are in and transform it with his glory.

We can't love like that without him first putting the love in our hearts and showing us how to express it in this moment. The best way to learn that is to watch how he treats you in a variety of circumstances.

Freely you have received; freely give.
MATTHEW 10:8

OCT 11 — Is Love a Feeling?

Many people see love as a feeling. I hear it when they say that they just don't feel that God loves them. And yet he does, to the core of their being.

Being loved and feeling loved are two different things. Anyone in a marriage can testify that sometimes our spouse doesn't feel the love we know we have for them. It is possible for people to miss love that is right there in front of them because it doesn't come in a package they recognize or want.

His love for us and ours for him must transcend feelings and touch us at a far deeper level than the capriciousness of our emotions. Love is a reality. Sometimes we feel it; sometimes we don't.

That's not to say he doesn't want us to feel his love with some regularity, but it will help us respond when we don't. Rather than use our lack of feeling to doubt his love or to push ourselves to try to earn it, it is far better that we ask him to reveal his love to us however he wants and look for how he is working in our lives in that moment.

His love is a given; we just need to find that place where we can see it. The default setting is always this: I'm loved and looking to see it. Be careful to avoid this trap: I'm not loved unless he proves it.

Let grace, mercy, and peace be with us in truth and love from God the Father and from Jesus Christ, Son of the Father!
2 JOHN 1:3 (MSG)

OCT 12 — All You Have to Do Is Love

Our new neighbors were not Christians and let us know in no uncertain terms that they didn't want that

"Jesus stuff crammed down their throats."

We assured them we would not talk to them about Jesus until they asked us.

"We never will," they responded.

As we got to know them better, we found out why. Their previous home had been located next to a church facility that wanted to expand and they were obnoxious in their attempts to get them to move. People parked in their driveway, trampled their flowers, and even one night marched around the house chanting. Because they are an elderly couple, it had scared them half to death.

They had held their ground for many years thereafter unwilling to give in. When they finally did move, they were embittered at how they had been treated and had rejected any sense of God's reality.

Do you know what finally opened the door to this elderly couple? One day I found out they were too ill to get their paper anymore and had to wait until the evening when their son would bring it to them after work. I told them I'd be happy to get theirs every morning when I got mine.

After four years of doing so, and lots of conversations in the exchange, they finally asked me to tell them about the Jesus I know. And they both decided to follow him.

To love him with all your heart, with all your understanding and with all your strength, and to love your neighbor as yourself is more important than all burnt offerings and sacrifices.

MARK 12:33 (NIV)

OCT 13 Loving Comes First

Jesus said, "If anyone loves me, he will obey my teaching" (John 14:23).

I used to think Jesus was saying that if I really loved

him, I would always follow his principles. I even taught that to other people when they wrestled with something in Scripture they didn't want to follow. "If you love him, you'll do it."

Except they didn't. They often chose their own course and hoped for forgiveness. But to be honest, I couldn't always live up to what I knew either. I thought I loved him, but my actions and responses often proved I didn't, at least by my interpretation of this verse.

I've since come to know that's not what he meant. That's how religious performance interprets those verses. What he was saying is that if we keep on discovering what it is to love him, we will end up keeping his teaching as well. The keeping doesn't prove the loving, but the loving will bear the fruit of our joyful obedience to him.

That's what Paul meant when he said that "love keeps the entire law." In Christ, we don't focus on keeping commands, which will always fail us. Instead, we learn to live in his love, and when we do that, we'll find ourselves following him to the ends of the earth.

> *But God demonstrates his own love for us in this:*
> *While we were still sinners, Christ died for us.*
> ROMANS 5:8 (NIV)

OCT 14 — A Love So Powerful

Paul was a man who had risen to the pinnacle of the religious institution of his day before he came face to face with the love of Jesus on that road to Damascus.

He knew what it was to fear God and the disapproval of his peers, so much so that he conformed his life by the strictest of codes. But he didn't know the power of love until that day.

When he discovered that the Lord of all was the Jesus

whose followers he was persecuting, I'm sure he expected to be destroyed. But he wasn't. In spite of it all, this Jesus, whom he was persecuting, loved him, and that proved to be the most powerful force Paul had ever encountered.

He had deserved to die and discovered that Jesus already had on his behalf. That love changed him. He no longer had anything to fear, nothing to earn, and no one to control. His life had been swallowed up by a love so great that there was nothing left for him to do except to live every day by what that love led him to do.

> *Christ's love has moved me to such extremes.*
> *His love has the first and last word in everything we do.*
> **2 CORINTHIANS 5:14 (MSG)**

OCT 15 — No Other Motive

Every day we are manipulated by a host of motives, some of which even look godly. There are expectations people put on us, fears that drive us, appetites that lure us, and guilt that badgers us.

Once we encounter the love of Christ, none of these can control us any longer.

The next time you feel torn in any situation, retreat to this simple test: overwhelmed by gratefulness for what he's done and secure in his acceptance and care for you, what does love invite you to do?

Paul discounted every other motivation, and so should we. That's the only motive that counts in this kingdom and the greatest gift of the cross.

Remain in my love.

Without that kindled fresh every day it is easy to find our spiritual lives sliding down an exhausting rut of demands and activities: we will be busy doing a lot of things for God, but absolutely devoid of his life and his joy.

> *You were taught, with regard to your former way
> of life, to put off your old self, which is being
> corrupted by its deceitful desires...*
> **EPHESIANS 4:22 (NIV)**

OCT 16 — Helping Others Live Loved

You can hear many voices talking about the love and grace of our Father and how the coming of Jesus changed everything about how we get to live in him. I love that no singular human is leading this parade and that many people are quietly discovering the power of love.

However, it's not writing and speaking about love that matters, but actually living in it. Living loved shows up in your relationships—not just the ones that benefit you, but the ones you consider the least or the last, or even with those you presume to be your enemies.

I am convinced that the depth of our character is most demonstrated by how we treat those who disagree with us when we're most certain that we are right. Do we treat them gently, give them the opportunity to engage, and offer them the same grace we talk about with others?

As Jesus said, it is wholly inconsistent for those who have received great love and forgiveness to grab anyone else by the throat and demand their satisfaction.

> *Live out this God-created identity the way our Father
> lives toward us, generously and graciously, even
> when we're at our worst.*
> **LUKE 6:35–36 (MSG)**

OCT 17 — Those Loved Well, Love Well

What I love about living loved, as opposed to just talking about it, is that it is transformational. Those who are well loved, love others well in good times and bad. They always value the relationship above their own perspective.

This is not something you can learn by principle, but by embracing God's affection at the deepest place in your soul. Until you know you are loved you will be sucked into every religious activity and performance treadmill that exists, hoping against hope that you can do the right thing to merit that deep affection from the heart of the Father.

Father, I know that there is nothing I can do to earn your affection. Show me how loved I am. Teach me to love my enemies and to give without expecting anything in return.

I tell you, love your enemies. Help and give without expecting a return. You'll never—I promise—regret it.
LUKE 6:35-36 (MSG)

OCT 18 — A Journey Lined with Love

A woman wrote me last week to tell me how God was bringing her out of spiritual bondage that resulted from prolonged abuse by her parents. He had given her simple steps to follow that drew her into increasing freedom from their influence.

I know a woman who have been caring for those living with AIDS for more than thirty years simply because God asked a woman to go back and care for her gay ex-husband as he was dying of that horrible disease.

I know a man who sang in a mostly gay civic chorus

in a conservative community because God asked him to demonstrate God's love to them when other Christians in the city were bashing them publicly.

I know deep and life-changing relationships that have started just because someone picked up a phone or made a visit in response to a nudge they thought came from God. All of these things and the fruit that flows from them came from incredibly small choices to be part of something God put on their heart.

> *Don't pick on people, jump on their failures, criticize their faults—unless, of course, you want the same treatment. Don't condemn those who are down; that hardness can boomerang. Be easy on people; you'll find life a lot easier.*
> **LUKE 6:37–38 (MSG)**

OCT 19 · The Next Person in Front of You

What if we just started loving the people God puts before us each day—can you imagine what would spill out of that in terms of opportunity, ministry, and even growing fellowship?

I think we have it all backward. Jesus didn't ask us to start ministries or projects. He didn't start any himself.

He didn't ask us to accomplish great things for him or seek fame and fortune.

He simply asked us to love the next person God puts in front of us. That put him in some of his most incredible moments—talking to a Pharisee in the dead of night, finding a shamed woman beside a well, forgiving an adulteress others wanted to stone, and talking to Pilate about some earth-shattering realities.

That will be enough for the whole world to know that we belong to him, and that they can too.

> *Give away your life; you'll find life given back, but not merely given back—given back with bonus and blessing. Giving, not getting, is the way. Generosity begets generosity.*
>
> LUKE 6:37–38 (MSG)

OCT 20 Finding Fellowship

People often ask me how they can start a house church or connect with other believers in their area on a more relational journey. Many have been frustrated at past attempts to find a good congregation or a healthy home group. While they can take advantage of internet forums, email lists, and directories to see if they can find local people growing in the same realities, that may not be the best way.

I now encourage people just to listen to Father every day and to love the people right in front of them. This has worked for Sara and me in our three recent moves. We have discovered a wealth of local relationships that have just grown out of taking an interest in the people around us and discovering others who are passionate for the God we love.

You don't have to start or join anything to find that, unless of course Jesus asks you to.

I am more convinced than ever that everything God wants to do in the world will flow from us learning to live in his love and listening to him as we walk through life. This allows the opportunities in our lives to grow organically, rather than through the artificial means of organizing, promoting, and manipulating others.

> *With all this going for us, my dear, dear friends, stand your ground. And don't hold back. Throw yourselves into the work of the Master, confident that nothing you do for him is a waste of time or effort.*
>
> 1 CORINTHIANS 15:58 (MSG)

OCT 21 — I Won't Let You Go Through This Alone

"I couldn't bear to let you go through it alone."

The first time I heard those words was from a good friend who walked beside me through the most painful experience of my life. We had previously shared some wonderful times for a season, but then he withdrew from our relationship. I missed him, but thought he must have his reasons.

I was so blessed when we reconnected in the midst of my trial.

One day I asked him why he had disappeared for so long. "I could see that you were going to get hurt badly and I just couldn't bear to watch it."

I know he'd been through a similar betrayal and how painful it would have been for him to walk through mine. I laughed, "But you're here now at the worst of it."

"I know," he grimaced. "I couldn't bear to let you go through it alone."

I don't know a better definition for community. It isn't always fun and games. Love will not let people go through their darkest days alone. As painful as it is to watch someone, love won't let us be anywhere else but right beside them.

> *The LORD himself goes before you and will be with you;*
> *he will never leave you nor forsake you.*
> *Do not be afraid; do not be discouraged.*
> **DEUTERONOMY 31:8 (NIV)**

OCT 22 — Running to Suffering

At my brother's funeral a number of years ago, one of his best friends stood up and told how he couldn't bear to visit my brother as he battled the final stages of multiple sclerosis. He wanted to remember him as he was, not as he had become. And yet, that was the time my brother needed him most.

The meaning of compassion is right in the word itself, "come (to) passion." Passion in the old English meant suffering, which is why we call Easter week, Passion Week. True compassion runs to suffering. We are there at someone's worst moment because they need us.

A good picture of that occurred on 9/11, when first responders were running into the World Trade Center as everyone else was trying to get out. Compassion means being there when it's incredibly difficult, painful, or even dangerous—not because we enjoy the circumstances but because we love the person in them.

No one enjoys walking with people through their darkest night, but love isn't about our comfort. I may not know what to do or what to say to help, but love says, "I just can't let you go through this alone!"

When Jesus landed and saw a large crowd, he had compassion on them, because they were like sheep without a shepherd.
MARK 6:34

OCT 23 Finding Your Way to Love

John Lynch is one of the authors of *Bo's Cafe*, one of the best books I've read about sorting through brokenness in a marriage to a real engagement with grace. Last Friday, as he was going out the door to do a wedding, he posted this on his Facebook status.

I perform another wedding tonight. I always wish I could show a DVD of what is coming up. How they'll deeply hurt each other, selfishly try to win, blaming the other for how their life is not working, how they'll want to run...until devastated, they each call out to God and learn to trust this new life He's given them. Then they'll begin to protect, love and enjoy each other. He adores them. He'll make it happen.

He pulled it down later. It's certainly not the kind of picture you want for a wedding night, but it is nonetheless true! Sara and I feel something similar every time we see a young couple installed as the new staff pastor at a large church. They are so excited to be offered the opportunity; they have no idea how brutally they will get hurt in that process.

Our greatest hurts come from the people closest to us and none more than our spouse. Marriage is the most critical relationship where we can truly learn to live selflessly because you can't hide yourself twenty-four hours a day.

It's probably a good thing none of us know how much pain will be involved, or else we would never go down that track to learn what we need to know to find real freedom.

> *Do nothing out of selfish ambition or vain conceit. Rather, in humility value others above yourselves...*
> **PHILIPPIANS 2:3 (NIV)**

OCT 24 You Don't Have to Look for Love

Most of us discovered while we were growing up that it is easier to manipulate people into giving us what we want or think we deserve, than it is to get them to love us. Even people who told us they love us would often prove by their actions that they only "love" us to the degree that we would do what they wanted.

There's nothing we can do to make people love us. If you have to earn someone's love, it really isn't love, it's just mutual accommodation of self-need. It's a good thing that God already loves you as much as anyone possibly can. We don't have to fight for his.

And when that becomes increasingly real to us, we won't need to try to make others love us either. Jesus didn't tell us to go "get love" from others; he told us to love others.

So, don't go about your day seeking for the love you may be craving from others. Look for ways to love others already in your life. They may or may not return it, but there's no freer way to live than to love freely and trust God to provide the love you need to get through your day, whether it's direct from him or he shares it with you through someone significant in your life.

> *Finally, all of you, be like-minded, be sympathetic, love one another, be compassionate and humble.*
> **1 PETER 3:8 (NIV)**

OCT 25 — Bound by Our Approval Needs

When the religionists of Jesus's day chided him for not fitting into their ways or respecting their authority, he was not swayed. He followed his Father's voice rather than the jealous cries of his threatened countrymen.

One of the hardest hurdles for any of us who grew up in a religious environment is to get past the need to live off of the approval of others. People caught up in religion use approval to manipulate people. If you conform to their ways, they shower you with acceptance and approval. But if you don't, they heap blame and accusations on you hoping to scare you back into their system.

Jesus pointed out that the Pharisees were constantly seeking the approval of people to affirm their identity and secure their sense of superiority. Paul reminded the Galatians that they wouldn't be able to follow Jesus if they were worried about the wrong people showering praise on them.

Our need for approval stems from our insecurities. Jesus knew who he was, where he had come from, and where he was going. No one could manipulate him. He couldn't be won into false ideas based on a need to be loved by other people.

He had the Father's love and approval and thus needed no one else's. As you yourself grow in that reality, not only will you be manipulation-proof, but you'll also find it easier to recognize what's true from what's false.

Am I now trying to win the approval of human beings, or of God? Or am I trying to please people? If I were still trying to please people, I would not be a servant of Christ.
GALATIANS 1:10 (NIV)

OCT 26 Dealing with Rejection

If you suffer rejection from others because you're genuinely seeking to follow Christ, Jesus said to count yourself blessed.

If, however, you are rejected because you are arrogant, bitter, or destructive, then that's a different matter entirely. Don't glory in the trouble caused by self; glory in Jesus's life, and love and rejection will just become another tool in his hands to make you more like him.

I know how scary and painful it can be to risk friendships like that, but it is the only way to follow him and to know who your true friends are. Some people in your life only want to use you for their own needs. Real friends will support your passion for Jesus even if they don't understand the way he's leading you.

To live in his fullness, we have to follow him instead of playing to the crowd—whether that's those caught up in the world, or those held captive by religious expectations.

> *If you are insulted because of the name of Christ, you are blessed, for the Spirit of glory and of God rests on you.*
> 1 PETER 4:14 (NIV)

OCT 27 — Betrayal Is Not the End of the Road

My good friend Tom Mohn says that betrayal is one of those amazing things God uses to shape his life in us. I know it doesn't feel like it. It more often feels like the end of the road when someone you love, and who you thought loved you, decides his own word is meaningless, and that you are of less value to him than what he can gain by lying to you or lying about you.

I've gone through this with three different people in my life and it is the absolute worst. The first time cost me everything—my involvement with a congregation I'd helped to plant, my salary, my health insurance, my reputation in a community, and countless friendships I treasured. I wasn't even offered a dime of severance pay, just an avalanche of lies about my family.

Those days were the darkest Sara and I have ever experienced. We thought we were following Jesus in it all, but we weren't sure. Jesus told us to *"count yourselves blessed every time people put you down or throw you out or speak lies about you to discredit me." (Matthew 5:11, The Message)*

I know that sounds crazy. It did when my dad read those words to me a few weeks into my betrayal. However, I began to let them sink into my heart and began to count myself blessed even when it didn't feel like it. That process drove us deeper into God and he opened some amazing doors we'd have never found otherwise.

Betrayal is not the end of the road. It can also open up other opportunities we might have missed otherwise.

*If an enemy were insulting me, I could endure it;
if a foe were raising himself against me, I could hide
from him. But it is you, a man like myself,
my companion, my close friend...*

PSALM 55:12–13

OCT 28 — The Friends You Choose

It is often true that we become like the people with whom we spend our time.

Have you noticed how much your heart covets the things of this world when we are around people who live for those things?

The same is true of those focused on eternal things. Real fellowship helps us see how God is working in our lives and will fill us with a greater passion for that which has eternal value. It will help you embrace the life that really is life rather than being sucked into the busyness of this world and the multitude of amusements it offers to seduce us back into its clutches.

And even our conversations with other believers can get sidetracked into political disputes, age-old theological controversies, speculations about the end times, or trying to find the right church model.

So, choose your closest friends wisely. Find people with their eyes on the eternal and you'll find yourself in the middle of fellowship that is real and invigorating. They will not only refresh you in God's presence, but you will also discover that he will make you an oasis of eternal life for people battered by our broken world.

*You use steel to sharpen steel,
and one friend sharpens another.*

PROVERBS 27:17 (MSG)

OCT 29 — A Mission Statement

I want to have conversations that matter with people who care.

I don't know who first wrote those words, but they said it as a personal mission statement for their own life. I've made it mine, too. They perfectly capture the cry of my own heart.

There's nothing better than being in a conversation that counts with people who are deeply invested. That may be a great definition for fellowship.

I didn't have many of those in my younger days. I came into conversations with a lot of agenda—the things I wanted to accomplish—and I'm sure people felt more manipulated than loved.

Now I aspire to just provide a safe place where people can notice what they need to notice, ask what they need to ask, and question what they need to question. Bringing out their most authentic self, even if it is difficult and conflicted, has become more engaging to me than any agenda I bring into it.

That's a conversation that matters. Where I am able to do that, I am able to be part of mending the brokenhearted, binding up the wounded, loving the outcast, and liberating the captive.

Use your heads as you live and work among outsiders...Make the most of every opportunity. Be gracious in your speech. The goal is to bring out the best in others in a conversation, not put them down, not cut them out.

COLOSSIANS 4:5–6 (MSG)

OCT 30 — Bringing Out the Best in Each Other

I got this email from someone I'd crossed paths with on a recent trip.

> *Thank you for talking with me the other night. I went home and thought about everything we discussed and somehow felt a little more at peace with my situation. I went to work with a different attitude and had a much better day. I felt as if God told me that He intends to answer my prayers in a little while, to hang on, that He has been working it out.*
>
> *This journey is so amazing. I have grown to not know what to expect. I assumed that God was being silent in some areas of our life and yet in talking with you, it's clear that it's not the case. I felt so loved and treated like a more mature person instead of a baby Christian.*
>
> *I am getting meat and a lot less milk. I hadn't thought of it that way and it's given me more freedom. It's caused me to heighten my attention to His leading and teaching…*

If that's what fellowship does in someone's life, who wouldn't crave it every chance they get?

> *And regardless of what else you put on, wear love.*
> *It's your basic, all-purpose garment.*
> *Never be without it..*
> **COLOSSIANS 3:14 (MSG)**

OCT 31 — You Have No Idea

We were just finishing our meal with my daughter and the grandkids at Bandit's, my favorite BBQ restaurant, when I noticed a young couple sitting at a table behind

Sara making goo-goo eyes at each other and doting over a one-year-old sitting in a high chair at the end of the table. I was touched by the sweetness of that young family.

I pointed them out to Sara and suggested we pick up their check. It's something we do occasionally ever since I was involved in a fight for the check at an ice cream parlour in Framingham, Massachusetts, twenty-five years ago. When our hosts pulled rank, demanding to pay it, I picked up the check of a young couple on the other side of the restaurant as an act of surrender.

Since then Sara and I occasionally pick up a check for random strangers. So, I told the waitress I wanted to pay the bill for the family near us. She asked if I wanted to keep it anonymous, which we usually do, but this time it didn't seem important.

When they finished, they got up to leave and walked by our table without a glance. They didn't know. They must have sought out the waitress, however, because two minutes later someone tapped me on the shoulder. I looked up, startled, and immediately the young mother broke into tears.

I stood up and introduced myself, and she hugged me while barely able to whisper in my ear, "You have no idea! You have no idea!" When she collected herself, she said, "That little boy was in a hospital Sunday night with a 105-degree fever. We almost lost him." She broke down again. Now I was tearing up. "You have no idea what this means to us, that Someone knows."

Sara and I left the restaurant with our hearts soaring. How fun was it to be part of something like that and watch someone be loved by God without us having to tag it with our own graffiti? And Julie said her kids talked about it all the way home, wanting to know what we did and why that woman was crying on Grandpa's shoulder!

Therefore, as we have opportunity, let us do good to all people, especially to those who belong to the family of believers.

GALATIANS 6:10

NOV 1 — Loving Others as Protection

I don't think anyone has sent me flowers before. But yesterday, I got an email from a friend in Oregon with a picture of two bouquets of roses. It was from a former pastor and former alcoholic who knows the dark side all too well.

His email was titled *Why I Take Flowers to Two 95-Year-Olds at the Retirement Center.*

> *I do not do these things to fill up something lacking inside my psyche or to simply be nice. I give and serve so I am not consumed by the hatred I see swirling around me and risk becoming what I see in others.*
>
> *Hatred runs rampant. The image of God placed inside me will be destroyed if I give in to the darkness. Over the years, many have hated me, many times people have tried to derail my career and, at times, my life. To save my own soul I cannot give in to the hatred.*
>
> *Serving and giving is a way of life for me. Jesus said we are to love our enemies, not for a misplaced sense of revenge or to prove our moral superiority, but so that we are not consumed by the same spirit that possesses them. For that I need His miraculous help. Then, I am able to say with Tiny Tim in Charles Dickens's The Christmas Carol, "...may God bless us, every one."*
>
> *Love wins. Every time. Especially in me.*

Love people who don't deserve it, and in places you're not obligated to do so. Your world will change. Jesus said it would.

Love your enemies, do good to them, and lend to them without expecting to get anything back. Then your reward will be great, and you will be children of the Most High, because he is kind to the ungrateful and wicked.

LUKE 6:35

NOV 2 — Love One Person at a Time

Isn't it interesting that you can spend all day wandering through the busy streets of Manhattan without anyone noticing you, yet anyone you pass on a hiking trail will not only notice you but usually will pause to find out where you've been and where you are headed?

The street is anonymous—people passing in a hurry to get somewhere else. There are far too many people to even consider engaging in a conversation, much less a greeting. You would never get anywhere.

Loneliness flourishes in large crowds. The camaraderie of a mountain trail is immediate, even if you are not likely to see each other again. For those brief moments the help and insight two people share can make a huge difference.

Maybe that's why Jesus asked us to love "one another." God loves in the singular. He doesn't love you because he loves all humans and you happen to be human. He loves you because he has yet to find a human he doesn't love.

There is no way to love masses of people, but we can learn to love the next one he puts in our path.

God sets the lonely in families, he leads out the prisoners with singing...

PSALM 68:6 (NIV)

NOV 3 — Where Love Can Take You

I am amazed at what love will invite people to do, and they won't even think it a sacrifice.

A number of years ago, I met a woman from the Midwest who got divorced after her husband told her he was gay, that he had AIDS, and that he wanted to live with his lover. A few years later, the disease had worsened and he and his partner were overwhelmed. During the same time, her life in God's love had grown and she felt God was asking her to help with his care.

She did just that. With her husband's permission she moved back in—not as wife, but as his sister—to help with his care. I can't imagine what it took for her to give of herself to someone who had hurt her so deeply.

I don't think her obedience should be a standard for others to meet, but she always talked about it as one of the greatest experiences of her life. What's more, after his death she took in other AIDS patients and cared for them in that home. During the past few decades, she has continued AIDS care for patients both in America and South Africa.

> But a Samaritan, as he traveled, came where the man was; and when he saw him, he took pity on him. He went to him and bandaged his wounds, pouring on oil and wine. Then he put the man on his own donkey, brought him to an inn and took care of him.
>
> LUKE 10:33–34 (NIV)

NOV 4 — Sharing the Gospel

Learning to live in freedom and watch God do things in far better ways than we ever could on our own is one of the great joys of this journey. Our evangelistic efforts are often contrived and manipulative, which is why few people do it. Living as a demonstration of his love in the world, however, and responding to the opportunities he creates is far better.

When evangelism is an obligation and we need to convince others how wrong they are, we are only pushing people away because of our religious agenda. But when the Gospel simply flows from our lives in the simplicity of how we love others, some amazing things result. The best conversations I have about the Gospel happen as a result of their desire, not mine.

Responding to his nudge in our hearts and the hunger of those we meet will allow us to see how the Spirit works. What he does is more incredible than anything our own efforts can achieve.

That's how the Spirit wins us into living freely in this kingdom. By convincing us that he works in ways our own efforts can't fathom we are more likely to let him do it.

> *Don't forget to pray for us, that God will open doors for telling the mystery of Christ, even while I'm locked up in this jail. Pray that every time I open my mouth I'll be able to make Christ plain as day to them.*
> **COLOSSIANS 4:2–4 (MSG)**

NOV 5 — A Life-Giving Description of Wrath

I got an email from a woman asking me to define God's wrath for her. Here's how I answered:

> *God's wrath is the consuming fire of his love that seeks to destroy the power of sin and rescue us into his love. Does it rest on an unrepentant sinner? Absolutely, in the desire to redeem them and burn out the sin that is destroying them. But when they come to Christ, he has*

already taken all that for us, so we are no longer objects of wrath, but children of God and part of his family.

That's why God's wrath is still coming at the end of the age, to consume sin and create a new heaven and new earth. But don't look at it as his hateful anger; it's not. It is the depths his love will go to purify his Creation. It's the mother bear coming out of the woods to protect her cubs. We're the cubs. We are rescued by wrath, not consumed by it.

Her response to that gave me a good laugh. "That's the most life-giving description of God's wrath I've ever heard."

And why wouldn't it be life-giving? It is not the opposite of God's love; it's an intense expression of it. It's what heals the broken Creation.

> *He who was seated on the throne said,*
> *"I am making everything new!"*
> **REVELATION 21:5**

NOV 6 — Bribed and Threatened

"If you died tonight do you know that you would go to heaven?" Many people come to this kingdom threatened with the torment of hell. Once you convince people that heaven and hell are both real, and God decides who goes where, the work of evangelism is done.

But how do you build a loving relationship with a God who would hurl you into eternal torture if you don't? Is there something so wrong with God that we have to be threatened with torture to come to him?

Others take the opposite approach to salvation: "God has a wonderful plan for your life…" And with that we conjure up images of a God who will keep us at peace, happy, and free from suffering if we'll just follow him.

So, some come to God in hopes of finding in him what they couldn't find for themselves in the world. But self is still at the center, joy is still defined in our terms.

In appealing to people to act in their own self-interest, both of these invitations may be counterproductive to the kingdom itself. If people chose God based on their fear of punishment or their greed for the good life, we only wrap them tighter in their bondage to self.

Jesus's invitation was this: "The kingdom of heaven is at hand. Repent and believe." God's reign is here, and he is so endearing that when you come to know him, you'll give up your agenda to embrace his.

> *We saw it, we heard it, and now we're telling you so you can experience it along with us, this experience of communion with the Father and his Son, Jesus Christ. Our motive for writing is simply this: We want you to enjoy this, too. Your joy will double our joy!*
> 1 JOHN 1:3 (MSG)

NOV 7 — Loved Not Manipulated

There is such a freedom in just getting to know another person for who they are—not as a "candidate" for conversion.

I met a man while golfing who was in his mid-fifties, single, did not believe in God. He had a variety of health problems, including drug and alcohol addictions over the years. I began to spend some time with him and have continued to do so. In the past, I would have felt a burden to witness to him, but Father has slowly changed me in this regard. I didn't feel that pressure at all.

As a result, we've had some interesting discussions about God, but it's based on his hunger. I don't have any agenda in that regard, just a simple love for him that I sense is a piece of how God feels about him.

One day, he told me that when we first met, he immediately sensed something "spiritual" about me. That launched us into a great conversation about who God is. I found far more openness with him because he felt loved, not manipulated onto the Roman Road.

God lives in me and his light will not be dimmed. As I trust him to open doors, I don't need to see the results I want to verify his work in them. I don't have to get them to the finish line—just help them see a bit further down the road.

> *As the Father has loved me, so have I loved you.*
> *Now remain in my love.*
>
> JOHN 15:9

NOV 8 — The Simplest Things

Here's the adventure I wake up to every morning:

Love whomever God puts before me on that day. Follow any nudges he gives me to express care for them and any insights he might want to give me. I don't have to bring any other agenda into the conversation.

Watch people light up with delight and watch your own heart recapture that childlike spirit that sees each day as an adventure in grace.

I let whatever conversations I have about God rise out of their curiosity, rather than trying to manipulate a moment to try to convert them. One approach opens doors wide, the other slams them shut before people even have a chance to know the God you love.

> *And that's about it, friends. Be cheerful. Keep things in good repair. Keep your spirits up. Think in harmony. Be agreeable. Do all that, and the God of love and peace will be with you for sure. Greet one another with a holy embrace.*
>
> 2 CORINTHIANS 13:11 (MSG)

NOV 9 — Relationships Make Us Rich

Fresh out of college and starting work on the staff of a growing congregation, the senior pastor warned me that I was not to have any friendships there. It would only breed jealousy.

I couldn't help myself. I can't be with people and not enjoy them. Jesus called his own followers friends, and that's the best way I know to share life with people. Now, after forty plus years, Sara and I have a rich heritage of friendships from every stage of our journey. Some of those span forty years, others only a couple. Because I've traveled the world and stay in people's homes when I do, those relationships cover the world.

For me, friendship doesn't inhibit ministry. If anything, it enhances it. Helping people grow happens more organically alongside them as a friend than it ever does above them as a so-called expert. And these relationships offer the truest joy of sharing in the Father's family. Various ones pop up from time to time with a phone call or a visit, and we always pick up right where we left off, as if no time had passed since we last saw each other.

The time you invest today in building relationships with others on this journey will be fruit you can feast on over a lifetime.

> *Friends love through all kinds of weather, and families stick together in all kinds of trouble.*
> **PROVERBS 17:17 (MSG)**

NOV 10 — I Just Gotta Listen Better

My daughter and two-year-old granddaughter were over for dinner. I was playing with her in the front room while my wife and daughter were preparing things in the kitchen. When it came time for me to light the grill, I told Aimee I'd be back and left the room.

My mind was already racing elsewhere when I saw Sara and Julie walk out of the kitchen with disapproving looks in my direction. "You can't hear that?" my wife asked.

Oops! Come to think of it I had heard something in the back of my mind but hadn't focused on it. "She's been yelling 'Grandpa, wait!' again and again." I turned and there was Aimee with sad eyes, completely bewildered as to why I hadn't responded to her.

I made amends with Aimee and this time brought her outside with me, lamenting the sorrow I'd caused her. As I got the grill ready I heard a faint chuckle in the back of my heart. "Wow! I know how that feels!"

Instantly I knew. How many times has the Spirit yelled, "Wayne, wait!" when I'm off to follow some idea or plan of mine. It was a gentle rebuke, but a great reminder.

I really do have to listen better. I don't want Aimee or God feeling neglected because my mind is too preoccupied to hear them.

God's voice…You'll do well to keep focusing on it. It's the one light you have in a dark time as you wait for daybreak and the rising of the Morning Star in your hearts.

2 PETER 1:19-20 (MSG)

The Golden Rule

It is so simple. It crosses theological, ethical, and cultural lines. Almost every religion has a similar sentiment in their text.

Jesus told us to just treat others the way you want to be treated. Whether or not they treat you the same way in return is not the issue.

It always disheartens me that people come to BridgeBuilder mediations ready to make their case by being angry, obnoxious, falsely accusing others by ascribing thoughts or motives, or simply maligning people who disagree with them.

How different would the world be if we extended the same rights, respect, kindness, and understanding that we want for ourselves. You don't have to learn that in a class on ethics or civility. We already know how we want to be treated—can we just extend that to others around us?

If we all did that, the world would change.

> *Here's my concern: that you care for God's flock with all the diligence of a shepherd. Not because you have to, but because you want to please God. Not calculating what you can get out of it but acting spontaneously. Not bossily telling others what to do, but tenderly showing them the way.*
>
> **1 PETER 5:1–3 (MSG)**

NOV 12 — Do It Anyway

There was a sign on the wall of Shishu Bhavan, a children's home in Calcutta, India. It reads...

- People are unreasonable, illogical, and self-centered. Love them anyway.

- If you are kind, people may accuse you of selfish ulterior motives. Be kind anyway.

- If you are successful, you will win some false friends and true enemies. Succeed anyway.

- The good you do today will be forgotten tomorrow. Be good anyway.

- Honesty and frankness will make you vulnerable. Be honest and frank anyway.
- What you spend years building may be destroyed over night. Build anyway.
- People need help but may attack you if you try to help them. Help them anyway.
- In the final analysis, it is between you and God. It was never between you and them anyway.

Don't let the actions of others diminish your humanity or quench your love. Much easier said than done, for sure, but do it anyway.

...If you see your enemy hungry, go buy that person lunch, or if he's thirsty, get him a drink. Your generosity will surprise him with goodness. Don't let evil get the best of you; get the best of evil by doing good.
ROMANS 12:20-21 (MSG)

NOV 13 Being Good-Hearted

Do you know the poor are the most generous people on the planet? They give more proportionately out of their need than wealthy people give out of their foundations.

It has a lot to do with having been there. They know what it is to be hungry, to not know where their next meal is coming from, despite them doing everything they know to do.

Throughout Scripture, we are reminded to help the poor, that they are often closer to Jesus than those distracted by their possessions and feeling superior to those who don't have as much.

There are lots of ways to be poor. One part is finances, but it's also possible to be poor in health, spirit, emotional need, and spiritual depth.

Keep your heart tuned to the poor and find ways to lighten their load with whatever you have in abundance. That will keep your heart soft, your perspective clear, and your mind engaged with Father's work in the world.

> *The good-hearted understand what it's like to be poor; the hardhearted haven't the faintest idea.*
>
> **PROVERBS 29:7 (MSG)**

NOV 14 Appeal to the Love of God

Nothing is more painful than a close relationship that goes awry, especially when a former friend thinks they have more to gain by turning on you than honoring the friendship. Love isn't easy over the long haul, which makes me appreciate my relationship with Sara for more than forty years all the more! We have found a way through every disagreement, every struggle, and every hurt to continue to forge an enduring relationship that means the world to both of us.

The greatest disappointments I've had on this journey have come in being separated from people with whom I've shared the work of the kingdom during a significant time. Conflicts and disagreements mar so many amazing things that God does in the world. Love is easy when everyone sees things the same way, but isn't it really tested when we don't?

If it's love, it will endure the pain and seek a course that serves everyone well. Scripture records many moments in the life of the early church where disputes and violent disagreements pitted brother against brother. The outcome wasn't always glorious, so I'm not surprised when it happens today.

> *This isn't the neighborhood bully mocking me—I could take that. This isn't a foreign devil spitting invective—I could*

> *tune that out. It's you! We grew up together! You! My best friend! Those long hours of leisure as we walked arm in arm, God a third party to our conversation.*
>
> PSALM 55:12–14 (MSG)

NOV 15 — Forgiveness and Reconciliation

The smallest bit of love and grace can restore any broken relationship.

Both parties have to be willing to take that risk, however. Someone asked me how much we are responsible for in mending a broken friendship, especially when someone has been judgmental or abusive toward us. I told her there isn't much anyone can do until the other party wants to reconcile too.

Forgiveness is one-sided. I can forgive anyone without their involvement. Genuine reconciliation, however, takes two soft and willing hearts. If the other person isn't interested, all you can do is keep her heart ready to respond in love when they open a door.

Paul appeals to the Philippians to agree and love each other if his love has made *any* difference in their life. It doesn't take much; it just needs to be channeled in the right direction.

I have a hard time with those who toss aside marriages or friendships so easily, or at least trade it away for some kind of temporal gain. Real open and honest friendships are some of the greatest treasures we get in this age.

> *If you've gotten anything at all out of following Christ, if his love has made any difference in your life, if being in a community of the Spirit means anything to you, if you have a heart, if you care—then do me a favor: Agree with each other, love each other, be deep-spirited friends.*
>
> PHILIPPIANS 2:1–3 (MSG)

NOV 16 Appeals to the Law

Law, politics, capitalism, and religion all seek to manipulate the law to gain an advantage over others.

Unless we're using the law to protect ourselves from abusive people, appealing to the law is simple cowardice. By letting an advocate represent our selfish side, we can still pretend to be kind and gracious—we are just following the advice of counsel, after all.

In my work with BridgeBuilders, a mediation service for religious liberty conflicts in public education, I have seen how our legal system disowns all that is important to God—love, grace, mutual respect, and relationship—and seeks to manipulate the letter of the law for whatever self-interest can be gained by either side.

The law sustains itself in an environment of distrust and suspicion. Rather than seeking common ground, it turns everyone into a winner or a loser. But it always sacrifices relationship on the altar of personal gain.

It is a system for adversaries, not an environment for the ministry of reconciliation. The heart of a relationship is not measured when times are good and we all agree, but in the times we disagree. How will we then treat one another?

Practically everything that goes on in the world—wanting your own way, wanting everything for yourself, wanting to appear important—has nothing to do with the Father. It just isolates you from him. The world and all its wanting, wanting, wanting is on the way out—but whoever does what God wants is set for eternity.

1 JOHN 2:15-17 (MSG)

NOV 17 Peacemakers

Hasn't there been enough division in this world between brothers and sisters without us adding to it? Look at all the church splits and lawsuits among Christians that make a mockery of Jesus's prayer that we all be one.

The first time I got separated from a good friend on this journey, the pain was so great, I told myself I'd never let it happen again. I'd do everything in my power—give up anything in my hands—to save a friendship.

Unfortunately, I couldn't do that alone. Whenever I have collaborated with others, I assured them how much I loved them and asked them to come to me before pulling some kind of power play.

I've found most people don't listen. While it takes two softened hearts and a significant amount of time to begin to taste the beauty of God's kind of community, it only takes one damaged heart and a split second to destroy it.

All we can do is forgive and hold our heart ready for reconciliation if it's ever given the chance. As much as it lies with you to be at peace with all men—this is how the writer of Romans put it—that's all we can do. We need more peacemakers in the world, not those who would exploit others.

> *Blessed are the peacemakers, for they*
> *will be called children of God.*
> MATTHEW 5:9 (NIV)

NOV 18 Grace Takes Time

I finished reading the novel *Les Miserables* by Victor Hugo, one of the greatest stories of redemption in literature. It was a bit of work at times. There are pages and pages of deviations from the story to fill in the back story of France's penal system, the French Revolution, the Waterloo campaign by Napoleon, and even a tour of the sewer system under Paris back in the day.

As with most stories, the book is so much richer than can be put into a movie or a play. Only a book allows you to get in the mind of the characters and experience their internal struggles. The poignant closing scenes of the relationship between Jean Valjean, Marius, and Cosette undid me.

Valjean was a young man who was so hungry he stole bread and served nineteen years in prison for it. He got out only to steal again from a bishop, but instead of demanding justice, the bishop showed grace by personal generosity.

This act of loving sacrifice weaves its way into the fiber of Jean's being throughout decades. He becomes a different person and eventually learns to love others and show grace to them even at great personal cost to himself.

> *We, though, are going to love—love and be loved.*
> *First we were loved, now we love. He loved us first.*
>
> 1 JOHN 4:19 (MSG)

NOV 19 Love Anyway

Jean Valjean's journey into loving in *Les Miserables* is often tragic. Because his first thought is not to protect himself, he gets used, abused, and tormented by even the people he treats with grace.

Rather than defend himself, he simply keeps loving, even when it costs him most dearly. He is misunderstood and doesn't defend himself. He forsakes his own personal happiness to ensure it for others.

What I love about this story is the tension between the

truth that those you love the most may misuse you for their own gain, and loving them anyway to put grace into the world to counteract all the selfishness already there.

In the end, only love changes lives and calls into question the way people live in their own self-interest. Grace is worth sharing, even when the objects of that grace don't understand it. In the end those with grace win—not everyone, of course, but enough to make it glorious all the same.

> *The command we have from Christ is blunt: Loving God includes loving people. You've got to love both.*
> 1 JOHN 4:21 (MSG)

NOV 20 Living by Law or Love

The law is a cruel taskmaster—it is often used by those who seek to exploit others to make themselves feel important. Law can so easily be manipulated by the wealthy and abused by those who lie without conscience. Its effects weigh heaviest on the most marginalized in society and is often abused to dehumanize them.

Love, however, is the antimatter to law! Love is the more powerful. It can find its way into the depth of human pain and transform people as it lifts them out of their misery. Live by the law and you become demanding and empty; live by love and even when painful, a greater purpose transforms everyone involved.

Into the misery of our world, God speaks his love in the language of grace. Only those who are truly changed by that reality become a light in the world and offer hope to those who are lost in the darkness.

> *We have come to know and have believed the love*

which God has for us. God is love, and the one who abides in love abides in God and God in him.

1 JOHN 4:16 (MSG)

NOV 21 — Character Isn't Complicated, Part 1

As living loved makes you less worried about yourself and freer to engage others, you'll find that real character isn't all that complicated.

- Be yourself, no more and no less. Pretense is not your friend and deceit darkens your own soul. Besides, if you have to pretend to be someone you're not in order to be liked, you still don't have a friend.

- Let your yes be yes and your no be no. Follow through on your word, even when you regret giving it.

- Value your relationships above all else. Be kind and gracious to everyone, especially with those you think don't deserve it.

- Live at the intersection of authenticity and compassion. You don't owe everyone all you know, but make sure that what you do share is honest while it also gives grace to the hearer.

Friend, don't go along with evil. Model the good. The person who does good does God's work. The person who does evil falsifies God, doesn't know the first thing about God.

3 JOHN 1:11 (MSG)

NOV 22 — Character Isn't Complicated, Part 2

Living loved changes you from the inside so that you can live differently in the world.

- Remember, character is measured by how you treat people with kindness when you're absolutely sure they are in the wrong, and even when they treat you contemptuously.

- Unless people are harassing or abusing you, you are better off hearing them out and working through their pain rather than cutting them off to protect yourself. Don't be so quick to cast off a relationship just because it becomes difficult. See if you can work through it. The best relationships are won through difficulties and misunderstandings.

- Life is so much easier when you treat people kindly, keep your integrity intact by not cutting ethical corners, and trust that God is bigger than any mistake you can make.

Lead with your ears, follow up with your tongue, and let anger straggle along in the rear. God's righteousness doesn't grow from human anger...
JAMES 1:19 (MSG)

NOV 23 — Living the Relational Journey

Those who live relationally make room for those God brings into our lives.

They get to know their colleagues at work and their neighbors down the street, and they find time to encourage their friends, even if they are not on a similar journey. And when they find brothers and sisters who share their passion and hunger for the kingdom, they take time to let those relationships grow.

They are also aware of people around them. They may only be able to offer a greeting in passing at an airport or a conversation in the grocery store line, but it says that the people who are important to Father are also important to them. They will make room in their lives for others and watch what God does with the relationships he gives them.

Live each day open-handed and gracious to everyone you can, without any agenda, and watch what God will do as you simply look to lighten the load of those around you.

> *Dear children, let us not love with words or speech but with actions and in truth.*
>
> 1 JOHN 3:18 (NIV)

NOV 24 Perspective

Can you look at need in the world without guilt and despair? If not, skip this. But I find it helpful, especially as an American, to maintain a perspective about the world I live in. It's easy just to see what is in front of us and miss the proportions that help us know how to live generously in the world.

I don't know how up to date these statistics will be when you read them, but I'm sure the proportions are at least similar. If you could shrink the earth's population to a village of precisely 100 people, with all the existing human ratios remaining the same, there would be

- 57 Asians
- 21 Europeans
- 14 from the Western Hemisphere
- 8 Africans

- 6 people would possess 59% of the entire world's wealth
- 80 would live in substandard housing
- 70 would be unable to read
- 50 would suffer from malnutrition
- 1 would be near death
- 1 would be near birth
- 1 (yes, only 1) would have a college education

Those of us who live in the developed west have such a skewed view of the world and its reality. I find statistics like this to be extremely helpful in seeing the world the way God does and finding ways to put some generosity in the world.

God brings death and God brings life, brings down to the grave and raises up. God brings poverty and God brings wealth; he lowers, he also lifts up. He puts poor people on their feet again; he rekindles burned-out lives with fresh hope, Restoring dignity and respect to their lives—a place in the sun!

1 SAMUEL 2:6–8 (MSG)

NOV 25 You Wouldn't Eat Like This

Again, please don't take this in if your response is guilt instead of being inspired to generosity.

A number of years ago, hunger banquets offered a powerful teaching tool. I've never been to one but reading about it makes my heart hurt in a good way. Only a handful of those who attend came away well-fed. Most go home hungry, and that's exactly what the organizers wanted.

These banquets are designed to highlight the vast disparity in the world around the globe. Fifteen percent were given a three-course meal on a linen-covered table, complete with silverware and utensils. Twenty percent were given "middle income meals," consisting of some beans, rice, and a glass of water. Like their wealthier counterparts they had chairs, but no table. Most of those attending, sixty-five percent, sat on the floor and were fed only some rice and water. They had to eat with their hands.

There is enough food in the world for everyone to eat, it's just that human greed and corruption keep it from being shared equally. You may not be able to fix the broken structures that perpetuate this, but just remember, your generosity is God's antidote to injustice.

> *Speak up for the people who have no voice, for the rights of all the down-and-outers. Speak out for justice! Stand up for the poor and destitute!*
> **PROVERBS 31:9 (MSG)**

NOV 26 Words to Live By

Lately my heart is drawn back to the words of the minor prophet, Micah. I used to dismiss the power of these words as old covenant demands that were superseded in Christ. In the increasing polarization of our world, however, I'm drawn back to their simplicity and power.

As Micah writes, he is overwhelmed by his own unworthiness before God. He wonders what he can give to God to make up for his failures, even contemplating child sacrifice to mitigate his pain. "Shall I give the fruit of my body to atone for the sin of my soul?"

Then God responds with what he desires most: to act justly, to love mercy, and to walk humbly. I used to think the "with your God" part only applied to "humbly." Now I see it belongs to all three. Fight for justice because God does. Love mercy for those who need it most because God does. And walk humbly in the world because God does.

When love transforms us enough, we will walk with God in justice, mercy, and humility. Those will serve you well wherever you travel in this world.

> *He has shown you, O mortal, what is good. And what does the Lord require of you? To act justly and to love mercy and to walk humbly with your God.*
>
> MICAH 6:8 (NIV)

NOV 27 — The #1 Lie of Affluence

"Do you have any conflict enjoying the money you have in a world with so much need?"

I had been invited by a friend to attend an investment seminar and there were some high rollers in the room. As I looked around, however, I was surprised to see so many faces seemingly confused by the question. Obviously, they didn't. I do. Every day.

When the speaker asked why not, most responded that they had worked hard for what they had and never thought twice about enjoying a disproportionate slice of the world's pie. The unspoken inference, of course, is that poor people don't work as hard, so they are only getting what they deserve.

That's only one of the lies wealthy people tell themselves so they can ignore people in need around them. We'll look at some other lies tomorrow—lies you can only believe if you don't actually know people who have very little without a lot of options to help them move beyond it. And I don't mean know *about* them, but actually know them individually.

These relationships have caused me to reassess many

of my lifelong conclusions. They have helped me come to grips with the lies affluent people use to justify their own comfort and suppress their generosity for people in need.

> *If a man shuts his ears to the cry of the poor,
> she too will cry out and not be answered.*
>
> PROVERBS 21:13

NOV 28 More Lies of Affluence

We looked at #1 yesterday. Let's look at some other lies the affluent use to close their hearts to people in need.

Lie #2: Every human is equally valued. By God, yes! Hopefully by you, but we have a long way to go to make this a reality.

Lie #3: Everyone has equal opportunities to apply themselves and succeed. You really believe there is no difference if you were born in the suburbs of Seattle or the inner city of Atlanta?

Lie #4: Inalienable rights apply only to American citizens. Our forbearers fought a revolution on the premise that our rights to life, liberty, and the pursuit of happiness is a gift of Providence, not government. Thinking that American citizens deserve more than others undermines our own ideals.

Lie #5: I did something deserving to be born in a developed country with a comfortable lifestyle. Those born already part way up the ladder of wealth can't understand the challenges of those who can't even find the ladder, much less have access to its lowest rungs.

Lie #6: Desperate people have choices. Many diligent people are simply victims of crime, war, famine, natural disaster, medical conditions, or psychological brokenness so that they have incredibly few choices.

Please don't let this breed guilt in your heart. Talk to

Jesus about these things as you embrace some realities that may make you uncomfortable for a season as he works compassion in your heart.

He who oppresses the poor shows contempt for their Maker, but whoever is kind to the needy honors God.
PROVERBS 14:31 (NIV)

NOV 29 Opening to Compassion

The reason so many wealthy people remain calloused to the plight of the poor is because they don't know anyone personally. Proximity changes everything. Until we see the whole world as our neighborhood and put faces and personalities to orphans growing up on the streets, children trafficked for sex, or families devastated by war or drought, those situations remain an abstraction to the exclusion of our love and compassion.

Get to know some of them, and your heart will change. Jesus told a story about a Good Samaritan to help us understand we are all part of a bigger family and cannot think only of ourselves. This is where the lies of affluence come to die, and some amazing acts of human compassion can begin. When you find people hurting, help them with whatever you have. If you don't know any, volunteer at a soup kitchen or a ministry in the inner city.

Don't just give money to them; befriend them and you will no longer be able to hide in those lies. You'll join them in looking for solutions that will help empower them to better their own lives rather than remain dependent on others. You will be a voice for a more compassionate society.

For he will deliver the needy who cry out, the afflicted who have no one to help.
PSALM 72:12 (NIV)

NOV 30 — The Gift of Honesty

"Don't you think that was the most manipulative sermon you've ever given?"

I couldn't have been more shocked. Dave loved everything I wrote or taught. I thought yesterday's sermon was one of my best. I had looked forward to our lunch, knowing how encouraging Dave would be.

"You're kidding, right?" I said, laughing it off. His face told me he wasn't. I told him how impactful I thought it was and the positive feedback others had given me.

"I could be wrong," he said, shrugging his shoulders. "But it looked to me like you were manipulating people with guilt to make them do what you wanted. I've learned that any time my success depends on another person's response, I will manipulate them."

His last sentence made me gulp. It sounded radioactive, knowing that if it were true it would expose so many things in me. After a few days of mulling over his words in prayer, I finally understood.

I called Dave to tell him so, adding in jest, "It probably wasn't the most manipulative sermon I've preached though. I can think of a few others far worse."

His honesty changed me that day, and his words about manipulating people still do.

> *Let a righteous man strike me—that is a kindness...*
> **PSALM 141:5 (NIV)**

DEC 1 — A Generous Conversation

Looking back at yesterday's story, I love that Dave thought enough of me to be honest, not knowing how I'd respond. We had the friendship that allowed me to process it.

He came as my friend, and not my judge. He had been a powerful encouragement in my life long before this one instance of helping me see something I was missing. As he saw me struggle with his conclusions, he took the pressure off, admitting that it just could have hit him wrong.

His graciousness opened a wider door in my heart. I didn't have to agree for our friendship to continue. From his standpoint, he was willing to trust that if he was right, God would make it clear.

That is admonishment—our willingness to be gently honest with people we see making hurtful choices for *their* benefit, not your own.

> *In the end, serious reprimand is appreciated far more than bootlicking flattery.*
> **PROVERBS 28:23 (MSG)**

DEC 2 Selfless Love

Take the best experience you've ever had with a friendship, where you experienced the mutuality of love, sharing, honoring, caring, and deep conversations that were enlightening as well as humorous. Now multiply that by a million.

You still aren't within a thousand miles of the absolute love that the Father, Son, and Spirit have shared for all eternity. Imagine a relationship with complete selflessness, each of them giving and serving without any thought for themselves.

Today, this kind of love is hard for us to grasp because what most people mean by love is usually nothing more than a mutually beneficial relationship. People say they love each other when each of them provides some benefit to the other. But as soon as one stops benefiting from the relationship, they usually withdraw to pursue other more satisfying relationships.

Such self-based love really isn't love at all. When we approach God in this way, we will find ourselves often disappointed when he doesn't do what we expect him to do.

Jesus invited us into the depths of relationship with the Father, the Spirit, and himself. This is where we learn what real love is. He knew the only way we could discover the depth of joy is to abandon the pursuit of our own self-interest because we know he will provide all that we truly need.

But that runs against everything we've ever known.

> *Greater love has no one than this: to lay down one's life for one's friends.*
> **JOHN 15:13 (NIV)**

DEC 3 Letting Others Have Their Journey

As you become increasingly secure in God's love and discover just how patient he is with your faults and misguided perspectives, it will begin to redefine every other relationship in your life.

Instead of demanding that others conform to what you think is best, you will find yourself letting them have their own journey. You will be able to walk alongside them even when they are being self-indulgent or believe things you know to be false.

By no longer manipulating them to do what you think is best, you can allow them the same freedom God gives you. And you can be there for them when they are open to wisdom and help with their struggles.

You'll trust that God is better able than you to get the truth to them and win them out of the dark places in their life. And you'll be there for them in the moments when God is opening their eyes and offering them greater freedom and security in his love.

> *Welcome with open arms fellow believers who don't see things the way you do. And don't jump all over them every time they do or say something you don't agree with—even when it seems that they are strong on opinions but weak in the faith department. Remember, they have their own history to deal with. Treat them gently.*
>
> **ROMANS 14:1 (MSG)**

DEC 4 How Do You Look at "Sinners"?

Misery loves company. The harder you think you have to work to earn God's approval, the more you'll look down on people who aren't paying the same price and giving up the same things you are.

That must have stuck in the throat of the Pharisees as they watched Jesus enjoy people they had rejected. It must have bothered them deeply when he forgave people they didn't think deserved it, or healed those who were not as spiritual as they were.

As best you can, stop thinking God loves you because you've earned it somehow, or you will require that of others. When you discover how loved you are, even in your failures, you won't despise people who are broken by sin. Instead, the depth of their bondage that holds them captive will touch you.

Instead of judging them, you'll feel compassion for their struggle. That's when you'll be able to discern with greater clarity how Father is responding to them. This will allow you to know how to love them best in their brokenness.

Sometimes that means you'll stand back and let the consequences of sin take their course as the Father did with his prodigal son. At other times they will invite you into their mess to help them find a way out.

> *Anyone who claims to be intimate with God ought to live the same kind of life Jesus lived.*
>
> 1 JOHN 2:5 (MSG)

DEC 5 — Love Opens the Door to Truth

Just being nice to people isn't the essence of loving them. In God, light and love travel together as love opens the way for truth to be revealed.

In true friendship, people don't just say what others want to hear. Friends can explore a gentle honesty in hopes that a door will open into what's true for them. Human love seeks people's comfort at the expense of truth. God's kind of love seeks people's freedom in response to truth. God doesn't avoid the difficult conversation or hold his peace just to make nice with you.

Jesus told his disciples that they would know the truth, and that truth would set them free. That doesn't mean truth is always welcome, because before truth frees us, it usually messes with us.

That's why love must first find a home before people will be at rest enough to embrace the truth. If not, truth will raise their defenses instead of opening their eyes.

> *The wounds from a lover are worth it; kisses from an enemy do you in.*
>
> PROVERBS 27:6 (MSG)

DEC 6 — Poking Holes in Our Illusions

I had just listened to some recordings of a teaching I'd done over a weekend in Pennsylvania. The weekend had gone particularly well, and had a touch of grace on it bigger than my abilities.

Sitting on the plane home, I was already doing computations in my head of the money we would make for Lifestream after we duplicated and sold them. Then a strange thought crept into my mind: *I want you to give them away.* My defenses went up immediately.

Oh that's just me trying to be generous, I told myself over the next few days. Still troubled by the thought, I shared it with a few friends. "Does that sound like God?" I asked.

"Well, it doesn't sound like Wayne," one of them responded. As we all laughed, I knew he was right. Ever since that day, that series of talks has been a free download on my website and has been accessed hundreds of thousands of times.

Jesus is good at poking holes in our illusions; it's how he brings us life. We often reject them immediately because we like our illusions. They offer us comfort and security. When he pokes a hole in them, we often get out our mental duct tape to mend over the hole so we don't have to think about it.

That's what he meant about exposing the evil behind the world's pretensions. Inside our lies, evil lurks. Looking through the hole he pokes in them is where freedom begins.

> *The world has nothing against you, but it's up in arms against me. It's against me because I expose the evil behind its pretensions.*
>
> JOHN 7:7

DEC 7 — Unless God Is Our Source

My twenty years of pastoring demonstrated repeatedly how much people looked to the church to fulfill their needs. People often got hurt because of something that was said or not said, or something done or not done. People would withdraw with hurt feelings or work even harder to exploit others to get what they felt they deserved.

When our relationships with others are need-centered, they will eventually disappoint our expectations and lead to disappointments and broken relationships. Instead, if we vest our hopes in God's ability to meet our needs, we won't have to manipulate our friends to do so.

By vesting our hope in God to be our provider, we won't need to manipulate our friends to get what we need. While his gifts and graces will often come through other members of his family, it's best that we not try to decide when or who they come through.

Then, instead of being hurt when someone doesn't respond the way we want, we are grateful however God chooses to give us his gifts.

> *There are different kinds of gifts, but the same Spirit distributes them.*
> **1 CORINTHIANS 12:4 (NIV)**

DEC 8 A Safe Place

"I don't think I've been in a room with more hurting people in my life," I commented, broken by the stories I'd just heard of the desperate situations people were facing.

My best friend in the room glanced around with a knowing smile. Others smiled back. Something was going on I didn't know anything about. "Should we tell him?" he asked the others.

All the people in the room had formerly been part of a congregation where I used to pastor. That was before a painful betrayal and a couple of incredibly challenging years. "You probably were and didn't know it," my friend continued.

"Wayne, people didn't want to share these kinds of circumstances with you years ago. You usually offered a pat answer, a quick prayer, and moved on. With all that has happened in your life, you've become a much safer place for people in pain."

It was embarrassing to hear, but I knew he was right. The next morning, I told God if all the pain I'd been through was just to have moments like this with people, it had all been worth it. And I meant it.

That's exactly what Jesus did. He didn't make it easy for himself by avoiding people's troubles, but waded right in and helped out. "I took on the troubles of the troubled,"

ROMANS 15:3-4

DEC 9 Treasuring Friendships

"We don't have any friends."

I was surprised he and his wife were feeling so lonely. We used to live near them and had spent hours enjoying their friendship. When we moved away, however, they hadn't invested time in others. They had lots of acquaintances, but no depth of friendship. When I asked him how much time he'd invested in friendships over the last few years, he admitted it was little.

His excuses are the same as most people: work, commuting, and responsibilities at home take up so much energy that he collapses in front of a TV before going to bed. They had let themselves be relationally impoverished.

Do you remember all those 9/11 phone calls from workaholic stock traders trapped in the World Trade Center? Their last thoughts and words reached out in gut-wrenching agony to affirm their love for spouses, children, and parents. No one dies wishing they had worked harder or watched more football games.

Other than God's presence, when all is said and done, the closest we'll touch eternal treasure in this world are the relationships we share with others. Make time for that however God leads you.

If you don't plant the seeds of friendship, you won't be there when needed most.

> *And let us consider how we may spur one another on toward love and good deeds...*
> **HEBREWS 10:24 (NIV)**

DEC 10 — Friendship Is the Foundation

We serve a relational God: I am convinced that almost everything Jesus does, he does through relationships—not programs, models, or projects.

Lots of strangers approach me about mentoring them or collaborating on some projects. My answer is almost always the same: if God has something in mind here, he is going to give us a relationship. Their request might be the door to that, but without a growing friendship of love I don't see how we can fruitfully collaborate together.

Of course, invitations like that can be the place where a new friendship begins. I am always looking for that, because a generous heart makes room for new people God might bring along and a new adventure he might begin.

It has also been a great tool to understand when Father is inviting me into a project or not. Father, Son, and Spirit are a community who collaborate in all they do, and where he works community happens among people who find the friendship every bit as engaging as the project.

> *The one who plants and the one who waters have one purpose, and they will each be rewarded according to their own labor. For we are co-workers in God's service; you are God's field, God's building.*
>
> **1 CORINTHIANS 3:8-9 (NIV)**

DEC 11 — Proximity and Compatibility

Friendships don't happen in a vacuum. I know many people who ask God to bring them friends and blame him if they don't happen.

We forget that our best friend today was at one point a stranger to us. What happened that made them a friend? It's usually two things—proximity and compatibility. We spend enough time with them to decide if there's a connection in our hearts. That's not always about gender, age, or outside interests. Friendships grow best from faith, passion, and purpose.

Sara and I sit down every week and talk about the people in our lives. Who has God put on our hearts to spend time with this week? We consider people all around us, whether it be at work, in our neighborhood, at our kids' activities, or even someone we met on the fly.

If something clicks, and they are interested as well, we pursue it. Some of our most amazing friendships today came out of inviting people out for a beverage or to our home for dinner.

> *Practice hospitality.*
> **ROMANS 12:13 (NIV)**

DEC 12 — Cast a Wide Net

"Something must be wrong with us," the young couple

admitted to my wife while we sat at dinner.

We asked what made them say that and they answered, "No one wants to be our friends." They had made an effort to get to know some people but found that they were more interested in a new friendship than others seemed to be. They had grown discouraged and assumed there must be something wrong with them. Having spent some time with them, we knew that part wasn't true.

I told them for every twenty or thirty relationships that Sara and I make ourselves available to, maybe two or three become friends over a significant time. They were shocked. "How do you handle that kind of rejection?" they asked.

I don't see it as rejection. People are busy and, regretfully, few people have the courage to pursue new relationships. That doesn't discourage me. I'm willing to cast a wide net and see what comes of it. Believe me, the two or three who do become friends are worth spending time with the other twenty-five who didn't.

The kingdom of heaven is like treasure hidden in a field. When a man found it, he hid it again, and then in his joy went and sold all he had and bought that field...

MATTHEW 13:44 (NIV)

DEC 13 — It's the Life Not the Gift

In the midst of a school day, my granddaughter thought to make me a card. She and her mom brought it over later in the day. The drawing on it and the words, "Grandpa, feel better," touched a deep place in my soul.

Of course, I would get well. Aimee wants me to.

You couldn't sell this card at any store in America, but Hallmark has never printed a card of more exquisite beauty or with a more soul-touching message. It is not the quality of the gift that defines the one who gives it; it's the quality of the one giving it that brings beauty and meaning to the gift.

That's why Aimee's card was a treasure to me. It represents the best gift she could give at that stage of her life. I'm sure a card she'll give me when she's fifteen or twenty-four will look quite different indeed. They will be special in their own way as well, but not because the artwork is better, the cut lines cleaner, or the printing more fanciful.

Many of the rich were making large contributions. One poor widow came up and put in two small coins—a measly two cents. Jesus called his disciples over and said, "The truth is that this poor widow gave more to the collection than all the others put together. All the others gave what they'll never miss; she gave extravagantly what she couldn't afford—she gave her all."

MARK 12:43–44 (MSG)

DEC 14 Deeper Fellowship

When my Christianity was more static—consisting of disciplines and trying to be good—my fellowship with others stayed shallow. I remember coming home many nights frustrated from having spent an entire evening with other Christians but somehow not having been able to find a conversation beyond the weather, sports, family, and current movies.

I wanted fellowship, but every time I would try to bring up something about God or Scripture the conversation grew stilted and awkward. Since my relationship with God has turned into a real adventure, with struggles and insights, it has brought me into ever-deepening levels of relationship and ever-widening spaces of freedom.

When you're on that journey you will naturally talk about it in virtually every conversation you have, without having to work it in or make other people feel put on the spot. As you share openly and honestly about your own journey, others often join in.

When you connect with someone else who wants to open up their journey as well, you'll find that fellowship is as natural as breathing.

> *We proclaim to you what we have seen and heard, so that you also may have fellowship with us. And our fellowship is with the Father and with his Son, Jesus Christ.*
>
> I JOHN 1:3

DEC 15 — Life at the Speed of Relationships

Damascus, Virginia, is a beautiful village where seven trails converge in the Blue Ridge mountains. While spending a few days there, my host John Coleman commented that he had discovered working at a retreat center for pastors that "life moves at the speed of relationships."

He meant *real* life, of course. Most people live at the frenetic speed of pursuing dreams, achievement, survival, or even fear. In doing so, they miss out on so much beauty. They end up violating relationships instead of enjoying them, and they find themselves alone.

Relationships move slowly. Life at that pace involves engaging people around you, taking time to understand their story and they, yours. Out of that process mutual concern begins to grow and you find your way to the enjoyment of each other, sharing laughter and tears.

Jesus lived that way, which is why he didn't accomplish what some think he should have and why he had such a profound impact on others. Learn this secret from him and slow down to make space for people.

When I live at the speed of relationships, my life is marked by joy and fulfillment even through difficult circumstances. Relationships make us rich.

If I speak in the tongues of men and of angels, but have not love, I am only a resounding gong or a clanging cymbal. If I have the gift of prophecy and can fathom all mysteries and all knowledge, and if I have a faith that can move mountains, but have not love, I am nothing. If I give all I possess to the poor and surrender my body to the flames, but have not love, I gain nothing.

I CORINTHIANS 13:1–3

SECTION 5
For the Road Ahead

DEC 16 The Deeper Freedom

The familiar voice on the phone brought back memories of our warm friendship, even though we hadn't spoken for almost two years. "What has God been doing in you?" he asked, exchanging pleasantries.

Words rolled off my tongue before I'd even had them in my mind: "God has defied to the nth degree every expectation I had for my life." I was so surprised at my own response and how easily it had slipped off my lips that I had to pause to think about it.

After a few seconds his tentative voice asked, "And is that a good thing?"

The last few years brought me through a painful betrayal by a close friend that decidedly changed the trajectory of my life and faith. Instead of thinking of God's love as something I needed to earn, I was learning to relax into the reality that I was already loved, even in my struggles.

"It's the best thing!" I answered with a hearty laugh. In every way, what Father has accomplished in me was far better than anything I had tried to produce for myself. What I realized in that moment was that none of those things I thought I wanted mattered anymore. Somehow, he had brought me toward a deeper level of freedom—a trust in God's ability to give me what he wanted.

> *And we know that in all things God works for the good of those who love him, who have been called according to his purpose.*
> ROMANS 8:28

DEC 17 Seeing How God Works

For most of my life I've tried to do God's work, instead of doing mine. Honestly, I wasn't very good at it. I've come to love the prayer Paul prayed for the Colossians and have made it my own:

> *We haven't stopped praying for you, asking God to give you wise minds and spirits attuned to his will, and so acquire a thorough understanding of the ways in which God works...As you learn more and more how God works, you will learn how to do your work. (Colossians 1:9–11 MSG)*

I wish someone had taught me that when I was younger. Not knowing, it led to so much wasted effort.

- When I was a pastor, I thought it was my responsibility to build the church, when Jesus said he would. (Matthew 16)

- In sharing Christ, I thought I was supposed to

bring the conviction of God, when Jesus said the Spirit does that. (John 16)

- I thought the body of Christ had to work at unity, when Jesus asked his Father to do it. (John 17)

- I tried hard to be better for God, instead of coming to the end of my human efforts and learning to trust his power. (John 15, Philippians 2)

Learning how God works changes everything! Now we can simply focus on what he is asking of us, which is far more fruitful.

> *As you learn more and more how God works,*
> *you will learn how to do your work.*
> COLOSSIANS 1:11 (MSG)

DEC 18 — Ask What You Need to Ask

A few years ago, I was teaching eight hundred Kenyan pastors in a hornet-infested building about the love of God. After sharing a bit of my story and laying the groundwork for living loved, I asked them what questions they might have about God's love that we could tackle in the next few days.

Immediately the atmosphere grew fearful and deathly quiet. It felt as if they had been threatened, and all eight hundred glared at me with a panicked look on their faces. Something had gone wrong, but I had no idea what it was. I told them to take a break so I could ask the facilitator what had just happened.

"They don't believe you," he said. Then he told me that the last American speaker who came through asked if anyone had any questions. Someone did, but it cost him. "How dare you ask a question!" the speaker responded. "I've explained everything you need to know and if you don't understand it's because rebellion is in your heart."

So, that's the problem. After the break, I assured them that I really wanted them to ask questions so we could learn in their time, not listen to me lecture. I promised not to get angry or defensive, but to create a safe place for us to explore God's love together. Tentatively at first, they began to talk, and eventually their hungry questions took us to some wonderful places and moments of discovery.

If we can't ask what we need to ask or struggle openly with the thoughts and questions that plague our minds, how will we ever come to know the reality of the life and love that God holds for us?

One day Jesus was praying in a certain place. When he finished, one of his disciples said to him, "Lord, teach us to pray, just as John taught his disciples."

LUKE 11:1

DEC 19 One Question at a Time

I met a man in New Zealand whose entire discipleship came about just by asking questions. He had been released from prison and at three o'clock the next morning, he found himself wandering in the rain looking for a dry place to sleep. A man walked up to him and invited him into his home for the night.

The man's generosity led him to Christ. When he wanted the man to mentor him, he just responded, "Every day we can sit down for a few moments and I will try to answer whatever questions you have about God." That was it. He didn't teach him a set of lessons but let his newfound friend set the course.

That man grew up in a deep and sincere faith that led to decades of growth. That's the best way to teach someone: inside their own questions and their own experiences.

Watch how much Jesus does that in the Gospels—not only responding to the questions of his followers, but also asking a few of his own to open their thinking to the wisdom and reality of God.

> *When Jesus looked up and saw a great crowd coming toward him, he said to Philip, "Where shall we buy bread for these people to eat?" He asked this only to test him, for he already had in mind what he was going to do.*
>
> JOHN 6:5

DEC 20 — The Freedom to Ask

I recently had lunch with a couple in their sixties who had attended a two-year Bible school in Florida a few years before. On the opening day of class, they were told questions wouldn't be allowed through their course of study. I was dumbfounded. How could any school, especially one based on the life of Jesus, not allow people to ask questions to understand what they needed to know.

As tragic as that was for people in their fifties and sixties, it's especially disgusting for students in their teens and twenties who aspire to teach others.

Jesus responded openly and warmly to the truth-seeking questions that were asked of him. Of course, some asked questions out of malice or seeking to trap him in some way, but Jesus was still patient with them. He didn't demean them for asking. And though he didn't always give them the answer they wanted, his answer would usually open a door into a wider world if they were willing to see it.

If you can't ask questions and struggle with what someone is trying to teach you about God, then you're not in an environment where the kingdom unfolds. If someone gets angry when you question them or dare to disagree with them, they are not leaders who can help you discover God's reality.

And if you're afraid to ask God any question that's in your heart, you have yet to discover just how loving and gracious he is and how much he wants to help you understand how to live in him.

> The disciples came to him and asked, "Why do you speak to the people in parables?" He replied, "The knowledge of the secrets of the kingdom of heaven has been given to you, but not to them."
>
> MATTHEW 13:10-11

DEC 21 Questions that Open Us to His Wisdom

There is a difference between asking God questions and questioning God's wisdom. There's a way to ask questions with humility that will open your heart to see in a fresh way what he wants to show you, and there's a way to challenge him defiantly that will blind you to what he wants to show you.

I've done both.

He can handle our defiance with a love that understands our pain, but until it gives way to humble surrender, we will not hear his gentle responses. Exhaust your anger as fast as you can with him, then set your heart at rest in his love. How do you do that? Begin to mistrust any conclusion about him that that doesn't lead you to love.

The enemy wants you to doubt his love and will pile on the evidence to support that lie. I've often said to God, "I don't know how you are loving me in this, but I know you do. Would you show me how?"

That's another prayer he answers—maybe not in twenty-four hours, but over the next weeks. God's love is bigger than our understanding. Don't let the enemy use that fact to undermine your trust in him. Everything he does is motivated by love.

> *God is love, and the one who abides in love
> abides in God, and God abides in him.*
>
> I JOHN 4:16

They Are Called Fruits for a Reason

You know the list: love, joy, peace, forbearance, kindness, goodness, faithfulness, gentleness, and self-control.

We call them the fruits of the Spirit, but isn't it so easy for us to turn them into New Testament law? How many times have you heard that we should act more loving, peaceful, or kind?

These are fruits, not commands. This is not a list of how we're supposed to act, but the offer of a different way of being. Jesus didn't come for a generation of actors who could pretend these virtues when they weren't in the heart.

The only way to truly be loving, peaceful, forbearing, and the like is to let the Spirit produce these over time as genuine reflections of his work inside you, not actions you will yourself to take in the heat of the moment.

You can't relax into his love over a lifetime and not come out more loving, joyful, peaceful, forbearing, kind, good, faithful, gentle, and in control of your "self."

> *But the fruit of the Spirit is love, joy, peace, forbearance,
> kindness, goodness, faithfulness, gentleness and self-
> control. Against such things there is no law.*
>
> GALATIANS 5:22–23 (NIV)

DEC 23 Another List, Same Chapter

Before Paul lists the fruits of the Spirit, he also identifies the deeds of the flesh. Most people skip over that list, fearing it might place an unhealthy focus on our failures. I don't, but I also don't let it over draw me into shame.

That's the joy of living a condemnation-free life in Jesus. You can look at the broken places in your old nature without taking it on as your identity. Instead, you can read through a list like this to see what Jesus is still doing from the inside to set you free.

> ...sexual immorality, impurity and debauchery; idolatry and witchcraft; hatred, discord, jealousy, fits of rage, selfish ambition, dissensions, factions, and envy; drunkenness, orgies, and the like.

Looking at this list now helps me recognize where my old nature still rears its ugly head. Since none of these are my true identity in Christ I get to pray, "Jesus, what is it about you I don't know that would displace this reaction from my heart?"

Do that, and your less-than-stellar moments won't draw you into condemnation, but simply remind you to lean in more deeply to his care. I may be powerless against them, but his love is not.

> *I warn you, as I did before, that those who live like this will not inherit the kingdom of God.*
>
> **GALATIANS 5:21**

DEC 24 — Jesus with Skin On

During a trip to the east coast in 2016, I was asked to meet with a couple whose twenty-something-year-old daughter had been recently killed in a car crash. A friend of a friend asked if I could, so I met them for lunch one day. I never know what to say to people who experience such loss, and I left wondering just how helpful I had been.

Four years later, I received this email:

You may not remember me, but I will never forget you. We were connected through a friend of a friend and met you at a restaurant on a rainy day. Our daughter had been killed in a catastrophic car accident about six months prior, and I was clinging with all I had to Jesus, my only hope. I can't say I remember what you said that day, but you made us feel loved. Especially meaningful to me, you showed my husband that men can talk about feelings and God's love in a real way.

A month after our meeting, a woman in my Bible study suggested we study He Loves Me. I loved your book and bought several copies to share with others. God has been so real, so good, and so over-the-top caring that he has literally blown me away! I would never be the person I am today without him, and I am grateful beyond words. I have occasionally been asked to speak to other bereaved parents. While challenging, I am willing because I want them to know God is their way through the valley.

I am a little embarrassed I have not written before. I have never had quite the words. I was moved today and decided I'll never have the right words. Thank you for being "Jesus with skin on." You are part of our raw but beautiful story. God is weaving a beautiful tapestry, and I am grateful for him, his love, and your threads in it.

Living loved will allow you, too, to live like Jesus with skin on, even when you're least aware of it.

> *My children, with whom I am again in labor until Christ is formed in you—*
> **GALATIANS 4:19**

DEC 25 — Every Morning a Gift

Waking up to a new day is like holding a Christmas present from a close friend. What delights will come my way as I unwrap it? Today gives God more opportunity to see what he might do, what wisdom he might give, and what provision he will put before me.

As Jeremiah said, his mercies really are new every morning.

Forgiveness allows us to start every day new, with all our unhelpful choices and their consequences now enfolded into a new plan that will still draw you toward his glory.

That's what I love about this journey—expectancy in his love with expectations that it come a certain way. How might he make himself known not only in those moments I'm surprised by joy but also in those moments where God appears in the midst of my pain and trials?

Will it come in a moment of prayer, a conversation with a friend, or a thought from out of the blue? Or might he underscore something he's showing me with a touching line in a book, a lyric from a song, or a scene from a movie?

The best part about his gift of a new day is that you'll spend all day unwrapping it and there will be a new one tomorrow.

> *Clean the slate, God, so we can start the day fresh! Keep me from stupid sins, from thinking I can take over your work...*
> **PSALM 19:11–14 (MSG)**

DEC 26 — Better Explored than Explained

Most things in life are better explored than explained: an alpine trail lined in wildflowers, the Basilica Sagrada Familia in Barcelona, the shoreline of Galilee, or even chocolate ice cream. Explanations just don't do them justice.

The same is true of a relationship to God. It can be explained to death, literally. We quote Scriptures, memorize pithy aphorisms, and read books trying to explain it. We have sought to understand him with our heads and missed the joy of exploring how God makes himself known, how his purpose unfolds around us.

Many who talk about God in eloquent terms have no idea how to live in him with grace and affection through difficult challenges. They have never explored his kingdom inside their world.

Make it a point to explore God in your life today. Talk to him about the circumstances you're in and the things you're wondering about. Watch for little ways God will drop things in your path that help you see what he is doing in you and around you.

> *The Son can do nothing by himself; he can do only what he sees his Father doing, because whatever the Father does the Son also does.*
>
> JOHN 5:19

DEC 27 — Don't Try to Figure It All Out

I've known so many people on the verge of truth who are trying to sort it all out in their head. It's like wanting a map of the whole world, just to walk down to the grocery store.

"I can't wrap my head around it," is a great excuse to ignore the bit of truth we see because we can't figure out how it fits with everything else. Change, however, comes in increments. It's like following a trail through the woods; it comes one step at a time.

That was Jesus's example. He didn't have an overriding agenda pushing him, which is why he could spend one afternoon with a woman at a well, and another on the hillsides above Galilee talking to a multitude. As far as we know, he never organized a single meeting, except for serving the Passover in an upper room.

He seemed to wake up every day and navigate the circumstances before him with an eye to simply doing whatever he saw the Father doing. He gave the kingdom away and encouraged his disciples to do the same. He didn't explain everything to them but invited them into experiences that began to shift how they saw and interacted with the world.

He was offering them a different way to live—in a Father's love, in power greater than their own efforts, in the growing simplicity of learning to trust his love. He wants you to explore that with him as well.

> You study the Scriptures diligently because you think that in them you have eternal life. These are the very Scriptures that testify about me, yet you refuse to come to me to have life.
>
> JOHN 5: 39-40

DEC 28 As Close as Today

What if the curriculum for your growing relationship with Jesus isn't in a book somewhere or a teaching series—not even the Bible?

What if his curriculum is in discovering how to deal with the person you got angry with yesterday, the fear you're feeling about not being enough for what you're facing, or the question about why God isn't doing what you think love would compel him to do. Look for opportunities to love people around you the way Father wants them loved. What is he showing you about himself that will unravel what causes you anxiety, or distract you from the life you want to live?

That's how you explore this kingdom. Take Jesus into the entirety of your life and think with him through the important things going on in your heart. When you're talking about something and are overcome with emotion, stop and let him show you what's going on in that moment. Close friends can help you process these things as well.

This is where the best growth happens. Rather than trying to force a random Scripture into your life, look at how your life is leading you to the Truth behind the Scriptures.

There remains, then, a Sabbath-rest for the people of God; for anyone who enters God's rest also rests from their works, just as God did from his.

HEBREWS 4:9–10 (NIV)

DEC 29 The Never-Ending Conversation

I've come to conclude that the best way to learn how to live in the Father's kingdom is by exploring it one day at a time.

Talk to him, not as a prayer ritual to be rewarded, but as a never-ending conversation with one who loves you deeply and wants to show you the best way to navigate all that lies before you. This is where Scripture becomes incredibly valuable, as you probe God's revelation in you with what he's already revealed of himself. Then, follow him as best you see him; by trial and error learn which are his thoughts, and which are your own ambitions.

Explore him and encourage others to do the same.

Rather than groping for explanations to give them, coach them as to how they can explore this kingdom with the help of the Holy Spirit.

How is he revealing himself to you today? What is he asking of you, if anything? Ask him to show you. Periodically carve out time to take you away from the noise and hurriedness of life to quiet your heart so his thoughts will percolate to the top of your own.

> *You received Christ Jesus, the Master; now live him. You're deeply rooted in him. You're well-constructed upon him. You know your way around the faith. Now do what you've been taught. School's out; quit studying the subject and start living it! And let your living spill over into thanksgiving.*
>
> COLOSSIANS 2:6–7 (MSG)

DEC 30 At Rest in Uncertainty

As I finish this book, we are living through the most tumultuous year of my lifetime with a pandemic ravaging the world, racial unrest that has to be addressed, and political polarization that threatens the future of our country. Much of this reminds me of John's prophecies in Revelation.

So, are these birth pangs of the Last Days? I have no idea. So many would-be prophets in my lifetime have been dead wrong trying to predict events. Nonetheless, my heart leaps at the thought. Yes, it would mean a rough ride ahead, but isn't this what our hearts have longed for—the consummation of this age in a kingdom that fulfills God's deepest desires for the Creation?

I know many people are afraid or at least find the uncertainty disturbing. I am not among them. A long time ago, Jesus began to teach me how little control I had over my own life, much less events around me. Ever-so-slowly, he began to win me into an ever-deepening security in his love and a trust in his plan for the world that has set me increasingly at rest in uncertainty.

Your whole life is in his hands—every breath—and he can enfold any circumstance into his purpose in the world. He promised you grace enough for each day and told us to look to the birds as encouragement because they live anxiety-free in the Father's care.

Your life is not in the stock market's daily movement or the politics of humanity. Your joy can be to wake up on this day, listen for his nudges, and follow his footprints. However he chooses to work all this out, fear is not your friend. It will only twist you into knots and make you respond in ways that will be destructive to you and to others.

When you find your certainty is in God himself, nothing can shake you.

Think of your sufferings as a weaning from that old sinful habit of always expecting to get your own way. Then you'll be able to live out your days free to pursue what God wants instead of being tyrannized by what you want.

I PETER 4:1–2 (MSG)

DEC 31 The Last Word

No matter who was picking grapes, harvesting raisins, or pruning vines on my father's vineyard, he was always the last one to walk the rows and make sure everything was as it should be. He always had the last word in his vineyard.

Jesus gets that in the Creation. Peter said he does.

That doesn't mean he's had the last word on everything yet. I've been cheated, shunned, blamed, excluded, and insulted unfairly by people who have taken out their brokenness on me. (By the way, I've done my share of that to others as well. When I'm aware of it, I've tried to own up to it by apologizing to the people it affected, but I'm sure there's more I haven't yet realized.)

Right now, it seems the wrong people get the last word but that's just because we're in the middle of a chapter and not at the end of the story. Every time I contemplate the unresolved circumstances or broken relationships in my life, I remember that Jesus will still be passing this way to set things right. It always brings a smile to my lips and an exhale from my heart.

After all, our circumstances don't get the last word, Jesus does. And there is no one better, for the struggles in my own life and for the whole of Creation.

> *Jesus has the last word on everything and everyone, from angels to armies. He's standing right alongside God, and what he says goes.*
>
> **1 PETER 3:22**

You can find Wayne on the following social media:
Facebook: https://www.facebook.com/wayneljacobsen/
Twitter: @LifestreamWayne
Instagram: @wayneatlifestream

Wayne's other books:

He Loves Me

So You Don't Want to Go to Church Anymore
(with Dave Coleman)

A Language of Healing for a Polarized Nation
(with Arnita Willis Taylor and Bob Prater)

Finding Church

Beyond Sundays

In Season

Authentic Relationships
(with Clay Jacobsen)

A Man Like No Other
(with Brad Cummings)

The Shack
(in collaboration with Wm. Paul Young
and Brad Cummings)

Acknowledgments

After spending a few days with a group of people across the United States, a newfound friend observed, "You're a repository for thousands and thousands of conversations you've had all over the globe with all kinds of people who are discovering what it means to live the life of Jesus."

I had never thought of it that way, but it does express what my life has been like. I've talked to some of the most amazing people on the planet caught up in their own Jesus journey. I have gleaned much from them as we have processed our journeys together to look into the mysteries of God.

So, for everyone I've ever had a conversation with, I'm grateful that you took the time to engage my life and add to my story. I hope I've added to yours as well.

Specifically, I want to thank Jessica Glasner, a college student when she came to work for me one summer. She culled through so many of my articles and blog posts to find those veins of rich gold that could encourage others on their journey. She began the initial compilation and edited them into smaller bites for a daily reflection. It has taken many years to get back to this project and update it with newer insights, but I am so grateful for her work and her friendship.

Kyle and Jess Rice of Blue Sheep Media were gracious enough to put this project together and make it available to all of you. Their partnership is magnified by the close friendship we share in life.

I'm also grateful to two people who've been beside me on many a book. I'm glad they were both free to jump on this project with me. Kate Lapin, editor extraordinaire, came into my life through a miracle and her touch on so many of my projects always makes them way more readable for you. And Nan Bishop came out of retirement to add the beauty of her eye to the presentation of this book both in cover design and page layout.

Finally, none of this would happen without Sara, my beloved wife of forty-plus years. She has lived all of this with me, encourages me more than I deserve, and is the one next to Jesus who knows me best and loves me most.